James H. Mauzy

Historical sketch of the Sixty-eighth Regiment, Indiana Volunteers:

With personal recollections by members of Company D, and short biographies of

brigade, division, and corps commanders

James H. Mauzy

Historical sketch of the Sixty-eighth Regiment, Indiana Volunteers:
With personal recollections by members of Company D, and short biographies of brigade, division, and corps commanders

ISBN/EAN: 9783337811051

Printed in Europe, USA, Canada, Australia, Japan

Cover: Foto ©ninafisch / pixelio.de

More available books at **www.hansebooks.com**

HISTORICAL SKETCH

OF THE

SIXTY-EIGHTH REGIMENT

INDIANA VOLUNTEERS.

WITH PERSONAL RECOLLECTIONS BY
MEMBERS OF COMPANY D;

AND

SHORT BIOGRAPHIES OF BRIGADE, DIVISION
AND CORPS COMMANDERS.

Edition 100—Privately Printed.

RUSHVILLE, IND.,
The Republican Co., Printers and Binders.
1887.

PREFACE.

Comrades:

A quarter of a century has passed since we rallied together and marched southward to help in putting down the rebellion. Since then, more events of interest have occurred for the well-being of the human race than in any century. How strange it all seems, now that we have been woven into the various callings of civil life, North, South, East and West, as farmers, merchants, lawyers, doctors, preachers and in the various trades. It is a romance in real life, a grand transformation scene. Wherever our lot has been cast, we all look back to the days when we marched shoulder to shoulder, and endured toils, trials and dangers together, and thus cemented ties of friendship which, we hope, will last into eternity.

> "Sometimes the friends who've left us,
> Joined the army gone before,
> Almost seem to bridge the river
> 'Twixt the near and farther shore."

Time has flown by so rapidly, and the daily duties and cares of life have so occupied our time, that many incidents have escaped our memories.

The following brief history and biographies have been compiled for presentation to you in order that all

may have in a convenient form the dates of our service and short sketches of the men who led us to victory.

> "Oh! it was glorious, grand, heroic,
>   Rushing over hill and plain;
> With its mighty recollections,
>   How the heart leaps up again!
>
> "How they cheered, and how they rallied,
>   How they charged 'mid shot and shell,
> How they bore aloft the banner,
>   How they conquered, how they fell.
>
> "Fell? Who shall tell the story?
>   There, among the brave and best,
> Who went down 'midst the battle,"
>   King, Price, Reese and the rest.
>
> "This the cost of human freedom—
>   Weary hearts that long and wait,
> Shadows on a thousand households,
>   Sanctified, but desolate."

The accompanying map of the Battle of Nashville and the portrait of Gen. Wood are presented by permission of the National Tribune, Washington, D. C., and from plates furnished by its editor.

The Roster of the regiment is copied from the official report of W. H. H. Terrell, Adjutant General of Indiana (1866).

J. H. MAUZY, Capt. Co. D.

RUSHVILLE, IND., August 19, 1887.

ERRATA.

The sketch of Major-General Thomas J. Wood should have included the statement that he was Chief Mustering Officer and Post Commander at Indianapolis, from May to October, 1861.

On page 61, line 19, for Hill Springs, read Mill Springs.

TABLE OF CONTENTS.

	PAGE.
Sixty-Eighth Indiana, by J. H. Mauzy	1
Indiana in the War	26
The Losses in the War	28
Enlistments by States	30
Losses in the Revolutionary War	31
Comparative Losses	31
The Battle of Missionary Ridge (with Map)	34
The Regimental Flag	38
Col. Edward A. King	40
Col. Daniel W. McCook	49
Gen. August Willich	51
Gen. James B. Steedman	53
Gen. Joseph J. Reynolds	57
Gen. Thomas J. Wood (with Portrait)	59
Gen. George H. Thomas	60
Anti-Compromise Resolutions	62
Regimental Roster—	
Field and Staff	64
Company A	64
Company B	66
Company C	68
Company D	70
Company E	74
Company F	76
Company G	78
Company H	80
Company I	82
Company K	84
List of Engagements	86

Reminiscences— PAGE.
J. H. Mauzy..99–126–143
Lee Goodwin.. 107
John M. Francis... 110
Harvey Caldwell.. 117
O. H. P. Mohler... 121
W. M. Souder.. 122
D. S. Fleehart...123–150
A. W. Earnest... 124
Samuel C. Pegg... 130
Samuel B. Jones.. 132
George Smith.. 135
Thomas T. Patterson.. 136
L. T. Stewart.. 136
W. F. Aldridge.. 137
S. C. Poppino... 138
Mason Maxey.. 140
Ed. A. Junkin... 141
Co. D at Chicamauga... 143
William Beale... 144
D. L. Thomas..147–171
Capt. Henry Romeyn.. 149
Charles Lester..153–155
Thomas E. Bramblett... 158
Enoch Whitely.. 160
James W. Richie.. 161
N. T. Ploughe... 162
John L. T. Wilson.. 166
Arthur J. Gates... 169

The Dead—
Major James W. Innis... 180
Samuel S. Bodine.. 180
Jefferson E. Trembley.. 182
William H. H. Danner.. 182
Manlius W. Pierce... 183

Memorial Address—Rev. E. H. Wood.................................. 184
Army of the Cumberland, September, 1863....................... 205
Confederate Army at Chicamauga....................................... 209
Fourth Army Corps, October, 1863..................................... 212

MAPS.

	PAGE.
Battle of Nashville...	1
Battle of Chicamauga..	143
Cyclorama of Missionary Ridge................................	34

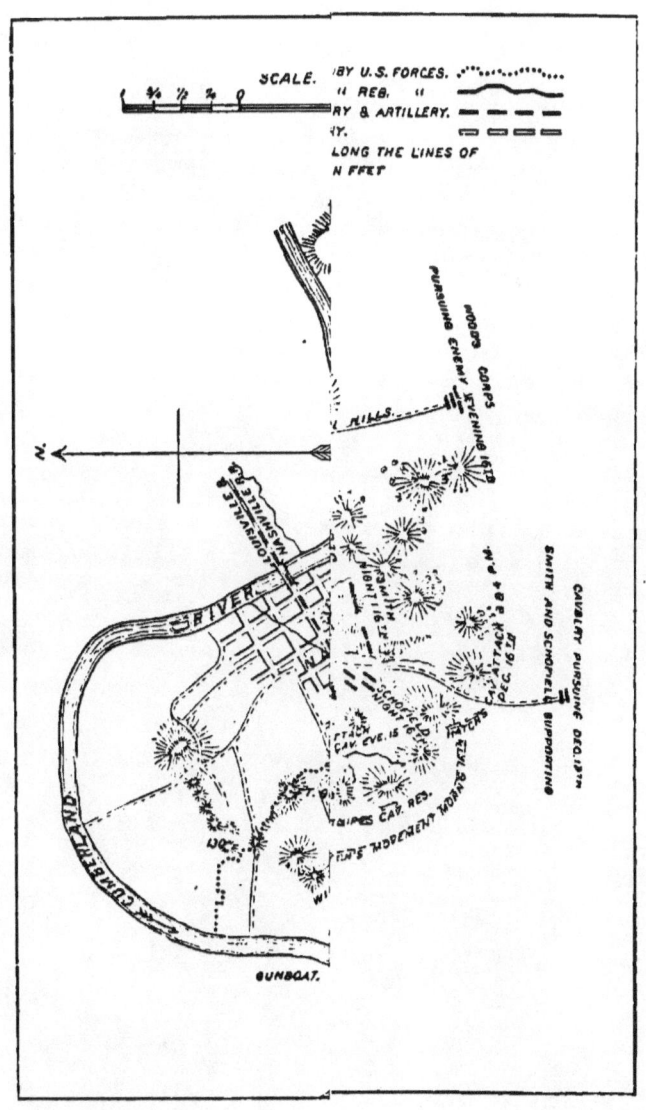

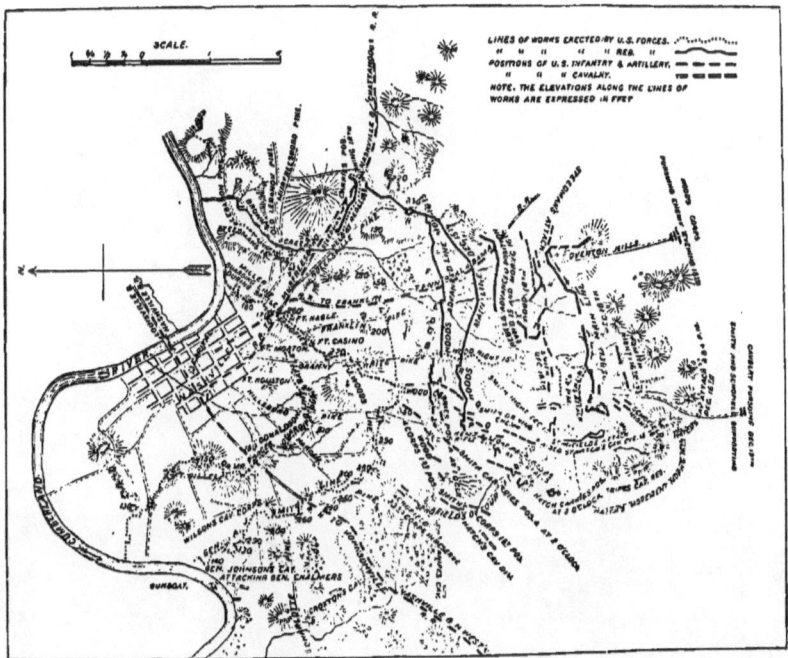

BATTLE OF NASHVILLE, DEC. 15-16, 1864.

68th Regiment Indiana Infantry.

OUTLINE HISTORY.

Not until the summer of 1862, when the rebels in large force were threatening to invade the Northern States at many places, was the Government or the people fully aroused to the magnitude of the Rebellion. Then all felt the necessity of prompt action to stay their onward course, and for the protection of our homes. Everywhere there was a "hurrying to and fro," and men organized into companies for short and long terms of service, and were hurried rapidly to the front. The 68th Regiment was organized at Camp Logan, near Greensburg, by Lieutenent-Colonel B. C. Shaw, and in less than seven days was confronting the enemy in Kentucky. Only a few outlines of the movements of the armies with which it served can be given in this short sketch, and all who wish can read in histories of the war the details of the campaigns, battles, and the general results of each. A regiment was a small part of the great machinery of war—conse-

quently its service is of interest to the general public only as part of a great army. To the survivors, after twenty-five years, their families and friends, it may recall many forms, faces and incidents, and of times and places nearly forgotten. At Camp Logan there was so much to do, the novelty of the situation, the coming and going of friends and relatives, the manner of living, and the exercise of "squad" drilling, made the few days there pass quickly away, and on Sunday night, August 17, we boarded the cars and arrived at Indianapolis in the night, and marched to the old State House, where we slept until morning. Governor Morton made us a speech next day, and asked us if we would go into Kentucky, as we were much needed there, without the bounty money in advance, as promised, and we agreed almost unanimously to go.

The 68th Regiment was mustered into the United States service next day, August 19, 1862, and, the Governor having made a loan, twenty-five dollars of the bounty money was paid to each man, and the regiment left at midnight on the cars for Louisville, Ky. There were forty-one commissioned officers and eight hundred and sixty-four men. During its term of service there were sent to it one hundred and four recruits. At Louisville, August 22, we received Springfield rifles and accoutrements, and were put to drilling almost all the time. Lieutenant-Colonel Edward A. King, of the 19th Regulars, was put in command as Colonel, and on the 25th of August we drew forty rounds of ammunition and marched southward. On

the 28th the "long roll" beat the first midnight alarm to us, near Bardstown. It was a false alarm this time; but the feelings it causes of a sudden attack and all that implies, makes this the most serious of all calls. September 1, at Springfield, the citizens gave us a dinner, the only time the regiment ever received such attention in the South. That evening we joined the forces under Brigadier-general E. Dumont, at Lebanon. There, and at Lebanon Junction, we cut down forests, and worked almost constantly, constructing fortifications and breast-works, and performing other duties to resist the attacks of the enemy, who were threatening us daily and nightly.

September 15, all of our regiment who were not on picket duty—five hundred and twenty-five in number—were ordered to take three days' rations and get into some box-cars which had been used to ship cattle in, and had not been cleaned. This being a new experience in our service, there were more comments than would have been made later on in our service, when, after long, weary, dusty or muddy marches, any chance to ride would have been hailed with delight. The train moved slowly along to Bacon Creek, where the rebels had burned the bridge and a train of cars, and the fires were yet blazing. Soon after, on our march, we met guards with the body of Major Abbett, of the 67th Indiana, who was killed at Munfordville the day before, and in the night we arrived there and slept on our arms in an open field. We learned afterwards the rebels had allowed us to pass through their troops,

knowing we were going into their trap. During the night we changed position into an old orchard between two small forts. About 9 a. m. the rebels opened up with artillery and musketry, and began to close in on us, when we were ordered into the western fort, to support the troops and artillery there engaged. All through the day cannon balls, pieces of shell, grape shot and small balls fell about us, but doing little injury. When a white flag of truce would appear, the firing would cease. and all would watch its approach with great interest. Greatly to the surprise of most of us, who did not understand the situation and thought there had been treachery, it was announced before daylight that we had surrendered. Early on the morning of the 17th, we marched out and laid down our arms "with the honors of war;" and when we saw the whole rebel army, and learned they had forty thousand men and sixty pieces of artillery in position, we became more reconciled to the situation. Colonels Wilder, King, Dunham, Owens and Murray refused to surrender unless they were allowed to see and know that there was no hope of a successful resistance, and General Bragg allowed them, after repeated demands and refusals to surrender, to send Colonel Wilder to see his arrangements for the assault. When he returned he advised an honorable surrender. Under the terms of capitulation we were to retain our side arms, haversacks. canteens and blankets. and were "paroled," agreeing not to take up arms until exchanged. Colonel King saved our flag by wrapping

it about his body, under his clothing; some of his rebel officer acquaintances remarking that he was getting aldermanic in the size of his body, but they did not suspect the cause.

What a ridiculous show was made of our preparations to put down the Rebellion, when we threw a large wagon-load of bowie knives, revolvers, dirks and pistols into a pile for the rebels to divide up as trophies. How foolish the carrying of such arms was considered by old soldiers. The troops surrendered were the larger parts of the 50th, 60th, 67th, 68th and 89th Indiana Infantry, two companies of the 74th Indiana Infantry, one company of the 78th Indiana Infantry, 204 recruits for the 17th Indiana, ten pieces of Indiana Artillery, one company of Kentucky Cavalry, and one company of the Eighteenth Regulars—in all four thousand one hundred and twenty-nine. The resistance at Munfordville for four days, served the purpose of retarding the enemy's march on Louisville, and allowed General Buell's army to come up with him. It also permitted such arrangements there for defense that, when he made the demand for its surrender and was refused, he marched his army away southward, and was overtaken at Perryville, October 8. September 18 we were given four days' rations out of our own captured stores, one cracker and one-third pound of side meat each, and we thought if they could go four days on that amount of food they would starve us out. Under a flag of truce and a small rebel escort, we marched out through the pickets of the rebels and into

General Buell's army, being delayed several hours by the pickets fighting. Colonel King made a strong effort to get our regiment exchanged, and we were delayed several hours while they were conferring with the rebel authorities. The soldiers almost universally censured General Buell for not attacking their rear in force while we were in Munfordville, but military critics say that it would not have done to jeopardize so much. If defeated, the enemy would be between him and the North.

We marched for eight days through a country which both armies had passed over and eaten out, through the sparsely-settled, woody hill region of Western Kentucky, suffering the pangs of hunger and the weariness of long marches, exposed night and day to rains and frosts. This exposure wrought more destruction on us than any other march we were called on to endure. Many of our strongest men were broken down, and shortly after discharged. Later on in our service we became used to hardships and exposures, but this came so soon after leaving comfortable homes that it was felt the more. Our route took us through Bowling Green, where seventeen brass bands, that had been discharged from Buell's army, joined us. We passed on through Brownsville, Litchfield and Tar Springs to Branderburg, on the Ohio River. Here we crossed and marched to New Albany and Jeffersonville, arriving there on the 28th. Governor Morton made a speech to us, which was both complimentary and cheering to our drooping spirits. That same even-

ing it was reported that he whipped General Boyle, and General Jeff. C. Davis shot and killed General Nelson. The rebel army under Bragg was near, and Buell's army was arriving. These events altogether made "exciting times then and there."

We arrived at Indianapolis on the 30th, and were furloughed to our homes until October 27. At that time we reported at the State capital and went into Camp Dumont, where we were kept busy preparing for further service when we should be exchanged. This occurred before December 26, and on that date a part of the regiment left for Louisville, the remainder following on the 30th.

January 7, 1863, we marched to Portland, and next day Companies C, D, E, and H went on board the steamer Ft. Wayne, and the other companies on the Horizon. A large fleet loaded with supplies was to be guarded up the Cumberland River to Nashville. The sides of the boats were boarded up, to protect the pilots, machinery and guards from the attacks of the enemy along the river banks. The water was low, and the delays on sand bars, heavy snows, guerrilla attacks, and finally heavy rains, made the voyage of thirteen days trying to our nerves and patience. A flock of geese that had been fired into would not make more stir in comparison, than did our fleet when, from behind rails and logs, the enemy fired into our boats. There was blowing of whistles, ringing of bells, backing and running wildly about, until we got our guns to work and drove them from their hiding places. But

this was done not until they had burned two of our steamers. The boats were lashed together in pairs, and one gun-boat went ahead and one behind, and the fleet would often be several miles in length.

On the 20th we left the boats at Nashville, and went into camp in the suburbs, in the slushy snow and mud. The weather was cold and foggy, and the change from boat life was so great that many sickened and died. On the 25th, while Company D was out on picket duty, the regiment was ordered to march at once, to hunt up some rebel raiders. The company was not relieved for two days, until their return. Such orders came often, and when not on such expeditions all were kept busy with picket drill and camp duties. While at Nashville we were attached to Colonel Dan. McCook's brigade.

April 2, the regiment marched to join the main army, under General Rosecrans. It arrived at Murfreesboro on the 3d, and was assigned to the 2d Brigade, 5th Division, 14th Army Corps. In June our division number was changed to the 4th, in the re-organization before the advance. The 2d Brigade was made up of the 68th, 72d, 75th and 101st Indiana regiments, the 105th Ohio, the 19th Indiana Battery, and the 80th Illinois, but the latter was on detached service, and never joined the brigade. Colonel A. S. Hall, of the 105th Ohio, commanded the brigade, Major-General J. J. Reynolds the division, and George H. Thomas the corps.

April 17, the regiment went on a general recon-

noisance with General Reynolds and a force of four thousand infantry and two thousand six hundred cavalry, which destroyed the railroad from Manchester to McMinville, and captured a large amount of supplies. The mounted troops took about two hundred prisoners and a large number of horses and mules. The regiment marched one hundred and thirty-three miles in eleven days, besides taking part in the work of destroying property. From this time until the army moved we were kept busy making necessary preparations. Shelter tents were issued and all things made ready for rapid marching. Colonel Hall died June 10, 1863, of a fever. He was a favorite, and had done brave service with his command, on the 18th of March, defeating General Morgan after a hard fight. Colonel M. S. Robinson, of the 75th Indiana, being the next officer in rank present, took command of the brigade. Colonel King was absent, sick.

On the 24th of June, the 14th Army Corps in the centre, joined in the grand forward movement, marching out on the Manchester turnpike, with our division in the advance. In the evening, at Hoover's Gap, a narrow passage way three miles long, between high hills, the enemy attacked our advance. Our regiment was rushed forward to support the 19th Indiana Battery, and there was some lively work for a short time. Our regiment lost one killed and six wounded. The next day we skirmished with the enemy, who gradually retired before us, as we pushed forward. On the 26th they again offered battle, but did not resist long.

They kept their retreat supported by heavy skirmish lines of infantry, artillery and cavalry. We were next in advance to the mounted troops into Manchester early in the morning of the 27th, and surprised the place, capturing their mails and some prisoners. During all this time the rain poured down in torrents; little streams had to be waded and mud pulled through, and it was a source of great rejoicing to all when, on the 30th, we marched into the rebel camps at Tullahoma, which they abandoned so hastily that much of their camp equipage was left behind. Pressing on in pursuit, we waded Elk River, July 4, and on the 6th went into Camp Winifred, among abundant blackberries. To the free use of this fruit here, many attribute their recovery from jaundice and diarrhœa, which had been brought on by being soaked so long in the rains of summer—steaming in the heat of the day time, and chilling in the coolness of the night, combined with the fatigues and exposures of the march. But a great number died, many were discharged, and others were sent to the Invalid Corps. After a few days rest the regiment was sent to Decherd, and set to work unloading cars and distributing supplies for the army. July 29 we marched to University Heights, and went into the most healthful and beautiful camp we ever had. July 30 Colonel King arrived, and assumed command of the brigade. August 17 we broke camp, moved out thirteen miles to Sweden's Cove, and thence, with little opposition, went to Jasper on the 21st, where we halted until the 30th. A large library was appropriated here,

and standard literature laid round loosely in the camps. On the 30th, the regiment crossed the Tennessee River at Shellmound, and during the night marched to Whiteside Station, supporting a cavalry raid. We found that the bridge there, 106 feet high, and a long one, had been burned by the rebels. The 2d East Tennessee ran the rebels to within five miles of Chattanooga. Next day we returned, and went into camp near the entrance to Nick-a-Jack Cave. September 3 we marched into Georgia, and slept in the narrow gorge in the road when the night became too dark to march. At daylight we moved on over the Raccoon Mountains, camping near Trenton. On the 10th our camp was near the Vulcan Iron Works.

Our objective point was the possession of Chattanooga, and the news of the evacuation of that city caused great rejoicing among the troops. Our forces were greatly scattered, and the point was to get them together and into that city. On the evening and night of the 11th, we climbed Lookout Mountain, and the road was so steep and rough the men had almost to carry up the artillery and wagons. We could hear heavy and rapid cannonading on the other side of the mountain, and next morning were rushed down the other side and camped in line of battle, beside General Negley's and Bayard's divisions, which had been forced back by overpowering numbers. On the 13th we were in line of battle until nearly dark, and early next morning marched to Pond Springs. Some skirmishing took place, the enemy being close. Our pickets re-

pulsed an attack on the night of the 15th. There was more skirmishing during the 16th. We were in line of battle all the 17th, and until the evening of the 18th. Then we marched, when not halting for obstructions ahead of us, all the night by the light of burning fences, logs, trees and brush. Next morning we could hear the sounds of the great battle which had commenced, and soon came into the woods where stray bullets fell about us. A little after noon we were in the thickest of the fray, and being overpowered by Liddell's division of Walker's Corps, had to fall back, leaving our dead and some of the wounded in the hands of the enemy. Our ranks were reformed, and about dark we took our places in the line of battle for the next day, Sunday, September 20. The night was cool, and the morning opened up smoky and foggy. About 9 a. m. the rebels began the contest, and the terrible carnage, the roar of cannon and musketry, with falling limbs from the trees above, made us feel like we were in the midst of a hurricane. The roar was continuous, and only the sound of the heaviest guns could be heard above the din of the conflict. Colonel King was killed about 4 p. m., a ball striking him in the forehead. He was brought off the field on a caisson. His courage and bravery won the admiration of all, and had he lived high promotion would have been his reward. Colonel M. S. Robinson, of the 75th Indiana, being next in rank, then took command of the brigade. Early in the night the scattered fragments of the army were concentrated at Rossville, and placed in position

for defense, the men sleeping in line of battle. The mere figures of the losses cannot make the terrors of the two days' battle of Chicamauga appear in the least to those who were never in a battle. We had comrades slain, and others wounded and left on the field, and the tortures of uncertainty in regard to their fate filled our minds with the saddest thoughts.

It was well the veil was not lifted for us to gaze upon the horrible scenes of suffering in those dark and gloomy woods during the next few days after the battle. There were three hundred and fifty-six officers and enlisted men of the 68th in the battle, and over one-third of them were killed or wounded. The loss of the regiment was one hundred and thirty-five. Lieutenant Robert J. Price, formerly editor of the Rushville *Jacksonian*, was among the number killed. Company D had thirty-seven men in the battle, under the command of 1st Lieutenant William Beale. (Captain J. H. Mauzy was in the battle as Brigade Inspector on the staff of Colonel King.) Of these, one was killed; one wounded, missing, never heard from; and twenty wounded, thirteen of whom fell into rebel hands. Several other companies had equal losses.

During the night of the 21st our army withdrew into Chattanooga. Our regiment and brigade, marching in the rear to cover the retreat, repelled all attacks by the enemy while we were withdrawing from Rossville.

Cist's History of the Army of the Cumberland thus sums up this battle: "All things considered, the battle of Chicamauga, for the forces engaged, was the

hardest fought and bloodiest battle of the rebellion. Hindman, who fought our right at Horseshoe Ridge, says in his official report that he had 'never known Federal troops to fight so well,' and that he 'never saw Confederate soldiers fight better.' The largest number of troops Rosecrans had, of all arms, on the field during the two days' fighting, was 55,000 effective men. Rosecrans' losses were: Killed, 1,687; wounded, 9,394; missing, 5,255—total loss, 16,336. Bragg had about 70,000 effective troops in line. His losses, in part estimated, were 2,673 killed, 16,274 wounded, and 2,003 missing—a total of 20,950. A full report of the rebel losses was never made."

In Chattanooga the work of strengthening our position was carried on night and day, until we felt secure from any assault. An entire brigade was sent on duty from our division each day. Until October 4 we had conversation and interchange of papers with the enemy's pickets on our front, the two picket lines being about one hundred yards apart. After that date orders forbade any communication. Almost every day the rebels would cause a stir in our lines by throwing in large shot and shell from their artillery on Lookout Mountain. On the 11th of October our brigade was broken up, and the 68th Indiana was assigned to the 1st Brigade, General Willich; 3d Division, General Woods; 4th Army Corps, General Gordon Granger, commander. The brigade was made up of the 15th Wisconsin, 8th Kansas, 25th, 35th and 89th Illinois, 32d and 68th Indiana, 15th and 49th Ohio—all infantry

regiments. After this we moved over and camped
with our new brigade, on the east side of the city, near
Ft. Wood. Often our pickets and those of the rebels
would get mixed up together in the dense fogs, when
going on duty, but each treated the other courteously,
and tried to point out their proper places. About the
the 1st of November our rations ran to the lowest
point, and mule meat became a luxury — the pangs of
hunger were felt by many as never before, and our
prospects seemed very gloomy. About the middle of
November the short line of communication with
Stevenson, Ala., was opened up by reinforcements
from other armies, and preparations were rapidly made
to break out of the pen in which we were confined.
There was only one way out — by crossing the river to
the North.

Almost every day our troops would drill in front of
the line of fortifications, and when we went out on the
23d, the rebels were somewhat surprised to see us
march steadily forward, drive in their pickets, and
never halt until we had possession of their rifle-pits.
Our brigade was in the advance, on the left, and half
our regiment on the skirmish line that night. The
forward movement was characterized in the official
reports as having been done "in the most gallant style."
That night we slept in line of battle. On the 24th we
remained quietly in our places, and from our position
could see both sides in the great battle near the top of
Lookout Mountain — "Hooker's fight above the clouds."
It was a beautiful sight. The sublimity and grandeur

of that living panorama will always be a memory of joy, for it was a "famous victory." About 10 a. m. on the 25th, our picket lines were ordered forward again, and it was a sight long to be remembered by those engaged, to see how the "Johnnies" went over their line of breastworks at the foot of Mission Ridge, like a drove of sheep on a stampede, and how disappointed we were when orders came for us to fall back and reform our lines. No mention of this part of the fight is given by General Grant or Van Horne in their histories, although it was certainly an important move. At 3:30 p. m., by the firing of six cannons in rapid succession on Orchard Knob, near us, an advance was ordered of our corps. We were in the center. Steadily we again drove them back to their line of works at the foot of the Ridge, and the storm of leaden hail, of shot and shell and grape, that came down upon and about us, thinned and disordered our ranks very much as we pressed on up the Ridge to the summit, about dark; and then on our front many fought to the death rather than surrender. Our regiment lost many brave men. Five officers and seventy-seven enlisted men were killed and wounded. 1st Lieutenant John Reese, of Company C, and Samuel S. Bodine, of Company D, were killed in the charge. Both were great favorites. Our division (Wood's) was the first to reach the top of the Ridge, losing one hundred and fifty killed and eight hundred and fifty-one wounded; total 1,001. Van Horne, in his History of the Army of the Cumberland, says:

"The peculiar features of the field revealed to the enemy the transcendent array of the National troops. The battle had opened with the splendid charge of Wood's division, and Lookout Mountain had been wrested from his hands in such a way as to change the martial tone of each army. Those assaulting Mission Ridge had Chicamauga to avenge and Lookout Mountain to surpass. The dashing, yet firm and resolute sweep of the assaulting column, for more than a mile, expressed in advance the resistless character of the attack. The loss of more than twenty per cent. in Sheridan's and Wood's divisions, in a contest of less than an hour, shows that the enemy did not yield his position without a struggle."

All our movements could be seen by them. When the top was gained, it took a little while to get together around our old flags. Notwithstanding our terrible losses, we cheered and sang and embraced one another for joy, while the tears filled our eyes for comrades slain. The scene was intensified by the rebels burning such stores and property as they could not get away with, so that the heavens were illuminated. We felt the prestige of victory again. The memory of Chicamauga was a sad one, and we all felt that it was nearly a defeat—a drawn battle. But this was a glorious victory, giving us renewed hope, and we marched on ever after in full confidence of a final victory. The rebels had the strongest position, and fought heroically to hold it, dying in heaps by their guns.

In the night our corps received orders to get ready and move at once to the relief of Burnside, at Knoxville, over one hundred miles away. He was there besieged by Longstreet with a large army. We went in the lightest marching order, carrying our rations in our haversacks, with one blanket for bedding, and one rubber poncho to each man for tent and protection against the winter weather. We marched all day and sometimes nearly all night, through rain and mud, resting by the roadside wherever the column was halted. Parched corn was a luxury, and was chiefly our diet for days together. The rebels, learning of our approach, made a most desperate assault on Fort Saunders, November 29, 1863, before we could get there. They were repulsed with terrible slaughter, and retreated. Our brigade marched beyond, to near Strawberry Plain, and went into camp in the woods among the rocks. Here we got a much-needed chance to wash and clean up, for we had worn and slept in our clothes for two weeks.

The "cold New Year's day" (January 1, 1864,) found us working on a high bridge over the Holston River, with short rations and sleeping in the pine thickets among the rocks. Often the snows and cold, chilly rains would make us think of better comforts. The exposure sent hundreds to hospitals with diseases. When the foraging parties returned, well loaded, there was much good cheer in camp. December 27, 1863, General Wheeler attacked a train of wagons under escort of Laiholt's brigade, at Calhoun, Tenn., but was

routed with great loss. 1st Sergeant James A. Smith, "the tall Orderly of Company D," (68th Indiana) was wounded while assisting in repelling the assault. On the 15th of January our division advanced and drove the rebels out of Dandridge, Tenn. But the enemy persisted in trying to bring on a general engagement, by massing a large force, and skirmishing was kept up for two days. On the evening of the 18th a brisk fight took place, and during the night our forces retreated, after a council of war, at which Generals Granger, Sheridan, Wood, Willich, Hazen, Beatty and others, were present. Next day we burned the bridge which we had undergone such hardships to build, and after a few days fell back to Marysville. Military jealousy between some of our prominent Generals was the cause of much trouble in the Department of the Ohio at this time, as they did not work harmoniously together.

In February, 1864, our command was again moved up to Morristown, and was kept busy with raids from the enemy and consolidating of regiments. The time of enlistment of many of the older regiments having expired, only the recruits of many remained. Company D had men assigned to it for muster from every regiment in the brigade, February 29. In April our command returned to Cleveland, Tenn., and at the consolidation for the Atlanta campaign, our regiment was one of eight selected to garrison Chattanooga. The responsibilities of the duty made us think very highly of the honor, it being the key position and containing more stores and valuable property than any

other post. The regiment reported to General James B. Steedman, at Chattanooga, April 28, 1864, and was assigned a place on the south front of that city. When Sherman's army advanced on the Atlanta campaign, General Steedman's command from Stevenson, Ala., was placed at the front, and called "The District of the Etowah." The duties required of us were of the most varied character. Besides picket, camp and garrison duty there were details to guard trains, to take bounty jumpers, cattle and supplies to the army at the front, and to Knoxville, and the taking of prisoners back and forth. Often all the regiment that was in camp would be ordered to march at once to repel an attack somewhere on our long line of railroad, and we would not get back for days. Details were made to take prisoners to Nashville, for provost duty, and to guard and help boats through the "Suck," a narrow place in the Tennessee River, a few miles below the city. Some of the men who had trades were put to work in the repair shops.

On the night of August 14, 1864, we were called to go to Dalton at once, where Wheeler's cavalry had driven our garrison into their fortifications and taken the town. At daylight General Steedman, in command of our force, ordered a charge to be made into the town, and, with a rush, swept the enemy from the place. Here Captain Charles C. Wheeler, of Company B, received a mortal wound, from which he died in a few days. All felt very sad for the loss of so brave an officer. Five enlisted men were wounded in the charge

of our regiment. Returning to Chattanooga on the 18th, the regiment was ordered to Athens, Tenn., but the rebels had left, and we returned on the 20th, very weary of marching so rapidly. September 1 the regiment went to Tullahoma, but returned in a few days, and in the same manner every few days to some point on the different roads threatened by Hood's advance cavalry, on their way to the North.

After Sherman left Atlanta for the sea, the regiment arrived back from one of these expeditions on the 26th, and before daylight on the 27th they were off for Decatur, Ala., where the regiment assisted in repelling the attack of Hood's army. Our regiment supported the 14th U. S. Colored Infantry, who made such a gallant charge on the 28th of October, 1864. The colored regiment lost forty men killed and wounded, among the number three officers killed. Our regimental loss was five wounded. After campaigning about the country for some time, we returned to Chattanooga, November 10. On the 12th our regiment received orders to go to Resacca, Ga., where it remained several days, guarding men tearing up the railroad tracks. November 29 the regiment went on picket duty at Chattanooga, in the morning, but was relieved, and left on the cars for Decatur, Ala. From then and until after the battle of Nashville, December 15 and 16, 1864, and until the pursuit of Hood's army had been abandoned near Tuscumbia, Ala., the regiment was with General Steedman's command, on the march all the time, receiving great credit with the other troops

of his in the battle at Nashville—the regiment losing one killed and five wounded. When the pursuit ceased many of our men were shoeless and ragged, being out forty-three days without any change of clothing. Many were without blankets and overcoats, fighting and marching through the cold rains and mud, and sometimes over frozen ground. At one time they were five days and nights on the cars—box cars—from fifty to sixty men in a car, without fire, and so closely packed they could not lie down without crowding one another. December 27 they waded a bayou, near Decatur, Ala., before daylight, which was hip deep.

The regiment returned to their camp at Chattanooga, January 11, 1865, and from that time until the close of the war, there was only enough vitality left in Hood's army to make a guerrilla warfare on our lines of communication, or on places that had few troops. January 29 the regiment went to Athens, Tenn., to repel a raid there, but the rebels left on our approach. February 4 we moved our camp over the river, at the end of the bridge, and were assigned to provost duty. The great floods which nearly submerged our camp and the boating experiences will long be remembered as something very unusual. The water ran through the streets and for miles over the valley.

April 10 the news of Lee's surrender was made the occasion of a wonderful demonstration. Every bell was rung, every whistle blew, the cannons roared, and men cheered until they were hoarse. The country people

came into the city or hid away in alarm at such a bedlam reaching through the mountains.

On the 14th, when the news of the assassination of Lincoln was received, the reaction was so great that men wept, and all wondered what would happen next. But the news of the capture of Jeff. Davis, the same day, caused our spirits to revive. On the 18th Cerro Gordo Williams and a large number of troops came in and surrendered. As they were flush with gold and silver from the Treasury of the Confederacy, which they were escorting out of danger, and which they paid out freely to the sutlers for luxuries they had not tasted for years, their money soon got into circulation, and we enjoyed the getting of a little hard cash very much, until the novelty wore off. And so until the end of our service there were events of thrilling interest, daily, because it was our side that was victorious. No one who has never experienced the despondency of defeat, can ever feel the full measure of joy in victory.

On the 17th of June General Steedman made us a farewell speech, in which he complimented us highly on our services to the country. We then left for Nashville, arriving there next day. On the 20th of June, 1865, we were mustered out of the service of the United States at that place. The recruits in our regiment were transferred to the 44th Indiana Infantry, with which they served until discharged, September 14, 1865.

We arrived at Indianapolis on the 22d of June, were furloughed for eight days, and took part in a public reception given at the Tabernacle to the returned

troops, which was addressed by Lieutenant-Governor Conrad Baker. After being paid off we at once resumed our places as citizens, each going his way in the pursuit of happiness, and to such duties as should fall to his lot in the ever changing cares of life.

Nearly a quarter of a century has passed since we first assembled together at Camp Logan, but I leave it to the comrades to reflect over the events which have occurred since then. How stranger than fiction have been the destinies of many; our hearts are now saddened when we think of those comrades slain, or who died in hospitals, or in those saddest of all places, the rebel prisons. Let us think of these things, and resolve to do all we can to honor their memory and for the country they died to save.

Our first service was in the Department of the Ohio. The Department of the Cumberland was ordered by the War Department, October 24, 1862, and was afterward organized with the 14th, 20th and 21st Army Corps, commanded in the order named by Major-Generals George H. Thomas, McCook and Crittenden. There were four divisions in the 14th Corps until after the battle of Chicamauga, viz.: 1st division, Baird's; 2d, Negley's; 3d, Brannan's; 4th, Reynold's. The 4th division was composed of the following brigades: 1st brigade, Wilder's; 2d, Ed. A. King's; 3d, Turchin's.

A reorganization of the entire army was made after the battle of Chicamauga, under the name of the Mili-

tary Division of the Mississippi, and commanded by General U. S. Grant. Under the new arrangement the Army of the Cumberland was composed of the 4th, 11th, 12th and 14th Corps, Major-General George H. Thomas commanding. The 4th Corps was made by consolidating the 20th and 21st, under Major-General Gordon Granger. The 11th was commanded by Major-General O. O. Howard, and the 12th by Major-General Slocum—the last two corps being under Major-General Hooker. The 14th was commanded by Major-General George H. Thomas, who was next in rank to General Grant, until the arrival of Major-General W. T. Sherman, with reinforcements, in November.

There were three divisions in the 14th Corps: 1st division, Major-General Palmer; 2d, Major-General Phil. H. Sheridan; 3d, Major-General Thomas J. Wood; and three brigades in Wood's division—1st Brigade, Brigadier-General August Willich; 2d, Brigadier-General W. B. Hazen; 3d, Brigadier-General Samuel Beatty.

After the battle of Chattanooga, on the march to Knoxville, General W. T. Sherman was in command of all the forces going to the relief of Burnside. After getting there, the enemy having retreated, all his command returned, except the 4th Corps, Major-General Gordon Granger, which remained, and while there was in the Department of the Ohio, Major-General J. G. Foster commanding, until the reorganization in April, 1864, for the Atlanta campaign, when we were assigned to the garrison of Chattanooga, Major-General

James B. Steedman, commanding. It was composed as follows: 1st Separate Brigade — 8th Kentucky Infantry, 15th, 29th, 44th, 51st and 68th Indiana Infantry, 3d and 24th Ohio Infantry. Engineer Brigade — 18th Ohio Infantry, 13th, 21st and 22d Michigan Infantry. Pioneer Brigade — 58th Indiana Infantry, 1st and 2d Pontoon Battalion. In addition there was a large number of batteries of U. S. and other artillery.

INDIANA IN THE WAR.

From the Adjutant-General's Reports of Indiana, we have the following figures in regard to the number of troops furnished by Indiana:

	30 Days.	60 Days.	3 Months.	100 Days.	6 Mo.	1 Year.	3 Years.	Totals.
Infantry..	1,874	587	6,308	7,415	539	21,331	133,640	175,776
Cavalry...					203	104	21,298	21,605
Artillery.						207	10,779	10,886
Totals.	1,874	587	6,308	7,415	742	21,642	165,617	208,367

These forces were organized into one hundred and twenty-nine regiments of infantry, thirteen regiments of cavalry, one regiment of heavy artillery, and twenty-six batteries of light artillery, besides independent companies.

MISCELLANY.

The 1st, 2d and 3d Indiana Infantry were raised under the administration of Governor Whitcomb, in 1846, to serve in Mexico; and in 1847 the 4th and 5th were raised for the same service. To avoid historical confusion, when the Rebellion came on the new regiments were numbered, commencing with the 6th, Colonel T. T. Crittenden, which went to West Virginia, and on the 3d of June, 1861, took part in the first battle of the war, at Philippi. So, also, did the 7th Regiment, Colonel Ebenezer Dumont, and the 9th Regiment, Colonel R. H. Milroy. There were six regiments of three months' troops raised in Indiana under the President's first call for 75,000 volunteers, and the 11th, Colonel Lewis Wallace, was the last. So great was the enthusiasm that after filling the quota, enough more troops remained for five regiments, which were organized into the service of the State, May 11, with a surplus of six companies in camp. The 16th, Colonel P. A. Hackleman, was one of these regiments, and it was the first to march through Baltimore after the firing on the 6th Massachussetts Regiment, in April. It served to the end of their one year's enlistment, in

the Army of the Potomac. The regiment was then reorganized and mustered into the three years' service, August 19, 1862. The 37th Indiana Infantry was mustered in September 18, 1861, for three years; the 54th Indiana Infantry, in October, 1862, for one year; the 68th Indiana Infantry, August 19, 1862, for three years; the 123d Indiana Infantry, March 9, 1864, for three years; the 134th Indiana, May 25, 1864, for one hundred days; the 19th Indiana Battery, August 5, 1862, for three years; and the 22d Indiana Battery, December 15, 1862, for three years.

THE LOSSES IN THE WAR.

The following extract from a speech delivered at Chattanooga, by General Joseph E. Wheeler, will serve to show the magnitude of the war of the Rebellion:

It takes but a few figures to show that it was one of the greatest and most momentous wars ever waged among civilized people. Official returns show that about 2,900,000 soldiers enlisted during the war, Reports show that the Northern and Southern armies met in over 2,000 skirmishes and battles. In 148 of these conflicts, the loss on the Federal side was over 500 men, and in at least ten battles over 10,000 men were reported lost on each side. The killed, wounded and missing on both sides, reported at Shiloh, numbered 24,000; Antietam, 38,000; Stone River, 37,000; Chancellorsville, 28,000; Gettysburg, 54,000; Chicamauga, 33,000.

Official statistics show that of all the men enlisted,

there were killed in battle, during the war, 44,238; died of wounds, 49,205; died of disease, 186,216; died of unknown causes, 24,184—total 303,843. To this number should be added, first, 26,000 men who are known to have died while in the hands of the enemy, as prisoners of war, and many others in the same manner, whose deaths are unrecorded, and thousands who died at home on furlough, and were buried in private cemeteries.

The Nation's dead are buried in seventy-three National cemeteries, of which only twelve are in the Northern States. Among the principal ones in the North are Cypress Hill, with its 3,786 dead; Finn's Point, N. J., which contains the remains of 2,644 unknown dead; Gettysburg, Pa., with its 1,967 known and 1,608 unknown dead; Mound City, Ill., with 2,505 known and 2,721 unknown graves. In the South, near the scenes of terrible conflicts, are located the largest depositories of the Nation's heroic dead, viz.: Chattanooga, Tenn., (seventy-five acres), 12,843, from 655 regiments and twenty-three States, of which 5,167 are unknown; Nashville, Tenn., 16,526, of which 4,700 are unknown; Stone River, Tenn., 6,121, of which 2,474 are unknown; seven cemeteries in Tennessee, (over 233 acres) in which are buried 56,817 soldiers. In all, the remains of *three hundred thousand men*, who fought for the stars and stripes, find guarded graves in our National cemeteries. Two cemeteries are mainly devoted to brave men who perished in the loathsome prisons of the same name—Andersonville, Ga., which contains

13,714 graves, and Salisbury, N. C., with its 12,126 dead, of whom 12,032 are unknown. In all the cemeteries 145,000 rest in graves marked unknown.

ENLISTMENT BY STATES.

The following table shows the number of men furnished by each State:

Maine	71,745
New Hampshire	34,605
Vermont	35,256
Massachusetts	151,785
Rhode Island	24,711
Connecticut	52,270
New York	455,568
New Jersey	79,511
Pennsylvania	366,326
Delaware	13,651
Maryland	49,730
West Virginia	30,003
District of Columbia	16,872
Ohio	317,133
Indiana	195,147
Illinois	258,217
Michigan	90,119
Wisconsin	96,118
Minnesota	25,024
Iowa	75,860
Missouri	108,778
Kentucky	78,540
Kansas	20,097
Total	2,653,062

LOSSES IN THE REVOLUTIONARY WAR.

As the following table will show, there were greater losses in one battle of the Rebellion than in all the battles of the American Revolution, on both sides:

	Dates and Months.	British Loss.	American Loss.
Lexington	April 19, 1775.	274	84
Bunker Hill	June 17, "	1,054	453
Flatbush	Aug. 12, 1776.	400	200
White Plain	Aug. 26, "	400	400
Trenton	Dec. 25, "	1,060	9
Princeton	Jan. 5, 1777.	400	100
Hubbardstown	Aug. 17, "	180	800
Bennington	Aug. 16, "	800	100
Brandywine	Sept. 11, "	500	1,200
Stillwater	Sept. 17, "	600	350
Germantown	Oct. 6, "	600	1,200
Saratoga	Oct. 17, "	*5,752	
Red Hook	Oct. 22, "	500	32
Monmouth	June 25, 1778.	400	130
Rhode Island	Aug. 27, "	200	211
Briar Creek	March 30, 1779.	18	400
Stony Point	July 15, 1780.	600	100
Camden	Aug. 16, "	375	600
King's Mountain	Oct. 1, "	950	96
Cowpens	Jan. 17, 1781.	800	72
Guilford C. H	March 25, "	532	400
Hobkirk's Hill	April 25, "	400	400
Eutaw Springs	Sept. "	1,000	550
Yorktown	Oct. 19, "	*7,072	
Total		24,851	7,897

*Surrendered.

COMPARATIVE LOSSES.

Waterloo was one of the most desperate and bloody fields chronicled in European history; and yet Welling-

ton's casualties were less than twelve per cent.—his losses being, 2,432 killed and 9,528 wounded out of over 100,000 men. At Shiloh one side lost in killed 9,740 out of 34,000, while their opponents report their killed and wounded at 9,616, making the casualties about thirty per cent. At Lodi, Napoleon lost one and one-quarter per cent., and at the great battles of Marengo and Austerlitz, sanguinary as they were, Napoleon lost an average of less than fourteen and one-half per cent. At Magenta and Solferino, in 1859, the average loss of both armies was less than nine per cent. At Kœnigratz, in 1866, it was six per cent. At Werth, Mars-le-Tour, Gravelotte and Sedan, in 1870, the average was less than twelve per cent.

At Perryville, Stone River, Chicamauga, Atlanta, Gettysburg, Mission Ridge, the Wilderness and Spottsylvania, the loss frequently reached (and sometimes exceeded) forty per cent., and the average of the killed and wounded on the one side or the other was over thirty per cent.

From the discovery of America to 1861, in all wars with other nations, the record gives the deaths in battle of but ten American Generals; while from 1861 to 1865, both sides being opposed by Americans, more than one hundred general officers fell while leading their triumphant columns.

In the battle of Hohenlinden, which was the ground work for the following stirring poetry, General Moreau lost but four per cent., and the Archduke John lost

but seven per cent., in killed and wounded. Americans would scarcely call this a lively skirmish.

* * * * * * *

> "Where rushed the steeds of battle driven,
> And louder than the bolts of heaven,
> Far flashed the red artillery;
> Where furious Frank and fiery Hun
> Were mixed in sulphurous canopy;
> Where rushed to glory or the grave,
> And Munich all her banners waved,
> And charged with all her chivalry;
> Where snow became their winding sheet,
> And every turf beneath their feet
> Became a soldier's sepulchre."

The following extract is from an oration by General J. D. Cox, at Chicago:

A full knowledge of all the circumstances of war will only make a civilized nation strive more wisely for peace: and as the improvements in the efficiency of arms make nations more careful how they invoke the judgment of the god of battles, so an acquaintance with all the cost and all the horrors which follow in the train of great military expeditions, may make a people more and more averse to strife unless the cause be one as holy as that which called upon us in 1861—the preservation of the Nation itself! With all our sad experience of comrades fallen, of a country desolated, of homes destroyed, of labors and sufferings of all kinds endured, and of unexampled burdens to be borne, I believe there is no veteran who would hesitate to draw the sword again to avert a like peril from our land.

THE BATTLE OF MISSIONARY RIDGE.

BY GENERAL H. V. BOYNTON.

A storming party twenty thousand strong, from the Army of the Cumberland, stood facing Missionary Ridge. For two days great battle scenes had been passing before the eyes of the men composing it. Half of them had taken part in that swift advance from Chattanooga, which, almost before the enemy had corrected the mistake of regarding it as a general review, swept a mile out into the plain and captured his entire line of advanced works. All of them had stood the day before watching and cheering as Hooker's line on Lookout, radiant with the flag they worshiped, swept around the point of the mountain, and seemed to roll over the lines of the stars and bars and crush them backward and down the steeps. The cheers of the armies below, the music of all their bands, and the rush and roar of the battle on the slopes above, were yet ringing in their ears, and to those living are ringing still. All of them at daybreak had gazed intently toward Lookout to see if it could be determined who held the summit. And all of them, with brimming eyes and thankful and exultant hearts, had cheered and cheered, and cheered till voices failed, that banner of stars, which, as the sun touched the point of the mountain, stood revealed on its highest crag.

And now, after this long and exciting waiting,

stirred to the depths of soldier feeling by the swift and magnificent sweep of the spectacle which they had witnessed, they stood a storming army facing the slopes of Missionary Ridge. From earthworks at its base, from a second line half-way to the summit, and from works along the crest, an army of rebellion waited under the shelter of half a hundred guns, and waved its battle flags in defiance. It was a mile across the plain to the lower line of earthworks. It was a half mile further up the rough and tangled slopes. Eighty-seven Union regiments, each with its flags, for most carried two, stood formed in two lines with proper reserves, most impatiently awaiting the signal for advance. At length it came—six guns from Orchard Knob—boom—boom—boom— boom — boom — boom! Who of those who heard will ever forget? As the firing progressed every soldier with that bated breath had counted one — two — three—four—five—six—with only pause enough to see that no seventh followed, and that this was really the signal of six guns, and instantly all rifles went up to the shoulder and flags to the belts of the standard-bearers. All officers cried "forward," and with mighty cheers those double lines of blue, so clearly marked and still further relieved by their beautiful flags and gleaming rifles, burst forward into the plain as if shot arrow-like from the terrible restraint which had held them so long. The Union front was two miles and a half. There were four divisions; in all eleven brigades. This magnificent array had scarcely advanced into the plain from the light

timber which partially concealed it, before the summit of the ridge was wreathed with the smoke of fifty guns, and the air was alive with missiles raining on the attacking columns. But there was no wavering in that long line of flags, or in the ranks of the army that was pushing them forward. In ten minutes the lines were under musketry fire from the works at the base of the ridge. Though the list of Union killed and wounded grew at every pace, those lines swept up to and over the earthworks at the foot of the slopes, and under the batteries above. With a brief pause at points for correcting the lines, the climbing of the heights began. Shell and canister, and the sleet of rifles poured down from the crest, but only the killed and wounded were halted by any or all of these. The lines swept on and up, and that wonderful and never-to-be-forgotten panorama of the flags unfolded itself in the clear sunlight. Let the reader look at it from among the wounded toward the base of the ridge, who seemed to forget even home and eternity, which was so near, as they lay there gazing on the wonderful scene and cheering their comrades on.

The lines had scarcely begun the ascent when far as the eye could reach the flag-bearers were rushing in advance, and each regiment crowding towards its colors, had taken the shape of an inverted V, the flags at the angle, and these wedge-shaped battalions were cleaving their way under murderous fire toward the summit. The eye could not run down the lines without seeing a flag-bearer fall. For some regiments five

or six were killed or wounded before the flag of stars took the place of stars and bar on the crowning works of the ridge. The whole face of the mountain — for it was little less — was soon covered with soldiers in blue. The front lines were rushing for the top. The second lines and the reserves broke against the entanglement at the base, and the rocks, ravines and fallen timber in their course. And yet the general formation was preserved. Baird's men on the left, were climbing where horses could not be ridden. Wood, to the left, was under the fiercest fire, but his flags went on with all the rest. Sheridan and his staff were in full view of both armies, riding in advance with his headquarter colors straight on the batteries near Bragg's headquarters; and the flags of Johnson on the extreme left showed that there also the flood-tide of the blue sea of Union men with all its flags advanced was about to pour over the crest.

One moment, and the rebel battle flags waved everywhere along the summit, the stars and bars floated from the staff at Bragg's tents; fifty guns poured death upon that storming army, and rifle pits, filled with the men who made those splendid assaults on the Union lines at Chicamauga, flamed unceasingly in the faces of the men who were pushing and supporting the flags. The next, Baird's troops had scaled the cliff which ran along the summit above them. Wood had carried the crest along his whole front. Sheridan with his staff and his lines was among the guns on top, and Johnson beyond stood in the rebel

works. From right to left the sun shone clear and bright only on the flags before which the banners of treason had fallen. Fifty-five minutes had passed from the firing of the signal guns. It was exactly an hour to the time when the cheers of victory had run down the Union lines — Only an hour with the flags! How the mind rushes on to all the other hours, and days, and months, and years in which the Union armies advanced their own banners and captured the emblems of treason!

More than one-fifth of that storming party were killed and wounded. A single division lost one hundred and twenty-three officers and 1,179 men. Another lost over 2,000. There were twenty-five rebel flags captured. Behold the cost! Is it strange that the men who took them, and the loyal communities who sent these soldiers forth and sustained and encouraged them, are stirred to the depth of their souls with emotions which can not be controlled when sacrilege is attempted with such trophies? It would be a sad day for the Republic if such feelings were dead.

THE 68TH REGIMENT'S FLAG.

Colonel John S. Scobey, in answer to a letter of inquiry, writes as follows from Greensburg, Ind., under date of June 2, 1887:

* * * "Of the flag of which you write (the one returned to Mrs. E. H. M. Berry), it was presented to the regiment by the ladies here, the presentation speech being made by Mrs. Berry, and she also made

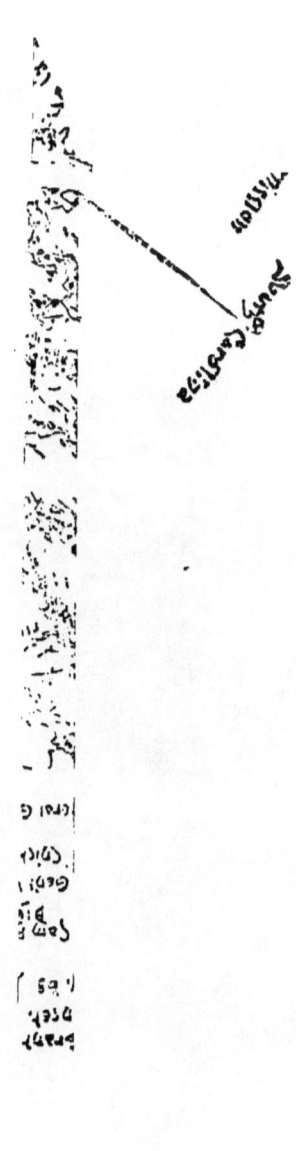

THE REGIMENTAL FLAG.   39

the reception speech on its return. I have no copy of the remarks I made, nor of hers. Her speeches were very nice and eloquent. At the capture of Munfordville, in September, 1862, Colonel King took the flag from the staff and wrapped it around his body, and there carried it until the regiment got to Indiana. And thus it was saved from going into the hands of the rebels. All honor to the memory of Colonel Edward A. King. He was a brave and good man."

Mrs. Berry, who has the flag in her keeping, says that the money to buy the flags for the 7th and 68th was made up by a popular twenty-five cent collection in one day, at Greensburg, and that Mr. Forsythe bought both the flags, paying out of his own money any balance.

BIOGRAPHY.

COL. EDWARD A. KING.

[From the Biographical Cyclopædia of Distinguished Men of the State of Ohio.]

BY J. FLETCHER BRENNAN.

Edward A. King, who, as Colonel commanding the 1st Brigade of a division of the 14th Army Corps, was killed at the battle of Chicamauga, was born in Cambridge, Washington county, State of New York, in 1814. He was a descendant of James King, who settled in Suffield, Connecticut, in the year 1678. In early life he emigrated with his father's family to Ohio, where he subsequently studied law at Columbus and Cincinnati. But his predilections were decidedly of a military character, and during the Texan struggle for independence, he raised a company in the city of New Orleans, reported with his command to General Sam. Houston, and served in Texas until her independence was acknowledged. In this service his health became seriously impaired, and he returned to the United States, and took up his permanent residence in Dayton, Ohio.

In 1844 he went to Europe, where he remained until the breaking out of the war with Mexico, when he returned and offered his services to his country. President Polk appointed him captain in the 15th Regiment, United States Infantry, in which he served with distinction until the close of the war. He was with a detachment of his regiment and other troops, under command of Colonel McIntosh, in the severe guerrilla fight at Tolome, on the 6th of June, 1847; and in the fight under General Cadwallader, at the National bridge, June 11 and 12, 1847. He afterward participated with his regiment in the several bloody battles in the valley of Mexico, under General Scott, resulting in the capture of the City of Mexico. Colonel George W. Morgan commanded the regiment, and General Franklin Pierce the brigade, to which he belonged. After the treaty of peace with Mexico, Colonel King returned to Ohio, and in the spring of 1849, crossed the plains to California. Returning again, he was appointed postmaster at Dayton by President Pierce, and after the election of President Buchanan the position was again conferred upon him. So general was the satisfaction given in the discharge of his official duties, there was no competing applicant for the place. For many years, both before and after the Mexican war, Colonel King took an active part in all important matters connected with the militia of Ohio, and at the outbreak of the late War of the Rebellion, was Colonel of the 1st Regiment of Ohio Volunteer Militia, at Dayton, which city sent several organized and equipped companies into the field.

On the 17th of April, 1861, the day of the proclamation of the Governor of Ohio, calling loyal men to the defence of their country, Colonel King reported to Governor Dennison, and was immediately placed in command of Camp Jackson (near Columbus), then in a chaotic state, but which he soon reduced to form and discipline. He was subsequently transferred to Camp Chase, where he remained in command until, without solicitation on his part, he was appointed by President Lincoln Lieutenant-Colonel of the 19th Regiment United States Infantry. His headquarters were established at Indianapolis, where he proceeded to organize and superintend the recruiting of the regiment. While thus engaged, in the summer of 1862, when Kirby Smith invaded Kentucky, he took, at the request of Governor Morton, the temporary command of the 68th Regiment Indiana Volunteers (all new recruits) to resist the enemy. After a brief but severe campaign, he was sent to the assistance of Colonel Wilder, at Munfordville, Ky., and participated in that severe engagement. He was surrendered with his regiment and the other bodies of Federal troops, to an overwhelming force. It fell to his lot to deliver the surrender to the enemy, and the rebel General Buckner, who, while a prisoner of war, had been in his charge at Indianapolis, treated him with marked consideration. A beautiful incident connected with this capitulation was afterward developed. When the 68th Regiment was sent to the field, the ladies of Greensburg, Ind., presented it with a rich silken flag. It was highly prized, and the regi-

ment was loath to part with it. When it was determined to surrender, Colonel King wrapped the precious colors around his body, under his clothing. He wore them thus for thirteen days, saved them, and the regiment bore them in the bloody fight at Chicamauga. After the 68th Indiana Regiment was exchanged, the command was again pressed on Colonel King, who (obtaining leave from the War Department for the purpose) accepted it.

In the Summer of 1863, his health, which had been seriously impaired, becoming somewhat re-established, he again took the field, and was placed in command of the 1st Brigade, General Reynold's division, 14th Army Corps, commanded by General Thomas, at the head of which he distinguished himself during the advance from Tullahoma to northwestern Georgia, and in the effective crossing of the Tennessee River (his brigade being the first troops to cross), and capture of Shellmont, in the face of the enemy. At the battle of Chicamauga his brigade was conspicuous for its high state of discipline and gallantry. He fell at the close of the second day's fight, shot in the forehead by a sharpshooter, when our army fell back upon Chattanooga. Colonel King's body was buried outside our lines, and the grave carefully marked, and after the battle of Mission Ridge his remains were recovered and brought home to Dayton for interment. On the 29th and 30th of January, 1864, his body lay in state at the courthouse, in a handsome casket, resting on a catafalque, prepared for the occasion by the members of the Day-

ton Light Guard, with which the deceased had long been associated. The four sides of the catafalque were respectively inscribed: "Contreras," "Molino del Rey," "Chepultepec," "Chicamauga." It was visited by thousands, who called to pay their respects to the memory of the gallant dead. On the 31st of January his body was buried at Woodland Cemetery with military honors, the 2d Regiment Ohio Volunteer Militia acting as escort. The pall-bearers were composed of officers of the Mexican War and the War of the Rebellion. The funeral was by far the largest ever before witnessed in Dayton.

Few men ever more thoroughly commanded the confidence and respect of all who knew him than Colonel Edward A. King. He was a gallant soldier, a ripe scholar, a good citizen, a man of noble character and high sense of honor, and whose love of country was so true that he laid down his life at her call. Just before his death he had been promoted to the Colonelcy of the 6th Regiment United States Regular Infantry.

The following tribute to Colonel King was written by his friend, General H. B. Carrington, of the Regular Army, on the receipt of the news of his death:

Edward A. King has fallen in battle. His memory should be held precious in Indiana as in Ohio. He was a soldier by taste as well as profession. In the Mexican War he held a Captain's commission in the 15th Infantry, and achieved distinguished mention. Return-

ing to his home at Dayton, Ohio, he identified himself with the State Militia, and organized the first complete and fully uniformed regiment under the State system. Its companies started for Washington, leaving Columbus, Ohio, within sixty hours after notice of the first call for 75,000 men. He was at once selected by the Ohio military authorities as the proper person to command Camp Jackson, the camp of rendezvous and drill for the nine regiments of Ohio three month's men, called into service by the act of the General Assembly of that State. At a time when experience in the management of large camps was a novelty, Colonel King earned just credit in the display of unusual talent for the position; and it is worthy of note that western Virginia was saved, and the lines of railroad to Grafton were occupied by these troops, assisted by the 1st Virginia, before the United States troops at Camp Dennison had even received arms. Colonel King's merit was rewarded by a commission as Lieutenant-Colonel of the 19th Regular Infantry, with headquarters at Indianapolis. In the Kirby Smith campaign, when the Ohio border as well as the State of Kentucky was in danger, Colonel King sought active duty. Leave of absence was obtained for the purpose, and Governor Morton gave him the Colonelcy of the 68th Regiment Indiana Volunteers. He took command on the evening of August 19, 1862; his regiment was mustered into service, received the bounty, and marched the same night. At Munfordville his cool gallantry was the theme of high encomium. During the parole of his

regiment, its camp was a model of discipline and good order, and he afterward joined the Army of the Cumberland with the eager desire to share its fortunes. Although just recovering from a severe attack of typhoid fever, he led his brigade into action with his usual address and spirit.

He has fallen! One who has been closely associated with him in military duties for seven years can share the grief of nearer friends in this bereavement, but cannot find words to fill the measure of the loss. Edward A. King was a true gentleman. His sense of honor was delicate and constant, and in every civil and social relation, he was true to family, friend and country. Instinctively generous and pure, no person ever came in his contact without feeling, at once, that a true man was found. Confidence in him was never misplaced. Appeals to his justice, his integrity, his honor, brought quick and true response. They who met him, honored, and they who knew him, loved.

Edward A. King was a soldier. Cool, dispassionate and clear-headed, he was no less prompt, keen and energetic. Danger only lifted him into the sphere of life he loved. No disaster disheartened; but, when most tried, his fitness for the profession of arms shone forth most clearly. He was a strict disciplinarian, an exact scholar, a martinet in the enforcement of regulations and tactics; but he had also a large heart, and commanded the affection of his men, while he shaped them by perfect models and incited them to personal development in the art of war. His personal character

gave weight to his authority, while his devotion to the comfort and well-being of his men, gave new zest to their obedience. Such was Edward A. King. They that knew him will fill up this faint outline with numberless characteristics that endeared him. Those little facts in his daily life that most of all mark the man, are lodged in the breasts of those he loved, and their balm will be grateful, while years go by; but the world's heart can only feel their preciousness through those uncounted tender memories that have made the interior life of departed ones most sacred to mourning friends.

The following is an extract from a letter of General Thomas J. Wood, concerning Edward A. King's death, written to his wife from Chattanooga, Tenn., September 23, 1863:

"It is with great grief I have to give you the sad intelligence of the death of your Uncle Edward. He was killed in the great battle of Sunday. I met General J. J. Reynolds on Monday, and learned from him the circumstances of his death. At the time he was killed there was a perfect cessation in the fighting. Your uncle walked to the front to look out for movements of the enemy, when he was shot by a sharpshooter. The ball struck him just above the right eye, passed through his brain, and of course killed him instantly. General Reynolds had his body brought away in the retreat Sunday night, and buried at Rossville, six miles from Chattanooga. The General told

me he had the grave distinctly marked, so that when there is an opportunity the body can be removed."

Extract from a letter of Chaplain David Monfort:
"The fearless, brave, noble, patriotic Colonel Ed. A. King, the glory of whose achievements should be a household word, the impress of whose masterly skill and discipline has given glory to our regiment. We who knew him, loved him. My children name the name of Colonel Ed. A. King with respect and affection; for he was a protector of their home and country I would teach others the debt of gratitude we owe such men, who have sealed the covenant of liberty with their blood."

The body of Colonel King was the only one brought from the fatal field of Chicamauga, on the night of the 20th of September, 1863. "He saved their flag, and they saved his body!"

The following is from the Dayton, Ohio, *Transcript*, of 1847:
"Captain King's Company of Volunteers from Dayton, had the honor of being the first company of the "ten regiments" which landed at Vera Cruz. The company arrived there on the 24th of May, and were to have taken up their march for Jalapa and Pueblo on the 26th."

COLONEL DANIEL W. McCOOK.

Colonel Daniel W. McCook commanded the brigade in which our regiment served, from January to May, 1863. He was the sixth son of Major Daniel W. McCook, who entered the service at the age of sixty-five, and was killed at Buffington Island, Ohio River, leading Ohio Militia in defence of his State against Morgan's raiders. The eldest son was Latimer McCook, surgeon of the 31st Illinois Regiment. He was badly wounded, and served until the end of the war. The next younger, Colonel George W. McCook, took three Ohio regiments to the field, and finally a fourth, which he commanded until the close of the war. The next son, John J. McCook, was a midshipman, and died on the U. S. ship of the line Delaware, and was buried at Rio Janeiro. The next brother was the famous General Robert L. McCook. In 1861 he was a partner at law with Judge J. B. Stallo, at Cincinnati, now Minister to Italy. He entered the army at the first call for troops, and raised and commanded the 9th Ohio. He commanded a brigade in the division of General George H. Thomas, was wounded in the battle of Mill Springs, Ky., and killed near Athens, Ala., by guerrillas, while sick, riding in an ambulance. The fifth son was Major-General Alexander M. McCook. He was a graduate from West Point in 1852, served in Indian wars on the frontier with distinguished bravery, and during the War of the Rebellion was five times brevetted in the Regular

Army for "gallant and meritorious conduct." Colonel "Dan.," the sixth son, was in 1861 a partner at law with W. T. Sherman and General Thomas Ewing, at Leavenworth, Kan. He was a Captain in the 1st Kansas Infantry in the three months' service, afterwards Captain and A. A. G. of the 2d Division, Army of the Ohio, during the Shiloh and Corinth campaign. In 1862 he was commissioned Colonel of the 52d Ohio Regiment, and at Perryville commanded a brigade in Sheridan's division. He was killed in the assault on Kennesaw Mountain, while leading his brigade on a charge. His was a brilliant career, as a soldier and a leader. He was made a Brigadier the day he was killed. The seventh brother, Edwin S. McCook, entered the army in 1861, as Captain in the 31st Illinois Regiment. He was afterwards Colonel and brigade commander in the Army of the Tennessee, and was wounded half a dozen times. The eighth son was Charles M. McCook. He left Gambier College and entered the army at the age of sixteen. He went with the 2d Ohio Regiment, and was killed at Bull Run in July, 1861. The ninth brother was John J. McCook. He left Gambier College and enlisted at the age of fifteen, as a private in the 19th Ohio Regiment, and served in West Virginia. Afterwards he was appointed a Lieutenant of Ohio Cavalry, and later Captain and Aid-de-Camp to Major-General T. L. Crittenden. He fought in the campaigns of the Army of the Cumberland and Army of the Potomac, and was wounded at Cold Harbor. Every one of these McCooks, father

and sons, was a Douglas Democrat, and every one served in the Army or Navy.

GENERAL AUGUST WILLICH.

He was born in 1810, at Gorzyn, Prussia. His father was a Captain of Hussars, in the Prussian service during the Napoleonic war of 1813 and 1815, was wounded and placed on the retired list, and died when August was three years old, when he found a home in the house of the famous theologian Schleiermacher, a distant relative. Twelve years old, he entered the school of cadets at Potsdam. At fifteen he graduated and went to the "School of War," at Berlin. When eighteen years old (1828) he received his commission as 2d Lieutenant of Artillery. In 1841 he was made Captain of Artillery. Up to 1848, when he resigned his commission, he had taken active part in all the campaigns for twenty years. In the Revolution of 1848 he joined with Sigel, Carl Schurz, Hecker, and others, and took a foremost part in that excited, bloody, courageous struggle to revolutionize Germany, and to proclaim and establish a Republic. The noble attempt failed, their armies were routed and its members fled to all parts of the world. Willich went to Switzerland, thence to England, where he remained until 1853, and then to America, where at the Brooklyn Navy Yard, he found employment as a carpenter. Soon his thorough knowledge became known, and he was enabled to enter the Coast Survey Service at Wash-

ington, under Captain Maffitt, who afterwards commanded the ironclad "Florida," in the Confederate Navy.

In 1858 he made the acquaintance of Judge Stallo, of Cincinnati, and was persuaded by him to come to that city and edit the *German Republican*, until 1861, when the war broke out, and he, with two hundred Germans, enrolled as privates in the 1st German Regiment of Cincinnati (9th Ohio.) Willich was appointed Adjutant by Colonel "Bob" McCook, and in May was commissioned Major. In August, 1861, he was appointed Colonel of the 32d Indiana Infantry, (a German regiment) by Governor Morton. At Rowlett's Station he met and defeated Terry's Texan Rangers in December. This victory brought him into public notice, and his career from then until the end of the war was as one of the heroes of the Army of the Cumberland. He was severely wounded twice, and was captured at Stone River. He was appointed Brigadier-General by President Lincoln, July 17, 1862. Willich remained with the Army of the Cumberland until the end of the war, in the last act of which drama—the "March to the Sea,"—he was as prominent an actor as he had been from the first. He returned to Cincinnati, where, in 1866, he was elected County Auditor, which office he held until 1869. At the outbreak of the Franco-German war, he was on a visit to his old home in Germany. He offered his sword and services to the King of Prussia; the same King, whom, when Crown Prince, he had twenty-one years before, actively opposed in arms

in the battle of Landau. His offer was not accepted, and he found consolation — then sixty years old — in attending a regular course of lectures on philosophy at the University of Berlin. He returned to this country, and went to St. Marys, Ohio, where he lived the quiet retired life of a philosopher until his sudden death, by paralysis, on the 23d of January, 1878, beloved, respected and mourned by all who knew him.

GENERAL JAMES BLAIR STEEDMAN.

James Blair Steedman was born in Northumberland County, Pennsylvania, July 29, 1817. While a boy his parents both died, and he was left with other children to struggle for their support. At fifteen he was apprenticed in a country newspaper office. In two years he became an efficient printer and went West. He was at work in the office of Prentice's Louisville *Journal* when the Texan War broke out, and he joined Sam. Houston's army in Texas. Afterward he returned to Ohio, bought a newspaper, married, was a contractor of work on the Wabash & Erie Canal, and also of the Toledo, Wabash & Western Railroad. In 1847 and 1848 he was elected for two terms to the lower house of the Ohio Legislature.

In politics he was a Democrat. The next year, when the gold fever broke out, he crossed the plains to California, but soon after returned to his old home in Ohio, and was elected a member of the Board of Public Works, for several terms. In 1857 he was

elected Public Printer by the Congress of the United States. In 1860 he was chosen a delegate to the National Democratic Convention, which first met at Charleston, South Carolina, and afterward adjourned to Baltimore, He was a firm supporter of Douglas throughout the long and bitter struggle. He was a Major-General in the Ohio Militia, and held the office until he took the field, at the head of a regiment in 1861. He was also the publisher of the *Times*, the only Democratic paper in Toledo, where he practiced law. The moment the news came that Fort Sumter had been fired on, his paper was ablaze with warlike ardor, and he began at once to raise the 14th Ohio Infantry, and within nine days after the surrender of Fort Sumter, his regiment was in camp at Cleveland, being drilled and organized. They fought at Philippi, Laurel Hill and Carrick's Ford in the three months' service. The regiment re-enlisted for the war, and in the Autumn of 1861 was sent into Kentucky. July 17, 1862, he was appointed Brigadier-General of Volunteers, and took part in the battle of Perryville. It was at the battle of Chicamauga that General Steedman displayed most conspicuously the energy, courage and tenacity which formed a part of his character. His division had been posted at Red House Bridge, and he was ordered to hold that point at all hazzards. The battle raged hotter and hotter, and no enemy appeared to threaten his position. He knew that the army was hard pressed. The fight on the 19th was indecisive. Next day Longstreet's Corps, fresh from Virginia, came

into action with fierce and relentless ardor. Soon the right of the Union Army was pierced, and the commander, carried away by the flying mass, retired to Chattanooga. The center and left, under General Thomas, held its own with indomitable tenacity. Again and again it repelled the fiercest assaults made upon it. At last, without any other orders than those which came to them from the sounds of battle, the Reserve Corps, Steedman's division leading, marched to the aid of the imperiled veterans, who were having a life and death struggle with the enemy. About 3 p. m. they came up on the right, where the contest was raging hottest, and at once, with loud cheers, rushed into the thickest of the fight. He drove the enemy from his position and occupied both the ridge and the gorge. Here the slaughter was frightful. The victory was won at a fearful cost, but the army was saved, and he won the title of "Old Chicamauga," and was promoted to be a Major-General.

In the reorganization which preceded the Atlanta campaign, General Steedman was assigned to the command of the District of the Etowah, including the lines from the Tennessee to the Etowah Rivers, with Chattanooga as the headquarters. It was a command which required the exercise of great energy, activity and skill; for on his success in maintaining the lines of communication depended not merely the welfare, but the very existence of the grand army under General Sherman. There was never a time during his four months campaign that the army wanted anything nec-

cessary for its operations. When it became evident, in November, 1864, that the rebel army under Hood, meant to invade Tennessee, General Steedman gathered together all the troops that could be spared in his district, and joined General Thomas at Nashville. In the battle of Nashville his troops opened the fight, and the next day was among the first to break over the enemy's works, when the rebel left gave way, in the afternoon, and pursued the retreating foe until after dark. His troops were made up in about equal numbers of white and colored regiments. He used to indulge in sarcastic laughter as he remembered his presence at the Charleston convention, and to wonder how his Southern Democratic friends would enjoy seeing him "fighting a nigger division." In the pursuit of Hood's army, he led his troops through a hard and difficult march to Tuscumbia, and then returned to Chattanooga. After the fighting was over, he was assigned to the command of the State of Georgia, holding his position until in July 1866, when he resigned. He was appointed by President Johnson Collector of Internal Revenue at New Orleans. After this he was elected for two years to the State Senate in Ohio. In 1873 he was a member of the constitutional convention of the State. In his last years he edited the Toledo *Democrat*, and was also chief of the police of that city at the time of his death.

Few men have had a wider or more varied public experience. His military career was especially brilliant, and whatever faults he may have had, he was, by nature, frank, generous, brave and earnest.

MAJOR-GENERAL JOSEPH J. REYNOLDS.

Major-General Joseph J. Reynolds, our Division Commander from March to October, 1863, and in the battles of Hoover's Gap and Chicamauga, was born in Kentucky. He graduated from West Point in 1843, and was an Assistant Professor there from 1846 to 1855. He was promoted 1st Lieutenant of the 3d Artillery in March, 1847; resigned, February 28, 1857; was Professor of Mechanics and Engineering in Washington University, St. Louis, from 1856, to 1860. When the Rebellion began he was in business at New Orleans, and his patriotism was aroused to the highest pitch by the scenes he witnessed. He was sought by Governor Morton, who appointed him Colonel of the 10th Indiana Infantry on the 27th of April. He was made a Brigadier-General of Volunteers by the President on the 17th of May, 1861, and Major-General of Volunteers, November 29, 1865.

General Reynolds was assigned to the command of the 1st Brigade of the Army of Occupation on the 24th of July, 1861, numbering about 6,000 men, and defeated General Lee in the Cheat Mountain Campaign. The great Confederate strategist was defeated in his combinations by the genius of General Reynolds. In November and December, 1862, he was in command of forces in Kentucky. In January, 1863, his division was ordered to Murfreesboro. In April, with a large force, he made a successful raid on the enemy, and in the

Summer and Fall campaign his division took a most active part. After the battle of Chicamauga, General Reynolds was Chief of Staff, with General George H. Thomas, in the Department of the Cumberland, from from October to December, 1863. He was assigned to the command of the 19th Corps, July 7, 1864, and organized the forces for the capture of Mobile and Forts Gaines and Morgan. He commanded the Department of the Arkansas from November, 1864, to April 25, 1866. March 2, 1867, he was brevetted Brigadier-General and Major-General in the U. S. Army, for services at Chicamauga and Missionary Ridge. He was made Colonel of the 26th U. S. Infantry, July 28, 1886, and transferred to the 3d Cavalry, December 16, 1870. He is now a General in the Regular Army.

MAJOR-GENERAL THOMAS J. WOODS.

Major-General Thomas J. Woods was our Division Commander from in October, 1863, to April, 1864. He was born in Munfordville, Ky., September 25, 1825. Graduated at West Point in 1845, being assigned to the Corps of Topographical Engineers, with orders to report to General Taylor at Corpus Christi, in Mexico. He took part in the battles of Palo Alto and Resaca de la Palma, and was especially commended in the official reports of General Taylor. At Monterey he was transferred to the 2d Dragoons. He was brevetted for gallant conduct at Buena Vista. From 1848 to

MAJ. GEN. THOS. J. WOOD.

MAJOR-GENERAL THOMAS J. WOODS.

1854 he served on the frontiers of Texas with his regiment—five years of the time as Adjutant. In 1855 he was transferred to the 1st Cavalry, as Captain, and served on the Western frontier and in Indian wars until 1859. Then, getting a leave of absence, he travelled a year in Europe. October 11, 1861, he was appointed Brigadier-General of Volunteers, ordered to report to General Sherman; and was given command of a division at Bardstown, Ky. He campaigned in eastern Kentucky and Tennessee. By rapid marching he was in the battle at Shiloh, on the 7th of April, 1862; was at Corinth, and campaigned in Mississippi, Tennessee and Kentucky, in pursuit of Bragg's army; at Perryville in the pursuit, his division holding its position at Stone River. The rebel General Polk, in his report of that battle, says: "The position was well selected and well defended by General Woods' division of the Federal army." General Woods was wounded by a rifle ball in the left foot about 10 a. m., on the 31st, but he remained on horseback, and did not leave the field until 7 p. m. He was then sent in an ambulance to Nashville, and detained from active duty about forty days. He was offered the command of that Post, but preferred to be with his division in active field duties. His division was the first to occupy Chattanooga, in September, 1863. At Chicamauga his horse was shot under him. Mounting an Orderly's horse, he placed himself at the head of his troops, and drove back the enemy, just before dark on Saturday. On Sunday, for six long hours the enemy assaulted his

division, and was repulsed. General Woods, with his division, advanced and captured Orchard Knob, November 23, 1863, being in the advance of the centre of the army until Missionary Ridge was gained, capturing many pieces of. artillery and hundreds of prisoners. Immediately after he went to the relief of Knoxville, and campaigned in east Tennessee during the winter, experiencing the severest weather, with limited protection and supplies, and undergoing many privations. In the Atlanta campaign, at Lovejoy's Station, September 2, 1864, General Wood was severely wounded by a rifle ball passing through his left foot. More than six months passed before he could walk without the aid of crutches. At Franklin, General Stanley being slightly wounded, General Woods took command of the 4th Corps, and in the great battle of Nashville he was assigned the most difficult work—that of attacking and carrying the enemy's centre. Never was an army so perfectly overthrown. The 4th Corps captured in the battle of Nashville twenty-four pieces of artillery and nearly 3,000 prisoners, and continued the pursuit over a hundred miles. He went with his corps to Texas in July, 1865, and later was given command of the Department of the Mississippi. Now, (July, 1887,) he is a Major-General in the United States Army, on the retired list, and resides at Dayton, Ohio.

MAJOR-GENERAL GEORGE H. THOMAS.

He was born in Southampton County, Virginia, July 31, 1816; and was appointed a Cadet to West

MAJOR-GENERAL GEORGE H. THOMAS. 61

Point from that State, in 1836. In 1840 he was commissioned 2d Lieutenant, 3d Artillery. He received brevets for gallantry in the wars against the Florida Indians in 1841 and 1849, and in the war against Mexico, in 1846-48, at Monterey and Buena Vista. He was instructor of artillery and cavalry in the Military Academy from 1851 to 1854; on frontier duty in California and Texas; and at the breaking out of the war, at the age of forty-five, he had arisen to the rank of Major of the 2d Cavalry. Albert S. Johnston was its Colonel, and Robert E. Lee, Lieutenant-Colonel. Earl Van Dorn was the other Major. How great should be his credit, that he stood fast by the Union amid such surroundings, and when his family and State ties had to be given up, and to take up arms against them?

He commanded a brigade July 2, 1861, in action at Hoke's Run, Virginia; was made Brigadier-General U. S. Volunteers, August 17, 1861, and sent to the Department of the Cumberland. January 19, 1862, at Hill Springs, Ky., he commanded and won the first complete victory of the war. He was commissioned Major-General April 25, 1862; commanded the right wing of the army before Corinth. His division was with Buell in Alabama, Tennessee and Kentucky. At Stone River he commanded the "centre," and in the middle Tennesse campaign; at Chicamauga the "left," and earned the title of the "Rock of Chicamauga." October 27, 1863, he was appointed Brigadier-General U. S. Army, and relieved General Rosecrans of the command of the department. He commanded the

"centre" in the battles about Chattanooga, taking Missionary Ridge. In the Spring campaign of 1864, Thomas' army comprised three-fifths of Sherman's active command, and assisted in the four months' fighting that ended when, at Jonesboro, his troops captured Atlanta. Sherman, when he decided to "march to the Sea," left him to contend with Hood's army. The battle of Nashville was his crowning glory. December 15, 1864, he was promoted to be Major-General in the United States Army.

From 1865 to 1869 he commanded several different departments. He wrote three weeks before he died, when asked to be a candidate for the Presidency: "My services are now, as they have always been, subject to the call of the Government in whatever military capacity I may be competent to fill, and will be cordially undertaken whenever called upon to render them. All civil honors and duties I shall continue to decline." He died at San Francisco on the 28 day of March, 1870, on duty in command of the Military Division of the Pacific.

ANTI-COMPROMISE RESOLUTIONS.

In February, 1863, nearly all the regiments of Indiana soldiers in Rosecrans' army adopted a strong series of resolutions against any armistice or compromise, to be sent to the General Assembly of Indiana, which was "wavering in the balance." For some reason the name of the 68th Regiment does not appear in the num-

ber signing the resolutions. February 22, 1863, at Nashville, Tenn., Major John S. Scobey read the resolutions to the regiment while on dress parade, and they were adopted without a dissenting voice. Colonel Edward A. King made an eloquent and patriotic speech, which was received with great applause, and our enthusiasm was aroused to a high pitch.

REGIMENTAL ROSTER.

68TH INDIANA INFANTRY.

Mustered Into the United States Service August 19, 1862.

FIELD AND STAFF.

Colonel—
    King, Edward A., mustered in Aug. 19, '62; from Lieut.-Col. 19th U. S. Infantry; killed in battle at Chickamauga, Ga., Sept. 20, '63.

Lieutenant-Colonels—
    Shaw, Benjamin C., mustered in Aug. 19, '62; was promoted from Major of the 7th Ind. Infantry; resigned June 1, '63, for disability.
    Scobey, John S., mustered in July 8, '63; resigned Nov. 13, '63, for disability.
    Espy, Harvey J., mustered in Nov. 14, '63.

Majors—
    Scobey, John S., mustered in Oct. 22, '62; promoted.
    Innis, James W., mustered in July 8, '63; resigned Aug. 13, '63.
    Finn, Edmund, mustered in Nov. 13, '63

Adjutant—
    Goodwin, Cyrus B., mustered in Aug. 19, '62.

Quartermasters—
    Miller, Elias W., mustered in Aug. 19, '62; resigned March 14, '64.
    Remy, William H., mustered in March 18. '64.

Chaplain—
    Monfort, David, mustered in Dec. 18, '62; resigned September 2, '63; disability.

Surgeon—
    Wooden, John L., mustered in Aug. 19, '62.

Assistant Surgeons—
    Hodgkins, Lewis W., mustered in Aug. 19, '62.
    Meredith, Marion, mustered in Dec. 6, '62.

COMPANY A.—From Decatur County

Captains—
    Scobey, John S., promoted Major.
    White, Giles E., mustered in Oct. 22, '62; promoted from 1st Lieut.

First Lieutenant—
    Jones, Reuben W., mustered in Oct. 22, '62; promoted from 2d Lieut.

Second Lieutenant—
    Bailey, Moses, mustered in Oct. 22, '62.

First Sergeant—
    Bailey, Moses, promoted 2d Lieutenant.

REGIMENTAL ROSTER.   65

Sergeants—
  Alley, Henry W., transferred to V. R. C.
  Vance, Edward A., mustered out June 20, '65, as 1st Sergeant.
  Paul, Francis M., mustered out June 20, '65, as private.
  Bird, William F., discharged Dec. 3, '62; disability.

Corporals—
  Sutfin, William P., killed at Chickamauga, Sept. 19, '63.
  Stagner, John W., discharged Oct. 28, '63; disability
  Alley, John S., mustered out June 20, '65, as Sergeant.
  McKinney, William, discharged Aug. 13, '63; disability.
  Drake, Gideon, discharged Dec. 9, '62; disability.
  Jones, John W., mustered out June 20, '65, as Sergeant.
  Cook, Ezekial R., mustered out June 20, '65, as Sergeant.

Musicians—
  Vance, William F., mustered out June 20, '65, Principal Musician.
  Swan, James C., mustered out June 20, '65.

Wagoner—
  Lemaster, Reuben, discharged Nov. 12, '62; disability.

Privates—
  Alley, James, discharged Dec. 8, '62, by civil authority.
  Armstrong, James W., transferred to U. S. A., Nov. 20, '62.
  Archcraft, Ivin, discharged Nov. 19, '62; disability.
  Barker, John, discharged Sept. 23, '63; disability.
  Belville, William, transferred to V. R. C., July 27, '63.
  Brooks, Nehemiah, discharged Dec. 23, '62; disability.
  Bruner, William, mustered out May 28, '65.
  Burns, John H., died at Richmond, Va., prison, Feb. 19, '64.
  Corl, Henry, discharged, disability.
  Chambers, George P., discharged May 30, '63; disability.
  Champ, Thomas, discharged May 30, '63; disability.
  Cheney, Frank, killed at Hoover's Gap, Tenn., June 24, '63.
  Clark, Albert, mustered out June 20, '65.
  Clever, Frederick, discharged March 24, '64; wounds.
  Cones, William H., mustered out June 20, '65.
  Dement, George G., died Dec. 14, '62.
  Dilks, Henry H., mustered out June 20, '65, as Corporal.
  Dilks, Leonard, discharged Sept. 9, '63; disability.
  Dougherty, Benjamin, mustered out June 20, '65.
  Davis, Isaac, mustered out June 20, '65.
  Druce, Levi, discharged Dec. 16, '62, by civil authority.
  Eggleston, John N., mustered out June 20, '65, as Corporal.
  Flowers, Thomas.
  Flowers, Alfred, discharged Sept. 25, '63; disability.
  Fortune, James, discharged Nov. 13, '62; disability.
  Gervon, Dudley, mustered out June 20, '65.
  Hannapry, James, mustered out June 20, '65.
  Hesler, Frank, mustered out June 20, '65.
  Hervey James H., discharged Nov. 14, ,63; disability.
  Hunt, Omer, mustered out June 20, '65, as Sergeant.
  Hurt, William, transferred to U. S. A., Dec. 19, '62.
  Jenkins, William, mustered out June 27, '65.
  Jones, David S., mustered out June 20, '65, as Corporal.
  Jones, Thomas W., mustered out June 20, '65.
  Kappas, John,
  Kitcher, William, transferred to V. R. C., Nov. 23, '63.
  Lane, Francis M., mustered out June 20, '65.
  Lawson, Nathan, mustered out June 20, '65.
  Lemasters, Fielding, transferred to V. R. C., April 22, '64; mustered out July 29, '65.
  Lewis, James, died at Deckard, Tenn., July 31, '63.
  Lewis, John, discharged Dec. 23, '62, by civil authority.
  Lowe, John, discharged Dec. 27, '62, by civil authority.

REGIMENTAL ROSTER.

Maple, Francis M., transferred U. S. A., Nov. 20, '62.
Maple, Jasper, mustered out June 20, '65.
Marlin, William, transferred Co. "F."
Matthews, John, transferred 19th U. S. Infantry.
McCune, George F., discharged Dec. 7, '62, by civil authority.
McCune, Robert, discharged Dec. 7, '62, by civil authority.
McShane, Frank, mustered out June 20, '65, as Corporal.
Miller, William, mustered out June 20, '65' as Corporal.
Mitchell, William B., discharged Nov. 19, '62; disability.
Myers, Harmon, discharged Dec. 26, '62, by civil authority.
Nisely, James R., mustered out June 20, '65, as Corporal.
Nolan, Joseph L., died at Louisville Ky., Sept. 26, '63.
Potter, William M. M., discharged Dec. 9, '62, by civil authority.
Renegan, John H., mustered out June 20, '65.
Rex, David, mustered out June 20, '65.
Scott, Joseph M., transferred 11th U. S. Infantry, Dec. 19, '62.
Sloan, James L., mustered out June 7, '65.
Spencer, James H., transferred 11th U. S. Infantry, Dec. 19, '62.
Wiley, Andrew J., mustered out June 7, '65.
Williams, John W., mustered out July 20, '65.
Williamson, Andrew, discharged Dec. 11, '62, by civil authority.
Wilson, Aaron, transferred V. R. C.
Woods, Cornelius, transferred 18th U. S. Infantry, Nov. 19, '62.
Woodford, Robert, died at Nashville, Tenn., Jan. 16, '84.
Wires, John, transferred 18th U. S. Infantry, Nov. 21, '62.
Recruits—
Bland, George W., transferred 44th Regiment, June 20. '65.
Eggleston, William H., mustered out July 5, '65.
Hooten, Thomas, died at Pennington Farm, Tenn., July 20, '63.
Hime, Samuel, died in Andersonville prison, July 14, '64.
Hainey, Thomas D., transferred 44th Regiment, June 20 '65.
Judd, George, mustered out June 20, '65.
Level, Solomon, mustered out July 5, '65.
McConnell, James, mustered out June 20, '65.
Rex, Emanuel, transferred 44th Regiment, June 20, '65.
Scott, William, transferred V. R. C.,; discharged Feb. 27, '65; disability.
Townsend, George W., transferred 44th Regiment, June 20, '65.
Thomas, William H., transferred 44th Regiment, June 20, '65.

COMPANY B.—From Ripley County, Versailles and Osgood.

Captains—
Boswell, Daniel, mustered in Aug. 19, '62; resigned March 24, '63; incompetency.
O'Connor, Hiram, mustered in May 1, '63; resigned Oct. 30, '63.
Wheeler, Charles C., mustered in Jan 1, '64; died Aug. 22, '64, of wounds, at Dalton, Ga.
Foreman, George W., mustered in Nov. 27, '64.
First Lieutenant—
Huffman, John W., mustered in Nov. 27, '64.
First Sergeant—
Dickerson, William S., discharged March 7, '63; disability.
Sergeants—
Sanders, John M., mustered out June 20, '65, as private.
Hyatt, James H., died at Nashville, Tenn., March 20, '63.
Jones, Joseph, transferred 1st U. S. Cavalry, Dec. 17, '62.
Mullen, Thompson D., transferred V. R. C.; wounds.
Corporals—
Wooley, Alfred M., mustered out June 20, '65.
Hancock, Francis M., mustered out June 20, '65.

REGIMENTAL ROSTER.

Foreman, George W., promoted 2d Lieutenant.
Albright, John, mustered out June 20, '65, as Sergeant.
Pendergast, Milton, mustered out June 20, '65, as 1st Sergeant.
Huffman, John W., promoted 1st Lieutenant.
Preble, James M., died at Indianapolis, Dec. 22, '62.
Hyatt, Calvin, mustered out June 20, '65.

Musicians—
Hair, William, mustered out June 20, '65, as Principal Musician.
Hair, Francis C., mustered out June 20, '65.

Wagoner—
Muir, Joseph H., mustered out June 20, '65.

Privates—
Atkinson, Andrew, discharged Dec. 5, '62, by civil authority.
Alcorn, John H., mustered out June 20, '65.
Atkinson, John M., discharged Dec. 17, '62; disability.
Boswell, Elijah, discharged March 5, '63; disability.
Black, William H., mustered out June 20, '65.
Borders, Augustus, discharged Dec. 18, '62, by civil authority.
Borders, Jacob, died at University Heights, Tenn., March 5, '63.
Boswell, William, mustered out June 20, '65, as Corporal.
Buckingham, Lewis, died at Nashville, Tenn., March 29, '63.
Bear, William, mustered out June 20, '65.
Black, Benjamin T., mustered out June 20, '65.
Brown, Oliver H., mustered out June 20, '65.
Brown, William, discharged May 20, '65; disability.
Breeden, Joseph A., killed at Chickamauga, Sept. 19, '63.
Cassidy, Stephen A., died at Indianapolis, Nov. 24, '62.
Cleaston, Harmon H., mustered out June 20, '65.
Colman, Daniel T., discharged; disability.
Carter, David, transferred to V. R. C., April 30, '64; mustered out June 30, '65.
Cady, David N., mustered out June 20, '65.
Cady, Andrew P., killed at Chickamauga, Sept. 20, '63.
Dermit, Josiah, discharged Dec. 18, '62, by civil authority.
Davis, Joshua, died Nov. 27, '63, wounds received at Chickamauga.
Fiedler, Ludwick E. H., died at Nashville, Tenn., Feb. 15, '63.
Folsom, James M., killed at Chickamauga, Sept. 19, '63.
Fergason, George H., died at Nashville, Tenn., March 5, '63.
Glaze, John W., deserted Nov. 3, '62.
Green, Richard L., transferred to V. R. C.
Gaddis, James G., discharged Nov. 19, '62; disability.
Hyatt, Starling, mustered out June 20, '65
Herndon, Thomas, mustered out June 20, '65.
Hardesty, Francis M., transferred to V. R. C.
Henderson, John died in prison at Richmond, Va.
Hontz, Godfried, mustered out June 20, '65, as Corporal.
Johnson, Wells, mustered out June 20, '65.
Jackson, Amos, discharged Sept. 5, '63; disability.
King, Cephas C., killed at Chickamauga Sept. 19, '63.
King, Peter B., died at Nashville, Tenn., June 4, '63.
Laswell, Thomas D., discharged June 20, '63; disabilty.
Lipperd, John W., mustered out May 31, '65.
Michael, Jacob, mustered out June 20, '65.
Moxley, Constant G., mustered out June 20, '65.
Martin, Patrick, mustered out May 31, '65
Martin, Jeremiah, died at Cowan, Tenn., Sept. 1, '63.
McCrede, William H., mustered out June 20, '65.
Morris, William, deserted Nov. 3, '63.
Miles, John L., mustered out June 20, '65.
Monroe, Allen W., discharged Nov. 10, '63; disability.
McKittrick, Robert, discharged April 19, '65; wounds.
Nicholas, Benjamin S., mustered out June 20, '65.

Nicholas, Philip P., mustered out June 20, '65, as Corporal.
Overturf, Samuel, transferred to 1st U. S. Cavalry, Dec. 17, '62.
Pullim, William, transferred to 1st U. S. Cavalry, Dec. 13, '62.
Parsons, Ephraim, mustered out June 20, '65, as Sergeant.
Rankin, Albert, died at Lebanon, Ky., Sept. 12, '62; accidental wounds.
Robertson, Mark, mustered out June 20, '65.
Robertson, Joseph, discharged March 22, '65; disability.
Rosety, Samuel, killed in railroad accident May 27, '65.
Rozzell, Elliott W., mustered out June 20, '65.
Ratakin, Jonathan, discharged Nov. 28, '64; disabilit.
Shaw, Wilson, discharged May 31, '63; disability.
Stark, William G., discharged Jan. 16, '63; di ability.
Stark, James, discharged Jan. 16, '63; disability.
Stewart, William, died at Murfreesboro, May 26, '63.
Simpson, Charles, died at Nashville, Tenn, Feb. 6, '65.
Stevens, Jacob, mustered out June 20, '65.
Smith, William F., transferred to U. S. Colored Troops Dec. 16, '62.
Stricklin, David, deserted Oct. 2, '62.
Sutton, Thomas W., mustered out June 20, '65, as Sergeant.
Turl, Joshua, killed at Chickamauga Sept. 20, '63.
Tyre, William, died at Indianapolis Dec. 19, '62.
Wooley, Daniel, died at Nashville. Tenn., Sept. 10, '63
Whitaker, Thomas, mustered out June 20, '65, as Corporal.
Wooley, Cory A., transferred to V. R. C, Feb. 15, '64.
Wooley, William B, transferred to V. R. C., Feb. 15, '64; mustered out June 30, '65.
Williams, Eli, mustered out June 20 '65.

Recruits—
Alcorn, William P., discharged Nov. 10, '63; disability.
Hyatt, James W., transferred to 44th Regiment June 20, '65.
Hyatt, Wilson, transferred to 44th Regiment June 20, '65.
Hodshier, Victor D., transferred to 44th Regiment June 20, '65
Jennings, Jesse, transferred to 44th Regiment June 20, '65.
Lattimore, John, transferred to 44th Regiment June 20, '65.
Short, Alfred P., transferred to 44th Regiment June 20, '65.

COMPANY C.—FROM FRANKLIN COUNTY, LAUREL AND METAMORA.

Captains
Smith, William H., mustered in Aug. 19, '62; resigned Nov. 17, '62.
Leeson, Richard L., mustered in Dec. 27, '62; promoted from 1st Lieutenant,
First Lieutenants—
Reese, John, mustered in Dec. 27, '62; killed in battle at Chattanooga, Tenn., Nov. 25, '63.
Kennedy, John R., mustered in Jan. 3, '64.
Second Lieutenants—
Kibbe, Moses H, mustered in Dec, 27, '62; resigned Feb. 18, '63,
Burkhart, John, mustered in May 1, '63; resigned Nov. 17, '63, for incompetency.
First Sergeant—
Kibby, Moses H., promoted 2d Lieutenant.
Sergeants—
Burkhart, John, promoted 2d Lieutenant.
Kennedy, John, promoted 1st Lieutenant.
Jinks, Richard, died at Nashville Tenn., April 9, '63.
Milton, Curry, mustered out June 5, '65, as Corporal.
Corporals—
Butsch, Thompson P., mustered out June 20, '65.

REGIMENTAL ROSTER. 69

McWhorton, Lynn, mustered out June 6, '65, as private.
Stally, Peter, mustered out June 6, '65, as Com. Sergeant.
Conner, Daniel H., died at Nashville, Tenn., March 16, '63.
Miller, Eliphalet B., mustered out June 20, '65, as Sergeant.
Burris, Charles W., mustered out June 20, '65.
Murry, Samuel J., transferred to V. R. C., ———, '63.
Doty, Daniel, mustered out June 20, '65.

Wagoner—
Ferris, James, discharged May 2, '63; disability.

Privates—
Allison, George W., deserted Nov. 28, '62.
Applegate, William H. H., deserted Jan. 10, '63.
Allison, William, discharged April 10, '63; disability.
Alley, Andrew, mustered out June 20, '65.
Abrahams, Benjamin, mustered out June 20, '65.
Applegate, James, discharged Dec. 16, '62, by civil authority.
Armstrong, William, discharged Dec. 8, '62, by civil authority.
Armstrong, Milton, discharged Nov. 12, '63; disability.
Bedoll, Alexander, discharged Dec. 30, '62, disability.
Blozier, George W., mustered out June 20, '65.
Bunyard, William W., mustered out June 20, '65, as Corporal.
Bunyard, Henry W., mustered out June 20, '65.
Brooks, David, transferred to V. R. C., ———, '63; mustered out July 5, '65.
Brooks, George, mustered out June 20, '65.
Brunger, Stephen, mustered out June 20, '65.
Brooks, Nicholas E., discharged Jan. 9, '64; disability.
Clark, Robert, transferred to V. R. C., ———, '64; mustered out June 30, '65.
Chapman, Neunham, discharged Dec. 11, '62, by civil authority.
Crowell, Harrison, mustered out June 20, '65.
Cooksey, James B., mustered out June 20, '65.
Collyer, Wesley, died at Indianapolis Aug. 8, '63.
Davis, Henry P., discharged Nov. 4, '62; disability.
Deamond, Conrad, mustered out June 20, '65.
Daniels, George W., mustered out June 20, '65.
Daniels, John W., mustered out June 20, '65.
Fey, Philip, mustered out June 20, '65.
Green, Jonathan, died at New Albany, Ind., Oct. 8, '62.
Gross, John, discharged July 23, '63; disability
Green, John, mustered out June 20, '65, as Corporal.
Gordon, William F., mustered out June 20, '65, as Q. M. Sergeant.
Green, George W., deserted Aug. 19, '62.
Gordon, Clinton, discharged Dec. 8 '62, by civil authority.
George, William, mustered out June 20, '65, as Sergeant.
Horsley, Isaac, mustered out June 20, '65, as Sergeant.
High, Edwin W., mustered out June 20, '65
Horny, Elisha, died at Chattanooga, Tenn., April 7, '64.
Hillman, Edwin, mustered out June 20, '65, as Corporal.
Johnson, Albert, discharged Nov. 24, '62, by civil authority.
James, William H. H., mustered out June 20, '65.
Johnson, James A., mustered out June 20, '65.
Jones, Samuel I., mustered out June 20, '65.
Kay, John L., died at Nashville, Tenn., Sept. 3, '63.
Langsley, Francis M., mustered out June 20, '65.
Lewis, Eliphalet, discharged Dec. 18, '62; disability.
Leish, Francis, died in rebel prison, Danville, Va., Dec. 7, '63.
Millan, John C., discharged Nov. 4, '62; disability.
Moslander, George, mustered out June 20, '65.
McGilin, James, mustered out June 20, '65.
Morford, Elisha, mustered out June 20, '65.
Milliner, Amos O., mustered out June 20, '65, as Corporal.

Osborne, James P., mustered out June 8, '65.
Pugh, George L., mustered out June 20, '65, as Sergeant.
Patterson, George E., deserted Nov. 12, '62.
Potts, Stephen M., mustered out June 20, '65.
Patterson, John, discharged Jan 15, '63; disability.
Patterson, William J., discharged March 26, '63; disability.
Ricord, Martin, mustered out June 20, '65.
Reed, Stewart, mustered out June 20, '65.
Smith, John H., discharged Dec. 30, '62, by civil authority.
Solyers, George D., discharged Dec. 20, '62, by civil authority.
Shafer, Claudius, mustered out June 20, '65.
Shafer, Ira, mustered out June 20, '65.
Sherwood, Francis M., mustered out June 20, '65, as Corporal.
Sutton, George, died at Chattanooga Jan. 26, '64.
Scott, Joel, mustered out June 7, '65
Swift, Richard, discharged Dec. 8, '62; disability.
Smith, Nathaniel, died at Chattanooga, Tenn., Jan. 20, '64.
Snyder, George, mustered out June 20, '65.
Vincent, William A., discharged May 31, '63; disability.
Walker, Alexander, discharged Dec. 18, '62, by civil authority.
Worden, Zenas M., mustered out June 25, '65.
Welsh, Joseph, died at Louisville, Ky., July 2, '63.
White, John L., died Sept. 25, '63; wounds.
Whitlock, Bailey J., mustered out June 26, '65,
Wilson, Squire H., discharged Nov. 24, '62; disability.
Wier, John, died Oct. 10, '62.
Wier, Jonathan, deserted Dec. 16, '62.
Worden, Isaac C., mustered out June 20, '65, as 1st Sergeant.
Wildridge, James, died at Indianapolis Nov. 24, '62.
Yates John P., discharged Dec. 18, '62, by civil authority.
Recruits—
Banes, Charles W., mustered out May 17, '65.
Bedoll, Alexander J., transferred to 44th Regiment, June 20, '65
Clark, James W., transferred to 44th Regiment, June 20, '65.
Chance, John W., transferred to 44th Regiment, June 20, '65.
Dunlop, John R., transferred to 44th Regiment, June 20, '65.
Dunlop, John, transferred to 44th Regiment, June 20, '65.
High, Jenks B., transferred to 44th Regiment, June 20, '65.
Murray, Coburn, transferred to 44th Regiment, June 20, '65.
Potts, James S., transferred to 44th Regiment, June 20, '65.
Reese, Ortho, transferred to 44th Regiment, June 20, '65.
Schillman, John, deserted May 1, '65.
Smith, William, deserted Jan. 12, '64.
Smith, George W., transferred to 44th Regiment, June 20, '65.
Tyner, George, transferred to 44th Regiment, June 20, '65.
Whitelock, Charles W., transferred to 44th Regiment, June 20, '65.

COMPANY D.—FROM RUSH COUNTY.

Captain—
Innis, James W., mustered in Aug. 19, '62; promoted Major June 2, '63; resigned Aug. 13, '63, and died soon after. He was Orderly Sergeant of Company F., 16th Indiana Infantry, in '61-2.
First Lieutenant—
Mauzy, James H., promoted Captain June 2, '63. Address: Rushville, Ind.
Second Lieutenant—
Beale, William, promoted 1st Lieutenant June 2, 63; wounded at Chickamauga Sept. 19, '63; honorably discharged May 20, '64. Address: Rushville, Ind.

REGIMENTAL ROSTER.

First Sergeant—
- Smith, James A., promoted to 1st Lieutenant, and transferred to Company F., 100th U. S. C. Infantry, in July '64; was wounded at Calhoun, Tenn., Dec. 27, '63; died in Tenn. since the war.

Sergeants—
- 2d. Cohn, Gabriel, mustered out. A money-making Jew, who removed south after the war, and assisted in restoring it to prosperity.
- 3d. Richie, George T., mustered out as private; killed by the falling of a tree March 20, '68. He was a Corporal in Company F., 16th Indiana Infantry, in '61-2.
- 4th. Burns, William, deserted Jan. 7, '63.
- 5th. Snider, George W., promoted Hospital Steward, Dec. 12, '62; mustered out as such. Address: Indianapolis, Ind.

Corporals—
- 1st. Richie, James W., mustered out as private; wounded and taken prisoner in the battle of Chickamauga, Ga., Sept. 19, '63; escaped from the rebels in South Carolina, while being transferred on the cars from Danville, Va., to Macon, Ga., and returned to his Company and Regiment at Chattanooga, Tenn., June 15, '64. He was in Company F., 16th Indiana Infantry, in '61-2. Address: Cambridge City, Ind.
- 2d. Innis, William, mustered out as private. Address: Milroy, Rush county, Ind.
- 3d. Woods, William, discharged Dec. 24, '62; disability.
- 4th. Smith, James W. C., discharged Nov. 18, '62; disability.
- 5th. Thomas, Daniel L., promoted 1st Sergeant Sept. 1, '64; 2d Lieutenant June 1, '65; not mustered; wounded at Chickamauga. Address: Rushville, Ind.
- 6th. Souder, William M., promoted Sergeant Nov. 1, '64; mustered out. Address: Kokomo, Ind.
- 7th. Caldwell, Harvey, wounded and taken prisoner in the battle of Chickamauga, Ga., Sept. 19, '63; was sent to Libby prison, Richmond, Va., Oct. 21, '63; exchanged Nov. 17, '63, and sent to St. Johns Hospital, Annapolis, Md.; the ball remains in his left lung; served the remainder of his time with Co. C., 17th V. R. C. Address: Rushville, Ind.
- 8th. Hurst, Isaac C., transferred to V. R. C., May 31, '64. Address: Frankfort, Ind.

Privates—
Aldridge, William F., mustered out. Address: Milroy, Rush county, Ind.
Alexander, James H., transferred to Invalid Corps July 1, '63; discharged Aug. 3, '63; disability. Address: Minneapolis, Minn.
Bramblett, Thomas E., transferred to 7th Regiment, V. R. C.; mustered out June 28, '65, at Washington, D C. Address: Milroy, Rush county, Ind.
Burns, Michael, deserted Aug. 20, '62
Brown, John D., promoted Corporal May 1, '65; mustered out.
Bosley, James R., wounded at Chickamauga and taken prisoner; mustered out. Address: Jonesport, Daviess county, Mo.
Bradburn, James, discharged May 18, '63, at Murfreesboro, Tenn.; disability.
Beetem, Hugh, wounded at Chickamauga; mustered out. Address: Detroit, Dakota.
Bodine, Samuel S., killed in battle at Mission Ridge, Chattanooga, Nov. 25, '63.
Bosley, Thomas, wounded in battle at Mission Ridge, Nov. 25, '63; discharged at Madison, Ind., Sept. 19, '64, on account of wounds. Address: Edinburg, Mo.
Billings, Abraham S., promoted Corporal Dec. 31, '62; missing in action in the battle of Chickamauga; he was shot in the abdomen, and likely died on the field.

REGIMENTAL ROSTER.

Baker, Pemberton S., deserted Sept. 7, '62.
Buzan, William H. C., wounded at Chickamauga, Ga., and taken prisoner Sept. 19, '63; discharged July 20, '64, at Columbus, Ohio. Address: Cicero, Hamilton county, Ind.
Chalfant, Wesley, discharged Sept. 8, '64, at Indianapolis; disability. Address: Elwood, Madison county, Ind.
Callender, John, died at Nashville, Tenn., April 21, '63; pneumonia.
Cobee, Benjamin F., mustered out. Address: Frankfort, Ind.
Conrad, Henry, discharged Aug. 23, '64, at Madison, Ind.; disability.
Delashmit, Noah, deserted Sept. 7, '62.
Dale, Isaac, wounded and taken prisoner at Chickamauga, Sept. 19, '63; mustered out; died about '85.
David, James B., wounded and taken prisoner at Chickamauga, Ga., Sept. 19, '63; died in rebel prison at Andersonville, Ga., March 19, '64.
Danner, William H., wounded and taken prisoner at Chickamauga, Ga., Sept. 19, '63; died in rebel prison at Richmond, Va., April 25, '64.
Delashmit, James T., deserted Dec. 1, '62.
Eagy, Charles, discharged Nov. 19, '62; disability; died about '68 or '69.
Earnest, Amos W., was detailed with Bridge's Battery, Illinois Light Artillery, in the Atlanta campaign; mustered out. Address: Arlington, Rush county, Ind.
Farlow, Alfred, discharged June 11, '63, at Nashville, Tenn.; disability. Address: Carthage, Mo.
Francis, John, promoted Corporal Nov. 1, '64; mustered out. Address: Sheridan, Hamilton county, Ind.
Fleehart, David S., promoted Corporal Sept. 1, '64; Sergeant Nov. 1, '64; mustered out; was in all the battles and all the marches with the Regiment. Address: Rushville, Ind.
Goodwin, Leander, promoted Corporal Nov. 1, '64; mustered out. Address: Curtis, Tipton county, Ind.
Griffin, William, killed in battle at Chickamauga, Ga., Sept. 19, '63.
Gates, Arthur J., promoted Corporal Dec. 31, '62; wounded at Chickamauga Sept. 19, '63; mustered out. Address: Homer, Rush county, Ind.
Grubb, Oliver J., discharged at Louisville, Ky., May 13, '63; disability. Address: Shelbyville, Ind.
Grisselback, Frank, wounded at Chickamauga; mustered out. Address: Alexandria, Madison county, Ind.
Hendricks, William, discharged March 21, '63, at Nashville, Tenn.; disability.
Junkin, Charles, mustered out. Address: Nebraska.
Junkin, Edward A., promoted Corporal; mustered out. Address: Arlington, Rush county, Ind.
Jones, Samuel B., wounded at Chickamauga; discharged July 29 '64; wounds and amputation. Address: Sweetwater, Tenn.
Lingenfelter, Deliscus, promoted Corporal Nov. 22, '62; Sergeant, Dec. 31, '62; 1st Lieutenant Aug. 28, '64. Address: Indianapolis, Ind.
Lester, Charles, promoted Sergeant Aug. 20, '62; mustered out. Address: Berea, Ky.
Lytle, John, discharged Dec. 9, '62, by civil authority; not of age— 18 years.
Lange, Walter S., died at Murfreesboro, Tenn., May 19, '63.
Liptrop, James R., deserted Dec. 27, '62.
Long, Charles, mustered out. Address: Milroy, Rush county, Ind.
Lee, Caleb C., died Sept. 21, '63; wounds received at Chickamauga, Sept. 19, '63.
Maxey, Mason, transferred to V. R. C., Jan. 14, '64. Address: Rushville, Ind.

REGIMENTAL ROSTER.   73

Mavity, Uriah J., discharged Nov. 19, '62; disability.
Mohler, John J., transferred to V. R. C., Feb. 11, '64.
Mohler, Oliver H., mustered out. Address: Peru, Ind.
Miller, Lemon, deserted Nov. 11, '62.
Nipp, William, discharged Dec. 9, '62, by civil authority; not of age—18 years.
O'Toole, John, discharged Oct. 25, '62; disability. Address: Morristown, Shelby county, Ind.
Pegg, Samuel C., mustered out. Address: Milroy, Rush county, Ind.
Pierce, Manlius W., appointed musician Aug. 25, '62; died since the war.
Poppino, Silas C., wounded at Chickamauga; mustered out. Address: Chanute, Kansas.
Patterson, Thomas T., mustered out. Address: West Liberty, Howard county, Ind.
Ploughe, Noah T., appointed musician Aug. 25, '62; mustered out. Address: Thompsonville, Jefferson county, Kansas.
Pierce, Llewellyn, died at Murfreesboro, Tenn., May 26, '63; chronic diarrhœa.
Roberts, James H., mustered out. Address: Cimarron, Kansas.
Roberts, John A., discharged June 25, '63; disability. Address: Hebron.
Robinson, John, deserted Nov. 14, '62.
Richey, Asbury, discharged Nov. 18, '62; disability. Address: Milroy, Rush county, Ind.
Rogers, Isaac, wounded at Decatur, Ala., Oct. 28, '64; shot through both thighs; discharged April 25, '65, at Jefferson Barracks, Mo.
Silvers, Isaac, wounded in battle at Nashville, Dec. 16, '64; mustered out. Address: Jolliette, Ind.
Simmonds, John, wounded at Chickamauga; transferred to V. R. C.
Stewart, Luther T., mustered out. Address: Milroy, Rush county, Ind.
Short, Frederick W., wounded at Chickamauga; transferred to V. R. C., Nov. 24, '63.
Sailors, Oliver H., mustered out. Address: Garfield, Chafee county, Colorado.
Smith, George, mustered out. Address: Harrodsburg, Monroe county, Ind.
Simpson, Daniel W., mustered out; was detailed by the Chief Commissary Military Division of the Mississippi, Col. A. Beckwith, and went with General Sherman's army on the great march. Address: West Liberty, Howard county, Ind.
Trimbly, Jefferson E., died at Chattanooga, Tenn., Oct. 22, '63, from wounds received at Chickamauga, Sept. 19, '63.
Trevillion, Martin, mustered out. Address: Knightstown, Henry county, Ind.
Wilson, Allen B., discharged Nov. 25, '62; disability. Address: Elwood, Madison county, Ind.
Wilson, John L. T., appointed Wagoner Jan. 1, '63; mustered out. Address: Charlottesville, Hancock county, Ind.
Walters, Payton H., shot through the left leg at Chickamauga and taken prisoner; transferred to Company K., 19th Regiment, V. R. C., May 31, '64, at Washington, D. C. Address: Indianapolis, Ind.
Widner, Jeremiah A., transferred to V. R. C., Sept. 16, '63; died since the war at the Soldiers' Home, Dayton, Ohio.
Widner, David S., transferred to 17th Regiment, V. R. C.
Whiteley, Enoch, promoted Corporal Sept. 1, '64; mustered out. Address: Jamestown, Boone county, Ind.

REGIMENTAL ROSTER.

Recruits—
Chalfant, Matthias, mustered in Nov. 1, '62; died at Nashville, Tenn., April 1, '63; typhoid fever.
Cox, David A., mustered in Nov. 3, '62; transferred to 44th Regiment, June 20, '65.
Forbes, John W., mustered in Nov. 3, '64; transferred to 44th Regiment, June 20, '65.
Smith, John, mustered in Nov. 3, '64; transferred to 44th Regiment, June 20, '65.
Vale, Leander, mustered in March 6, '65; transferred to 44th Regiment, June 20, '65.
White, Henry C., mustered in Nov. 3, '64; transferred to 44th Regiment, June 20, '65.
[From Co. B., 6th Ind. Inf.; assigned to Co. D., 68th Ind., March 6, '65.]
Murphy, Joab P., mustered in Aug. 26, '62; transferred to 44th Regiment, June 20, '65.
Mullen, Otis, mustered in Jan. 7, '64; transferred to 44th Regiment, June 20, '65.
Ogden, Joshua D., mustered in Dec. 26, '63; transferred to 44th Regiment, June 20, '65.
Peacock, Moses D., mustered in Dec. 26, '63; transferred to 44th Regiment, June 20, '65.
Rust, Francis M., mustered in Dec. 26, '63; transferred to 44th Regiment, June 20, '65.

In January and February, '64, there were transferred to Co. D., 68th Ind., by order of Col. N. Odine, 36 Sergeants, Corporals and privates from the 15th Ohio Inf., 8th Kansas Inf., 15th Wisconsin Inf., 32d Indiana Inf., and 49th Ohio Inf., and 28 of them were present and mustered with the Company at Morristown, Tenn., Feb. 29, '64.

COMPANY E.—FROM DEARBORN COUNTY.

Captains—
Beckman, Alexander, mustered in Aug. 19, '62; resigned Nov. 23, '62.
Bryant, Charles H., mustered in Nov. 24, '62; promoted from 1st Lieutenant.
First Lieutenants—
Sheldon, George W., mustered in Nov. 24, '62; resigned Jan. 31, '63.
Price, Robert T., mustered in April 1, '63; killed in battle at Chickamauga, Ga., Sept. 19, '63.
Liddell, Oliver B., mustered in Nov. 11, '63.
Second Lieutenant—
Glardon, Peter F., mustered in Nov. 24, '62; resigned June 3, '63.
First Sergeant—
Liddell, Oliver B., promoted 1st Lieutenant.
Sergeants—
Crist, Hiram C., transferred to 1st U. S. Cavalry, Dec. 4, '62.
Robbins, Jeremiah, died at Lawrenceburg Oct. 3, '62.
Neff, Charles, mustered out June 20, '65, as private.
Terhune, James, transferred to V. R. C.; mustered out Aug. 19, '65.
Corporals—
Smith, George W., mustered out June 20, '65, as musician.
Lewis, Albert, transferred to 1st U. S. Cavalry, Dec. 4, '62.
Babcock, Worden, transferred to V. R. C., May 1, '64.
Alfred, Simeon, discharged Jan. 24, '65; disability.
Stockman, Lewis C., died in Andersonville prison, Aug. 14, '64.
Eckert, Michael, discharged April 22, '63; disability.
Wade, Cullen J., mustered June 2, '65, as Sergeant.
Wardell, Francis, deserted Oct. 27, '62.

REGIMENTAL ROSTER. 75

Musician—
  Goebler, Adair, transferred to V. R. C., Sept. 12, '62.
Wagoner—
  McCright, Austin, mustered out June 20, '65.
Privates—
  Alfred, Joseph, died at Dillsboro, Ind., Nov. 1, '62.
  Baines, James, transferred to V. R. C., Feb. 11, '64; wounds.
  Babcock, Lemuel, died at Nashville, Tenn., March 28, '63.
  Beggs, Lafayette, died at Louisville, Ky., Oct 1, '63.
  Bolander, Chris. W., deserted July 9, '63.
  Borden, Michael, deserted Aug. 19, '62.
  Bearnes, Henry, deserted Oct. 27, '62.
  Callahan, William, discharged May 7, '64; disability.
  Clark, Hiram R., died at Indianapolis, Nov. 29, '62.
  Claspil, Martin, discharged Jan. 16, '63; disability.
  Cady, Robert M., transferred to 18th U. S. Infantry, Dec. 9, '62.
  Campbell, James S., died at Nashville, Tenn., March 28, '63.
  Donner, John, transferred to 18th U. S. Infantry, Dec. 17, '62.
  Davern, Michael, deserted Nov. 10, '62.
  Darrogh, Charles, mustered out June 25, '65.
  Daniels, Richard, deserted Nov. 10, '62.
  Eubank, Robert J., discharged Nov. 29, '62; disability.
  Eubank, John A., mustered out June 20, '65, as Corporal.
  Goodwin, John, transferred to V. R. C., Feb. 15, '64.
  Godfrey, Jacob, mustered out June 20, '65.
  Glarden, Peter F., promoted 2d Lieutenant.
  Gould, Richard H., mustered out June 20, '65, as Corporal.
  Gould, Joseph, discharged Dec. 23, '62, by civil authority.
  Graham, Alonzo, discharged Sept. 6, '63; disability.
  Gibbs, Asa, mustered out June 20, '65, as Sergeant.
  Gibbs, Theodore, transferred to V. R. C.; wounds.
  Gruber, Joseph, transferred to 18th U. S. Infantry, Dec. 27, '62.
  Haynes, Jesse, drowned at Lawrenceburg, Ind, Oct. 15, '62.
  Hohn, Joseph, mustered out June 20, '65.
  Hamel, Nelson, mustered out June 20, '6 .
  Hendrickson, Abram, transferred to V. R. C., April 10, '64.
  Hall, Thomas L., mustered out June 20, '65, as Sergeant.
  Hall, William, died at Nashville, Tenn., June 9, '63.
  Klineman, William, mustered out June 20, '65, as Corporal.
  Koh, John W., discharged Nov. 19, '62; disability.
  Knowler, Amasa C., died at Louisville, March 10, '63.
  Lyon, Charles, mustered out June 8, '65.
  Moore, Marcus, transferred to V. R. C., July 27, '63.
  Morley, John, transferred to 18th U. S. Infantry, Dec. 3, '62.
  Neff, Rudolph, mustered out June 20, '65, as Sergeant.
  Probst, Jacob, mustered out June 20, '65.
  Rudieson, Michael, mustered out June 20, '65.
  Rinerson, John, died at Chattanooga, Nov. 6, '63.
  Ross, John, deserted Nov. 15, '62.
  Rockaway, William, deserted Oct. 27, '62.
  Sohn, Rudolph, deserted Aug. 19, '62.
  Skelton, John, mustered out June 20, '65.
  Shafer, Michael, discharged Dec 22, '63; disability.
  Smith, George, mustered out June 20, '65.
  Sullivan, John R., transferred to 1st U. S. Cavalry, Dec. 4, '62.
  Smith, William F., died at home, Aug. 11, '63.
  Snell, Charles, mustered out June 20, '65.
  Smith, James A., mustered out June 20, '65, as Corporal.
  Schmidt, Jacob, mustered out June 20, '65, as Corporal.
  Schmidt, George, mustered out June 20, '65.
  Swan, Levi B., transferred to V. R. C., Jan. 15, '64.
  Spell, Abram, discharged Dec. 8, '62; disability.

Texter, Christopher, transferred to V. R. C.
Tuley, William, died at Nashville. Dec. 27, '64.
Taylor, Elias, died at Murfreesboro, June 27, '63.
Tuley, James, mustered out June 20, '65.
Walters, Hiram G., deserted Dec. 18, '82.
Walters, William G., deserted Nov. 10, '82.
Welgart, Benjamin F., mustered out June 20, '65.
Wyneman, Jacob, transferred 18th U. S. Infantry, Dec. 17, '62.
Ward, William, deserted Aug. 19, '62.
Wilson, John, mustered out June 20, '65, as Sergeant.
Recruits—
Bennett, James, mustered out March 27, '65.
Crawford, John R., transferred to 44th Regiment, June 20, '65.
Dutton, Stephen A., mustered out June 20, '65, as 1st Sergeant.
Dyke, William H., mustered out June 20, '65.
Ewbank, Robert W., transferred to 44th Regiment, June 20, '65.
Grove, John W., mustered out June 20, '65.
Irish, Charles, mustered out June 20, '65.
Laine, Jesse L., discharged Feb. 27, '65; disability.
Mavity, John A., mustered out June 8, '65.
Noble, Robert J., mustered out June 8, '65.
Parker, Deforest, transferred to 44th Regiment, June 20, '65.
Smith, John L., transferred to 44th Regiment, June 20, '65.
Tull, Isom, transferred to 44th Regiment, June 20, '65.
Weatherford, David, transferred to 44th Regiment, June 20, '65.
York, Caswell, transferred to 44th Regiment, June 20, '65.

COMPANY F.—FROM NAPOLEON, RIPLEY COUNTY.

Captains—
Espy, Harvey J., mustered in Aug. 19, '62; promoted.
Hicks, John, mustered in Jan. 1, '64; promoted from 1st Lieutenant.
First Lieutenant—
Culver, Moses A., mustered in Jan. 1, '64.
Second Lieutenants—
Bankirk, Jemison, mustered in Aug. 19, '62; resigned Feb. 18, '63.
Arnold, Joseph W., mustered in May 1, '63; resigned Oct. 6, '63.
First Sergeant—
Showers, David D., discharged Feb. 4, '63; disability.
Sergeants—
McKee, James, transferred to V. R. C.
Standiford, James A., mustered out June 20, '65, as Corporal.
Culver, Moses A., promoted 1st Lieutenant.
Eaton, Hiram, died Oct. 3, '63; wounds recieved at Chickamauga.
Corporals—
Thackery, James B., mustered out June 20, '65.
Parker, James, deserted Dec. 6, '62.
Eaton, David L., mustered out June 20, '65, as Sergeant.
Arnold, Joseph W., promoted 2d Lieutenant.
Bare, Thompson, deserted Nov. 19, '62.
Johnson, Benjamin C., discharged Nov. 25, '62; disability.
Brunt, William H., killed at Nashville Dec. 16, '64.
Nicolai, Henry, mustered out June 20, '65, as Sergeant.
Musicians—
McFatridge, Henry C., died at Indianapolis, Nov. 27, '62.
Lyons, David, discharged Dec. 6, '62, by civil authority.
Privates—
Arnold, James, mustered out June 20, '65.
Arnold, Yewlls, mustered out June 20, '65.
Beasle, Celestine, discharged Nov. 18, '62.

REGIMENTAL ROSTER. 77

Belanger, William, mustered out June 20. '65.
Brunt, Samuel, transferred to V. R. C., July 27. '63.
Betener, Charles, mustered out June 20, '65, as Corporal.
Becroft. John T., died at Nashville, March 3, '63.
Castor, Robert, mustered out June 20, '65, as Corporal.
Castor, Gabriel, discharged Nov. 28, '63; disability.
Castor, William, mustered out June 20, '65.
Castor, Lorenzo D., discharged April 16, '63; disability.
Castor, Benjamin, discharged Dec. 8, '62; disability.
Crowe, Henry, discharged May 26, '63; disability.
Cole, Henry H., mustered out June 20, '65, as Corporal.
Dubois, Benjamin F., discharged May 31, '63; disability.
Davis, Isaac, transferred to Co. "A.," Jan. 1, '63.
Denny, Ambrose, discharged Nov. 25, '62; disability.
Day, David A., mustered out June 20, '65.
Eaton, Arnold P., discharged Oct. 14, '63; disability.
Fulmer, David, died at Murfreesboro, May 29, '63.
Glaus, Nicholas, transferred V. R. C.
Gursling, George, deserted Sept. 2, '62.
Hausman, Charles, died at Chattanooga, Jan. 14, '65.
Hiner, John, discharged Dec. 29, '62; disability.
Harrel, Joshua, deserted Nov. 19, '62.
Houck, Franklin, mustered out June 20. '65.
Hardy, Henry, discharged Dec. 8, '62, by civil authority.
Holloway, James L., transferred V. R. C., July 27, '63.
Jones, James, mustered out June 20, '65.
Kermickle, John, died at Indianapolis. Dec. 18, '62.
Lewis; Nathan W., discharged Dec. 8, '62, by civil authority.
Lines. David O., discharged Nov. 15, '62; disability.
Lewis, Isaac, transferred V. R C., Aug. 11, '63.
Lines, Enoch, mustered out, June 7 '65, as Sergeant.
Lozia, Martin B., deserted Nov. 19 '62.
Lutz, Michael, mustered out June 20, '65.
Lyons, William H., deserted Jan 10, '63.
Luxx, George, deserted Aug. 26, '62.
Lamb, Michael, discharged Nov. 24, '62; disability.
McQuane, Andrew, mustered out June 20, 65.
McKee, Homer B., died at Indianapolis, Dec. 7, '62.
McLaughlin, John U., mustered out June 20, '65, as Sergeant.
Moore, Stephen J., mustered out June 20, '65, as Corporal.
Mace, Fleming, discharged ——, '63; disability.
Pollman, John, discharged May 25, '63; disability.
Parker, Stephen A., killed at Chicamauga, Sept. 19, '63.
Porter, Robert L., died at Murfreesboro, July 8, '63; accidental w'ds.
Parker, Harvey J., mustered out June 20, '65, as Corporal.
Peteman, Lewis, discharged June 18, '63; disability.
Ralph, George W. A. J., died in Andersonville prison, Aug. 19, '64.
Reinier, James L., died at Indianapolis, Nov. 25, '62.
Runion, John H., mustered out June 20, '65, as Corporal.
Shill, Joseph, mustered out June 20, '65, as 1st Sergeant.
Shackleford, Erastus, discharged May 31, '63; disability.
Showers, Benjamin, transferred V. R. C., Sept. 12, '63.
Stackhouse, George H., discharged Dec. 20, '62, by civil authority.
Skinnims, James, mustered out June 20, '65.
Skinner, Joseph, discharged Dec. 8, '62, by civil authority.
Thackery, Thomas B., mustered out June 20, '65
Thackery, Thomas E., mustered out June 20. '65.
Thackery, Jacob C., mustered out June 20, '65
Thackery, Stephen, discharged April 3, '63; disability.
Toy, Ephraim, discharged May 17, '63 disability.
Victory, John, mustered out Jun 20, '65.
White, Seth, mustered out June 20, '65.

Williams, William G., deserted Nov. 19, '62.
Waters, John, transferred V. R. C.
Wantling, William, discharged Dec. 2, '62, by civil authority.
Winkleman, John K., mustered out June 20, '65.
Williams, William, transferred V. R. C.
Recruits—
Adkins, George W., transferred 44th Regiment, June 20, '65.
Elliott, John B., transferred 44th Regiment, June 20, '65.
Fortune, Lewis, transferred 44th Regiment, June 20, '65.
Leeman, Charles, died at Nashville, Sept. 15, '63.
Martin, William M., transferred 11th U. S. Infantry, Dec. —, '62.
Steele, John S., mustered out June 20, '65.
Stackhouse, David, died at Indianapolis, Nov. 17, '62.

COMPANY G.—From Franklin County, Brookville and Fairfield.

Captains—
Lynn, Lawrence V. G., mustered in Aug. 19, '63; resigned March 4, '63.
Claypool, George W., mustered in May 1, '63; promoted from 1st Lieutenant; dishonorably dismissed April 27, '65; cause: conduct unbecoming an officer; dismissal revoked Aug. 18, '65, and honorably discharged to date April 27, '65.
First Lieutenants—
Clark, Joseph R., mustered in May 1, '63; promoted from 2d Lieutenant; dishonorably dismissed Aug. 9, '63.
Holsted, Oliver B., mustered in Aug. 29, '64.
Second Lieutenants—
Webb, Austin, mustered in Aug. 19, '62; resigned Nov. 29, '62.
Moore, Climpson B., mustered in May 1, '63; resigned Dec. 2, '63.
First Sergeant—
Clark, Joseph R., promoted 2d Lieutenant.
Sergeants—
Wilson, George, discharged June 20, '63.
Moore, Climpson B., promoted 2d Lieutenant.
Smith, Edward C., discharged Dec. 22, '62.
McReady, Samuel, transferred V. R. C.; mustered out July 5, '65.
Corporals—
Best, William, died at Nashville, Tenn., Oct. 29, '63; wounds.
Burnett, Thomas J., killed at Chicamauga, Sept. 19, '63.
Stephens, Isaac, Jr., discharged Nov. 8, '62.
Hubbard, James A., mustered out June 20, '65.
Dukate, James, died at Nashville, Tenn., Jan. 27, '63.
Trusler, John N., discharged Sept. 19, '63.
Ryman, Alanson, mustered out June 20, '65, as 1st Sergeant.
Swift, Franklin, died at Chicamauga, Sept. 20, '63; wounds.
Musicians—
Lynn, Prince Albert, discharged Dec. 11, '62, by civil authority.
Hibbard, Marion B., mustered out June 20, '65.
Wagoner—
Bright, Ezekiel A., mustered out June 26, '65.
Privates—
Bell, Thomas H., died at Brookville, Dec. 26, '63.
Barton, Caleb S., transferred to V. R. C., Jan. 14, '64.
Bresler, William H., discharged June 26, '63.
Craver, George, mustered out June 20, '65, as Sergeant.
Cheney, Edmund J., mustered out June 20, '65, as Sergeant.
Castle, James, mustered out June 20, '65.
Davis, George M. D., discharged Dec. 11, '62, by civil authority.
Dukate, John B., discharged Dec. 11, '62, by civil authority.

REGIMENTAL ROSTER. 79

Donough, Andrew, mustered out June 20, '65.
Filer, Charles E., discharged Dec. 3, '62.
Higgs, James M., mustered out June 20, '65, as Corporal.
Halstead, Oliver, promoted 1st Lieutenant.
Hickson, Charles H., discharged Sept. 30, '63.
Hayward, Elihu, died at Indianapolis, Jan. 3, '63.
Hayward, Thomas B., mustered out June 20, '65.
Hall, Theodore, mustered out June 20, '65.
Jones, William, mustered out June 20, '65, as Corporal.
Jamison, Jacob, died at Nashville, Tenn., Sept. 15, '63.
Larimore, Isaac, mustered out June 20, '65.
Line, Dennis B., transferred to 19th U. S. Infantry, Dec. 12, '62.
Loper, Elmere, died at Jasper, Tenn., Aug. 27, '63.
Monroe, Libius, discharged May 29, '63.
Macombs, James, discharged Dec. 12, '62, by civil authority.
McCready, Jacob A., mustered out June 20, '65, as Corporal.
Minson, Entiles, mustered out June 20, '65.
Moore, James C., discharged Dec. 12, '62, by civil authority.
McCormick, Theodore, deserted Oct. 31, '62.
Miller, Lewis C., discharged Dec. 6, '62.
Marlatt, Charles E., mustered out June 20, '65.
Masters, Jacob K., mustered out June 20, '65.
Moore, Andrew, mustered out June 20, '65.
McFall, John, discharged Nov. 8, '62.
Masters, David W., died at Knoxville, Tenn., Jan. 24, '64.
McIlvaine, James P., discharged Dec. 12, '62, by civil authority.
Masters, John W., died at Knoxville.
McDonald, Ambrose, died at Louisville, Jan. 7, '63.
Marlatt, Hezekiah R., mustered out June 20, '65, as Corporal.
Oliphant, Francis M. J., mustered out June 20, '65.
Ogden, Charles W., died at Murfreesboro, May 27, '63.
Pippin, Joseph, discharged April 25, '64.
Pierson, John R., died at Decherd, Tenn., July 26, '63.
Poe, Chester, mustered out June 20, '65.
Parrott, Nimrod, mustered out June 20, '65.
Ryman, Jarrad C., discharged Dec. 12, '62, by civil authority.
Risk, Charles B., discharged Dec. 12, '62, by civil authority.
Roberts, William P., died at home Nov. 2, '62.
Remy, William H., promoted Quartermaster.
Ryman, Cineas, mustered out June 20, '65, as Sergeant.
Rose, Hezekiah, discharged Nov. 20, '62.
Roberts, Lafayette, mustered out June 20, '65.
Staut, John, died at Evansville, Ind., Jan. 23, '64.
Stilwell, David, mustered out June 20, '65, as Corporal.
Skinner, Theodore, mustered out June 20, '65.
Shepperd, Thomas C., promoted Quartermaster 146th Regiment.
Stephens, Isaac J., mustered out June 20, '65.
Sims James L., discharged Sept. 6, '62.
Templeton, Oliver G., discharged Sept. 30, '63.
Van Metre, Joseph N., died at Murfreesboro, July 13, '63.
Warne, Elijah, died at Louisville, April 14, '64.
Wallace, William J., mustered out June 20, '65.
White, Melville B., discharged Dec. 7, '62.
West, Andrew H., mustered out June 20, '65.
Weaver, William H., transferred to 11th U. S. Infantry, Nov. 22, '62.
Wright, Fuller, discharged Feb. 4, '63.
Yates, Thomas B., mustered out June 20, '65.
Yates, Daniel, mustered out June 20, '65.

Recruits—
Armstrong, William F., transferred to 44th Regiment, June 20, '65.
Bird, William A., discharged Dec. 8, '64; wounds.
•Coil, John L., transferred to 44th Regiment, June 20, '65.

REGIMENTAL ROSTER.

Glover, Lafayette, transferred to 44th Regiment, June 20, '65.
Gall, Raphael, transferred to 44th Regiment, June 20, '65.
Higgs, George W., transferred to 44th Regiment, June 20, '65.
Howard, Thomas J., transferred to 44th Regiment, June 20, '65.
Lewis, Isaac, transferred to 44th Regiment, June 20, '65.
Moulton, George W., mustered out July 21, '65.
McCarty, William, mustered out June 20, '65, as Sergeant.
Reed, Zachariah, transferred to 44th Regiment, June 20, '65.
Smith, Jeremiah W., transferred to 44th Regiment, June 20, '65.
Swift, Richard M., transferred to 44th Regiment, June 20, '65.
Smith, Henry, transferred to 44th Regiment, June 20, '65.
Smith, James, transferred to 44th Regiment, June 20, '65.

COMPANY H.—FROM FRANKLIN COUNTY, BROOKVILLE AND MT. CARMEL.

Captains—
Finn, Edmund, mustered in Aug. 19, '62; promoted Major.
Wilkinson, Francis M., mustered in Jan. 1, '64; promoted from 1st Lieutenant.
First Lieutenant—
Davis, John M., mustered in May 28, '64.
Second Lieutenants—
Buckingham, Levi W., mustered in Aug. 19, '62; resigned Feb. 18, '63.
Case, Elijah H., mustered in May 1, '63; resigned March 14, '64.
First Sergeant—
Washburne, William S., mustered out June 20, '65, as private.
Sergeants—
Case, Elijah H., promoted 2d Lieutenant.
Stringer, Shadrack, mustered out June 20, '65, as 1st Sergeant.
Davis, John M., promoted 1st Lieutenant.
Jeffries, Lycurgus, mustered out June 7, '65, as private.
Corporals—
Blew, Samuel, transferred to V. R. C., April 28, '64.
Johnson, Nicholas V., discharged Nov. 15, '62; disability.
Davis, Nathan, discharged Nov. 22, '62; disability.
Jones, John M., died at home, Dec. 9, '62.
Backhouse, Theo. P., mustered out June 20, '65.
Bradburn, Henry, deserted Nov. 12, '62.
Harrell, John C., died at Nashville, Tenn., July 20, '63.
Lyons, Zachariah, mustered out June 20, '65, as Sergeant.
Musicians—
Harper, Rufus, mustered out June 20, '65.
Baker, Samuel R., discharged March 9, '63; disability.
Privates—
Alvey, William, deserted Sept. 1, '62.
Baker, David G., died at Chattanooga, Oct. 2, '63; wounds.
Budemeyer, Dietrich, mustered out June 20, '65, as Corporal.
Bickle, Henry, transferred to V. R. C., May 31, '64; wounds.
Baker, William M., discharged Nov. 23, '62; disability.
Baker, David, Jr., discharged Dec. 18, '62, by civil authority.
Barber, John, died at Knoxville, Tenn., Jan. 16, '64.
Best, William H., mustered out June 20, '65, as Corporal.
Barrieman, Martin C., deserted Dec. 29, '62.
Burns, Thomas, mustered out June 20, '65.
Burtn, John, transferred to V. R. C., July 27, '63.
Campbell, George W., mustered out June 20, '65.
Cummins, Cheef M., transferred to V. R. C., May 31, '64; wounds.
Carson, James E., mustered out June 20, '65.

REGIMENTAL ROSTER.

Crocker, Wesley, discharged April 21, '63; disability.
Cregar, Elmore W., died at Nashville June 2, '63.
Dunham, Aaron, mustered out June 20, '65, as Corporal.
Feary, Charles, mustered out June 20, '65.
Farmer, John A., transferred to V. R. C.; mustered out June 28, '65.
Ferguson, Thomas A., transferred to 18th U. S. Infantry, Oct. 9, '62.
Gleason, William, mustered out June 20, '65.
Gage, Benjamin, mustered out June 20, '65, as Sergeant.
Greger, John H., discharged April 2, '63; disability.
Grimes, Patrick, transferred to 18th U. S. Infantry, Oct. 9, '62.
Grimes, William, discharged Nov. 25, '62; disability.
Harris, William H., discharged Dec. 10, '62; disability.
Howell, George W., discharged Dec. 6, '62; disability.
Holliday, John, transferred to V. R. C., July 25, '64.
Hopkins, Isaac, mustered out June 20, '65.
Heep, John, died at Chickamauga, Sept. 19, '63; wounds.
Jacques, Joseph, discharged May 27, '63; disability.
Jenkins, Alhanan W., mustered out June 20, 65, as Sergeant.
Kilgore, Elwood, mustered out June 20, '65, as Corporal.
Kennedy, John S., mustered out June 20, '65.
Long, Joseph, mustered out June 20, '65.
Larue, Brison, mustered out June 20, '65.
Laforge, James L., discharged Sept. 14, '63; mental imbecility.
Lee, Gabriel, died at Indianapolis, Dec. 18, '62.
Lee, William, discharged June 11, '63; disability.
Morford, Joseph, mustered out June 20, '65.
Maley, Michael, mustered out June 20, '65, as Corporal.
Miller, Henry H., discharged Dec. 24. '62; disability.
Meyncke, Christopher C., died at home, Dec. 1, '62.
Mullin, Joel, died at Nashville, March 23, '63.
Millspaugh, Peter B., mustered out June 20, '65.
Maley, Patrick, mustered out June 20. '65.
Parvis, Jonathan, mustered out June 20, '65.
Price, Robert J., promoted 1st Lieutenant.
Proctor, John, discharged Nov. 14, '62; disability.
Quick, James M., mustered out June 20, '65.
Runyan, John R., died at Indianapolis, Dec. 1, '62.
Raymond, Lewis, discharged Dec. 16, '62, by civil authority.
Rogers, Martin, deserted Nov. 28, '62.
Rogers, Peter, deserted Nov. 28, '62; mustered out Dec. 2, '65.
Roe, John P. A., mustered out June 20, '65.
Robeson, John, discharged Nov. 21, '62; disability.
Rust, Herbert L., discharged Jan. 4, '64; disability.
Scoonover, Benjamin F., mustered out June 7, '65.
Serring, Silas W., mustered out June 20, '65, as Corporal.
Serring, William H., transferred to V. R. C., May 31, '64.
Sprodling, William N., died at Indianapolis, Dec. 8, '62.
Smith, Benjamin A., discharged Nov. 22, '62; disability.
Sprodling, Elisha, discharged Nov. 15, '62; old age.
Sickler, Nehemiah, died at Palestine, Ind., Nov. 23, '62.
Taylor, Charles A., mustered out June 20, '65, as Sergeant.
Teegarden, Daniel, transferred to V. R. C., July 1, '63.
Taylor, John W., mustered out June 20, '65, as Corporal.
Valandigham, Lewis J., discharged Nov. 7, '63; disability.
Vessendorf, Henry, died at Chattanooga, Oct. 1, '63; wounds.
Withers, Jerome J., discharged Nov. 6, '62, by civil authority.
Washington, Isaac, discharged Dec. 18, '62, by civil authority.
Woolworth, Adelbert C. C., discharged Dec. 2, '62, by civil authority.

Recruits—

Chamberlain, Francis M., transferred to 44th Regiment, June 20, '65.
Hensler, Albert, transferred to 44th Regiment, June 20, '65.
Koehler, August, transferred to 44th Regiment, June 20, '65.

REGIMENTAL ROSTER.

Meyncke, James, died at University, Tenn., Aug. 4, '63.
Newman, Jacob, transferred to 44th Regiment, June 20, '65.
O'Byrne, George F., transferred to 44th Regiment, June 20 '65.
Peterman, Henry C., discharged Feb. 13, '65; wounds.
Raymond, Lewis, died at Dalton, Ga., Aug. 15, '64; wounds.
Smart, William F., transferred 44th Reg't, June 20, '65.
Williams, David, transferred 44th Reg't, June 20, '85.
Washington, James E., transferred 44th Reg't, June 20, '65.
Washington, Isaac, transferred 44th Reg't, June 20, '65.

COMPANY I.—FROM RUSH AND DECATUR COUNTIES, RICHLAND AND SARDINIA.

Captains—
Patterson, Reuben F., mustered in Aug. 19, '62; resigned April 20, '64.
Patton, Nathaniel S., mustered in Aug. 28, '64; promoted from 1st Lieutenant.
First Lieutenant—
Carson, George, mustered in Aug. 28, '64; promoted from 2d Lieut.
Second Lieutenant—
Brehenney, William, mustered in Aug. 19, '62; resigned April 2, '63.
First Sergeant—
Carson, George, promoted 1st Lieutenant.
Sergeants—
Showalter, Franklin F., died at University, Tenn., Aug. 8, '63.
Hankins, George G., killed at Chicamauga, Sept. 20, '63.
Wood, John W., mustered out June 20, '65, as 1st Sergeant.
Stout, Joab H., discharged March 7, '63; disability.
Corporals—
Bolton, Robert W., transferred to 19th U. S. Infantry, Dec. 8, '62.
May, Thomas T., discharged Aug. 3, '63; disability.
Alexander, Israel C., mustered out June 20, '65, as Sergeant.
Smisor, Jacob, transferred V. R C., April 6, '64; mustered out June 30, '65.
Alexander, Elbert S., discharged Jan. 11, '64; wounds.
Wynn, James, died at Nashville, Tenn., March 26, '63.
Stage, Hiram P., mustered out June 20, '65, as Sergeant.
Webb, William B., discharged Dec. 30, '62; disability.
Musician—
Shumm, John P., died at Nashville, Tenn., April 20, '63.
Wagoner—
Plough, John, discharged Nov. 4, '62; disability.
Privates—
Byons, John H., transferred to 19th U. S. Infantry, Dec. 10, '62.
Burous, Newton J., mustered out June 20, '65.
Booth, William A., mustered out June 20, '65.
Brehenney, James, mustered out June 20, '65, as Corporal.
Clendenning, Thomas, died at Nashville, Tenn., March 6, '64.
Childers, Jesse, mustered out June 20, '65.
Childers, Joseph H., transferred to 19th U. S. Infantry, Dec. 10, '62.
Cox, James H., mustered out June 20, '65.
Christy, Henry P., mustered out May 19, '65.
Critcher, John, transferred to 19th U. S., Infantry, Dec. 10, '62.
Carson, Joel, mustered out May 27, '65.
Davis, Thomas C., mustered out June 20, '65.
Fieber, William M., discharged June 3, '63; disability.
Grant, Giles, transferred to 19th U. S. Infantry, Dec. 10, '62.
Gard, Oliver P., deserted Dec. 28, '62.
Gard, William J., deserted Dec. 1, '62.
Gard, Samuel M., died at Indianapolis, Nov. 11, '62.
Gilmore, John W., missing, Mission Ridge, Nov. 25, '63; supposed killed.

REGIMENTAL ROSTER.

Gilmore, Andrew J., died in the field, Tenn., July 10, '63.
Goldsmith, William H. O., transferred to Regular Army, Dec. 13, '62.
Humes, Worthington, mustered out June 20, '65.
Humes, John C., mustered out June 20, '65, as Sergeant.
Hood, James N., mustered out June 20, '65, as Corporal.
Hughes, David M., discharged Dec. 20, '62, by civil authority.
Hiaberlin, Andrew J., transferred to 19th U. S. Infantry, Dec. 20, '62.
Hibbard, Clayburn W., discharged Dec. 30, '62; disability.
Heckinger, John, mustered out June 20, '65.
Herring, Isaac, mustered out June 20, '65.
Howell, Charles W., mustered out June 17, '65.
Higgs, George W., died at University, Tenn., Aug. 8, '63.
Irwin, Ovid, discharged Dec. 23, '62; disability.
Klapp, William, M., died Oct. 4, '63; wounds received at Chickamauga.
Littell, Elias, transferred to 19th U. S. Infantry, Dec. 11, '62.
Lefforge, Ephraim, mustered out June 7, '65.
Lyon, John V. T., transferred to V. R. C., April 10, '64.
Lansberry, William V., mustered out June 20, '65.
Matherly, William W., mustered out June 20, '65, as Musician.
McIlvain, Ira, mustered out June 20, '65, as Sergeant.
McIlvain, William W., mustered out June 7, '65.
Murray, John D., died at Murfreesboro, Tenn., May 8, '63.
McMann, Wellington, deserted Dec. 25, '62; died in Canada.
Moncrief, Wilson L., mustered out June 20, '65.
Moncrief, John C., mustered out June 20, '65, as Corporal.
Moncrief, Perry, discharged Jan. 20, '63; disability.
Mitchell, Newton, mustered out June 20, '65.
Manson, Patrick, mustered out June 20, '65.
McCune, John W., mustered out June 30, '65.
May, Jeremiah, transferred to V. R. C., Sept. 26, '63; mustered out June 28, '65.
McCorkle, Alexander P., discharged Jan. 25, '64; wounds.
Moor, Peter, mustered out June 20, '65.
Moor, George, died at Nashville, Tenn., March 5, '63.
Moor, Anderson S., discharged Jan. 21, '64; disability.
Moor, Edmond M., discharged Sept. 10, '64; wounds.
McDowell, Oliver P., mustered out June 20, '65.
Ogden, William R., discharged Dec. 26, '62, by civil authority
Patrick, Andrew J., mustered out June 20, '65.
Patrick, Solomon H., killed at Chickamauga, Sept 19, '63.
Plymote, Alfred H., discharged March 19, '63; disability.
Reed, Henry, deserted Dec. 28, '62; died at Nashville, June 6, '64
Runyan, Reuben A., died at Nashville, March —, '63.
Roberts, Calvin T., discharged Dec. 26, '62, by civil authority.
Reed, David C., mustered out July 1, '65, as Musician.
Reed, Reason, transferred to V. R. C., ——, '63.
Reed, John H., mustered out June 25, '65.
Stage, Paul R., discharged March 21, '65; disability.
Stafford, John W., died in Andersonville prison, June 25, '64.
Shafer, John W., mustered out June 20, '65.
Sheara, William, died at Nashville, July 8, '63.
Sherra, James, mustered out June 20, '65, as Corporal.
Spriggs, Riley, mustered out June 20, '65, as Corporal.
Swope, Russell, mustered out June 20, '65.
Thompson, John F., died at Cowan, Tenn., Aug. 15, '63.
Thompson, John W., mustered out June 20, '65, as Corporal.
Viley, Joseph, transferred to V. R. C., Sept. 1, '63; mustered out July 21, '65.
Webb, James G., mustered out June 20, '65, as Corporal.

REGIMENTAL ROSTER.

Wright, Joy, transferred to V. R. C., Feb. 11, '64; mustered out June 30, '65.
Wynn, William, discharged Aug. 5, '63; disability.
Wiley, Francis M., transferred to 19th U. S. Infantry, Dec. 10, '62.
Recruits—
Covert, Lucas, transferred to 44th Regiment, June 20, '65
Eglin, Francis M., transferred to 44th Regiment, June 20, '65.
May, John Q. A., transferred to 44th Regiment, June 20, '65.
Pool, James R., transferred to V. R. C., March 17, '64; wounds

COMPANY K.—FROM DEARBORN AND RIPLEY COUNTIES, MOORE'S HILL.

Captain—
Moore, Hanson D., mustered in Aug. 19, '62; Moore's Hill.
First Lieutenants—
Brewington, Robert F., mustered in Aug. 19, '62; resigned May 25, '63; Knightstown.
Wood, Edward W., mustered in Aug. 1, '63; Milan.
Second Lieutenant—
Gould, George H., mustered in Aug. 19, '62; resigned June 4, '63.
First Sergeant—
Pierce, William O., discharged Dec. 3, 62; disability.
Sergeants—
Dawson, John H., mustered out June 20, '65, as 1st Sergeant.
Wood, Edward W., promoted 1st Lieutenant.
Arnold, Omar A., mustered out June 20, 65.
Wood, Robert W., mustered out June 20, '65, as Sergeant Major.
Corporals—
Johnson, Edward P., mustered out June 20, '65, as Sergeant.
Kelley, Constantine, discharged Aug. 20, 63; disability.
Abbott, Monroe, discharged May 20, '62; wounds.
Wilson, Oliver C., died at Murfreesboro, Tenn., May 2, '63.
Moore, Benjamin F., mustered out June 20, '65, as Sergeant.
Duncan, Joshua, mustered out June 20, '65, as Sergeant.
Gualt, David H., discharged June 20, '65; disability.
Todd, Robert, mustered out June 20, '65.
Musicians—
Riggin, Mellvin M., mustered out June 20, '65.
Moore John W., discharged June 20, '63; disability.
Wagoner—
Loyd, Harvey S., mustered out June 20, '65.
Privates—
Arnold, George C., mustered out June 20, '65, as Corporal.
Arnold, William S., mustered out June 20, '65.
Arnold, Milton, transferred to V. R. C., Aug. 11, '63.
Arnold, Italel S., mustered out June 20, '65.
Auston, Samuel L., mustered out June 20, '65.
Austen, William, discharged Dec. 10, '62; disability.
Abbott, Isaac M., mustered out June 20, '65, as Corporal.
Buhrlege, George L., discharged Dec. 26, '62, by civil authority.
Beggs, William G., mustered out June 20, '65.
Bowen, William W., died at home, Oct. 26, '62.
Brooks, John E., discharged Sept. 16, '63; disability.
Burlingame, Stephen, discharged April 21, '63; disability.
Bohmer, Henry, discharged Dec. 10, '62; disability.
Cannon, Charles.
Cornell, William H., mustered out June 20, '65.
Carr, Thomas, discharged April 3, '63; disability.
Craven, Allen, died at Murfreesboro, Tenn., Jan. 1, '63.
Childs, Benjamin, discharged Nov. 1, '62; disability.
Darby, Thomas, discharged Dec. 10, '62, by civil authority.

REGIMENTAL ROSTER.   85

Frazier, William H., discharged May 30, '63; disability.
Grow, Michael, mustered out June 20, '65.
Gray, Josiah, discharged Nov. 23, '62; disability.
Gualt, Elton H., discharged Dec. 6, '62; disability.
Gualt, James H., died at Murfreesboro, Tenn., April 15, '63.
Halt, Samuel, discharged Dec. 10, '62, by civil authority.
Herndon, Jonathan, discharged Dec. 10, '62, by civil authority.
Hancock, Curtis, discharged Dec. 9, '62, by civil authority.
Johnson, John W., discharged Dec. 10, '62, by civil authority.
Jones, John H., killed at Mission Ridge, Nov. 25, '63.
King, Geo., transferred to Mississippi Marine Brigade, March 11, '63.
Knott, John P., mustered out June 20, '65.
Kidwell, John W., mustered out June 20, '65.
Laughlin, David, discharged Dec. 9, '62, by civil authority.
Lewis, William S., mustered out June 20, '65.
Losey, William F., transferred to V. R. C., Jan. 14, '64.
Lippard, Columbus, discharged Dec. 11, '62; disability.
McGehan, William, died at Chickamauga, Sept. 19, '63; wounds.
Mulvaney, John M., transferred to V. R. C.; mustered out June 30, '65.
Mills, Benjamin, discharged Nov. 1, '62; disability.
Mackey, John, transferred to Mississippi Marine Brigade, March 11, '63.
McKinley, James H., discharged Nov. 26, '62; disability.
Nelson, Samuel B., mustered out June 20, '65.
Punnal, William, mustered out June 20, '65, as Corporal.
Robbins, Monterville, mustered out June 20, '65.
Shuman, Thomas S., transferred to V. R. C., Sept. 26, '63.
Shafer, Conrad, mustered out June 20, '65.
Shockley, John, mustered out June 20, '65.
Stevenson, William T., mustered out June 20, '65, as Corporal.
Smith, John, discharged July 16, '63; disability.
Strastinger, Henry, mustered out June 20, '65.
Sutton, Henry P., mustered out July 20, '65.
Soper, Francis A., discharged Dec. 9, '62, by civil authority.
Sitzger, Joseph, mustered out June 20, '65.
Stautsman, Adam F.
Sedwick, William F., discharged April 30, '62; disability.
Todd, John, mustered out June 20, '65, as Corporal.
Tanner, Martin L., killed at Charleston, Tenn., Dec. 28, '63.
Tower, Alvah W., mustered out June 20, '65, as Corporal.
Taylor, Robert K., transferred to Mississippi Marine Brigade, March 11, '63.
Truet, Thomas J., mustered out June 20, '65.
Wilson, Arvah D., discharged Oct. 4, '62; disability.
Wilson, Moses P., discharged Nov. 10, '63; wounds.
Wood, Henry E., mustered out June 20, '65, as Corporal.

Recruits:--
Curry, Archibald, transferred to 44th Regiment, June 20, '65.
Hall, Jared W., transferred to 44th Regiment, June 20, '65.
Malott, William H., transferred to 44th Regiment, June 20, '65; Sergeant.
Stautsman, Adam F., transferred to 44th Regiment, June 20, '65.
Smith, James H., mustered out June 20, '65.
Tucker, William H., mustered out June 20, '65.

UNASSIGNED RECRUITS.

Hester, Frank.
Hixon, Charles H.
Kiser, William.
McArty, William.
*Speake, James E., promoted Adjutant 148th Regiment.

List of Engagements

In Which Indiana Troops Participated, with a List of Regiments and Batteries Participating Therein.

ATLANTA, Georgia, (Siege,) July 21, to Sept. 2, '64.—Infantry—6th, 9th, 10th, 12th, 22d, 23d, 25th, 27th, 30th, 31st, 32d, 33d, 35th, 37th 38th, 40th, 42d, 53d, 57th, 63d, 65th, 66th, 70th, 74th, 75th, 79th, 80th, 81st, 82d, 83d, 84th, 85th, 86th, 87th, 88th, 91st, 97th, 99th, 100th, 101st, 120th, 123d, 124th, 128th, 129th, 130th. Light Artillery—5th, 7th, 11th, 15th, 18th, 19th, 20th, 22d and 23d Batteries.

APPOMATTOX C. H., Va., April 7-8, '64.—Cavalry—Right Wing Third (45th) Regiment.

ANTIETAM, Maryland, Sept. 17, '62.—Infantry—7th, 14th, 19th, 27th. Cavalry—Right Wing Third (45th) Regiment. Light Artillery—16th Battery.

AVERYSBORO, North Carolina, March 16, '65.—Infantry—22d, 33d, 38th, 42d, 85th. Cavalry—Eighth (39th) Regiment.

ASHBY'S GAP, Virginia, November 2, '63.—Infantry—7th.

ATCHAFALAYA, Louisiana, July 28, '64.—Infantry—8th, 47th.

ALLEGHENY, Virginia, Dec. 13, '61.—Infantry—9th, 13th. Light Artillery—26th Battery.

ARKANSAS POST, Arkansas, Jan. 11, '63.—Infantry—16th, 46th, 49th, 54th, 60th, 67th, 69th, 83d.

ATHENS, Alabama, Oct. 1-2, '64.—Infantry—73d.

ABERDEEN, Arkansas, July 9, '62.—Infantry—34th.

AUSTIN, Mississippi, August —, '62.—Infantry—8th.

ANDERSON TURNOUT, Virginia, August —, '62.—Cavalry—Right Wing Third (45th) Regiment.

ADAIRSVILLE, Georgia, May —, '64.—Infantry—80th, 101st. Light Artillery—5th Battery.

BEVERLY FORD, Virginia, July 9, '63.—Cavalry—Right Wing Third (45th) Regiment.

LIST OF ENGAGEMENTS. 87

BEAVER CREEK FORD, Maryland, July 9, '63.—Cavalry—Right Wing Third (45th) Regiment.
BARBER'S CROSS ROADS, Virginia, November 4, '63.—Cavalry—Right Wing Third (45th) Regiment.
BOONSBORO, Maryland, July 8, '63.—Cavalry—Right Wing Third (45th) Regiment.
BLOUNTSVILLE, Tenn., Sept. 22, '63.—Infantry—65th. Cavalry—Fifth (90th) Regiment.
BEAN STATION, Tenn., Dec. 14, '63.—Infantry—65th, 117th. Cavalry—Fifth (90th) Regiment. Light Artillery—24th Battery.
BLUE SPRINGS, Tenn., Oct. 10, '63.—Infantry—115th, 116th.
BIG SHANTY, Georgia, June 14, '64.—Infantry—7th, 22d, 97th, 99th.
BUFFALO MOUNTAIN, Indian Territory, Oct. 25, '63.—Light Artillery—2d Battery.
BRISTOW STATION, Virginia, Oct. 14, '63.—Infantry—14th.
BLACK RIVER BRIDGE, Mississippi, May 17, '63.—Infantry—8th, 16th, 18th, 49th, 54th, 60th, 67th, 69th. Light Artillery—1st Battery, 6th Battery.
BROWNSVILLE, Mississippi, Sept. 17, '63.—Infantry—93d.
BENTONVILLE, North Carolina, March 19, '65.—Infantry—12th, 22d, 23d, 25th, 33d, 38th, 42d, 48th, 53d, 75th, 82d, 83d, 85th, 88th, 97th, 99th, 100th. Cavalry—8th (39th) Regiment. Light Artillery—19th Battery.
BETHESDA CHURCH Virginia, May 30-31, '64.—Infantry—7th
BALL'S BLUFF, Virginia, Oct. 21-22, '61.—Infantry—16th.
BUFFINGTON ISLAND, Ohio River, July 19, '63.—Cavalry—Fifth (90th) Regiment.
BAYOU DE GLAISE, Louisiana, May 18, '64.—Infantry—89th.
BRANDY STATION, Virginia, Aug. 22-24.—Light Artillery—16th Battery. Cavalry—Right Wing Third (45th) Regiment.
BATON ROUGE, Louisiana, Aug. 5, '62.—Heavy Artillery—1st (21st) Regiment.
BROWN'S FERRY, Tennessee, Oct. 27, '63.—Infantry—6th.
BLOUNT'S FARM, Alabama, May 2, '63.—Infantry—51st, 73d.
BUZZARD Roost, Georgia, May 8, '64.—Infantry—6th, 9th, 82d, 88th.
BATON ROUGE, Louisiana, (Siege) Jan. —, '64.—Infantry—18th.
BALD KNOB, Georgia, May —, '64.—Infantry—81st.
BELLE PLAIN ROAD, Georgia, June —, '64.—Infantry—17th.
CHAPIN'S BLUFF, Virginia, ——, ——.—Infantry—13th, 20th
CROOKED CREEK, Alabama, April 30, '63.—Infantry—51st, 73d.
CORINTH, Mississippi, (Siege) April 11 to May 30, '62.—Infantry—6th, 9th, 10th, 11th, 15th, 17th, 22d, 23d, 24th, 25th, 29th, 30th, 31st, 32d, 36th, 44th, 48th, 51st, 52d, 53d, 57th, 58th, 59th. Cavalry—Second (41st) Regiment; Left Wing Third (45th) Regiment. Light Artillery—4th, 6th, 7th, 8th, 9th, 10th, 11th, 12th, 14th Batteries.
CASSVILLE, Georgia, May 19, '64.—Infantry—9th, 33d, 79th, 85th, 87th 101st. Cavalry—Sixth (71st) Regiment. Light Artillery—5th, 18th, 19th Batteries.

LIST OF ENGAGEMENTS.

CULP'S FARM, Georgia, June 22, '64.—Infantry—33d, 85th.

CORINTH, Mississippi. (Defense) Oct. 3-4, "62.—Infantry—48th, 59th.

CHICAMAUGA, Georgia, Sept. 19-20, '63.—Infantry—6th, 9th, 10th, 17th, 29th, 30th, 31st, 32d, 35th, 36th, 37th, 38th, 40th, 42d, 44th, 58th, 68th, 72d (mounted), 74th, 75th, 79th, 81st, 82d, 84th, 86th, 87th, 88th, 101st. Cavalry—Eighth (39th) Regiment, Left Wing Third (45th) Regiment, Fourth (77th) Regiment. Light Artillery—4th, 5th, 7th, 8th, 11th, 18th, 19th, 21st Batteries.

CHICAMACOMICO, North Carolina, Oct. 4, '61.—Infantry—20th.

CRAIG'S MEETING-HOUSE, Virginia May 5, '64.—Cavalry—Right Wing Third (45th) Regiment.

CHESTER STATION, Virginia, May 10, '64.—Infantry—13th.

CEDAR CREEK, Virginia, Oct. 19. '64.—Infantry—8th, 11th, 18th. Cavalry—Right Wing Third (45th) Regiment. Light Artillery—17th Battery.

CHEAT MOUNTAIN, Virginia, Sept. 12-13, '61.—Infantry—13th, 14th.

CUMBERLAND GAP, Kentucky, June 18, '62.—Infantry—33d, 49th.

CARRICK'S FORD, Virginia, July 12, '61.—Infantry—6th, 7th, 9th.

CHESTER GAP, Virginia, July 22d, '63.—Cavalry—Right Wing Third (45th) Regiment.

CARRION CROW BAYOU, Louisiana, Nov. 3, '64.—Infantry—34th, 60th.

COLD HARBOR, Virginia, June 3, '6-,—Infantry—7th 13th, 14th, 19th, 20th.

CHANTILLY, Virginia, Sept. 1, '62.—Infantry—20th.

CLOVER HILL, Virginia, April 9, '65.—Infantry—20th.

CHANCELLORSVILLE, Virginia, May 2-3, '63.—Infantry—7th, 14th, 20th, 27th.

CEDAR MOUNTAIN, Virginia, Aug. 9, '62.—Infantry—7th, 27th. Light Artillery—16th Battery.

CHARLESTOWN, Virginia, Oct. 18, '63.—Light Artillery—17th Battery.

CAMP STERLING, Louisiana, Sept. 29, '63.—Infantry—26th.

CROSS KEYS, Virginia, June 8, '62.—Light Artillery—26th Battery.

CAMDEN, Arkansas, April 17, '64.—Infantry—43d, 50th. Light Artillery—2d Battery.

COTTON GAP, Arkansas, Sept. 1, '63.—Light Artillery—2d Battery.

CANE HILL, Arkansas, Nov. 27, '62.—Light Artillery—2d Battery.

COTTON PLANT, Arkansas, July 7, '62.—Infantry—8th, 18th.

COLLIERVILLE, Tenn., Oct. 11, '63—Infantry—Detachment of 16th.

CHATTAHOOCHIE RIVER, Georgia, July 7, '64.—Infantry—17th, 22d, 33d, 37th, 40th, 74th, 86th, 100th.

CONCORD, Tennessee, Nov. 16, '63.—Light Artillery—15th, 24th Batteries.

CAMPBELL'S STATION, Tenn., Nov. 16, '63.—Light Artillery—15th, -24th Batteries.

LIST OF ENGAGEMENTS. 89

COLUMBIA, Tennessee, Nov. 26, '64.—Infantry—9th, 33d, 65th, 128th, 129th. Cavalry—Fourth (77th) Regiment. Light Artillery—15th, 21st, 22d, 23d, 24th Batteries.

CHICKASAW BAYOU, Mississippi, Dec. 27-31, '62.—Infantry—16th, 49th, 44th, 69th, 83d.

CHAMPION HILLS, Mississippi, May 16, '63—Infantry—8th, 11th, 12th, 18th, 23d, 24th, 34th, 46th, 47th, 48th, 49th, 59th, 60th, 67th, 69th, 83d. Light Artillery—1st Battery.

CORNET BRIDGE, Louisiana, Dec. —, '62.—Heavy Artillery—1st (21st) Regiment.

COUCHERVILLE, Louisiana, May —, '64.—Light Artillery—3d, 9th Batteries.

CANE RUN, Louisiana, May —, '64.—3d, 9th Batteries.

CLINCH VALLEY, Tennessee, Jan. —, '64.--Infantry—79th.

COOSAVILLE, Georgia, Oct. —, '63.—Infantry—17th.

COURTLAND, Tennessee, Dec. —, '64. Cavalry—Tenth (125th) Regiment.

DUG GAP, Georgia, Sept. 11, '63.—Infantry—37th, 74th, 88th. Light Artillery—4th Battery.

DANDRIDGE, Tennessee, Jan. 17, '64.—Cavalry—Fifth (90th) Regiment. Light Artillery—18th, 24th Batteries.

DAVIS' MILLS, Mississippi, Dec. 21, '62.—Infantry—Detachment of 25th.

DOBBINS' FORD, Tennessee, Dec. 9, '62.—Infantry—35th.

DALTON, Georgia, August 15, '64.--Infantry—68th.

DECATUR, GEORGIA, July 19, '64.—Infantry—91st, 99th, 100th, 123d, 124th, 129th, 130th.

DALLAS, Georgia, May 27, '64.—Infantry—6th, 9th, 10th, 12th, 22d, 30th, 32d, 35th, 37th, 40th, 63d, 65th, 66th, 74th, 75th, 79th, 81st, 82d, 83d, 84th, 85th, 88th, 97th, 99th, 100th, 101st, 128th, 129th.

DUVAL'S BLUFF, Arkansas, June 10, '63.—Infantry—46th.

DECATUR, Alabama, Oct. 26-30, '64.—Infantry—68th, 73d. Cavalry—Detachment Tenth (125th) Regiment.

DESERTED FARM, Virginia, Jan. 30, '63.—Infantry—13th.

DES ALLEMANDS, Louisiana, Sept. 8, '62.—Heavy Artillery—1st (21st) Regiment.

DEEP BOTTOM, Virginia, Sept. 18, '64.—Infantry—13th, 20th.

DAY'S GAP, Alabama, April 30, '63.--Infantry—51st, 73d.

ELKWATER, Virginia, Sept. 12-13, '61.—Infantry—13th, 15th, 17th. Light Artillery—26th Battery.

EDGEFIELD JUNCTION, Tennessee, Aug. 20, '62.—Infantry—Detachment of 50th.

EBENEZER CHURCH, Alabama, April 1, '65.—Infantry—17th, 72d (mounted). Cavalry—Fourth (77th) Regiment. Light Artillery—18th Battery.

EGYPT STATION, Mississippi, Feb. —, '64.—Cavalry—Seventh (119th) Regiment.

LIST OF ENGAGEMENTS.

FLINT RIVER, Tenn., Dec. —, '64.—Cavalry—Tenth (125th) Regiment.
FLAT ROCK, Georgia, Oct. —, '63.—Infantry—17th.
FORT FISHER, North Carolina, Jan. 14-15, '65.—Infantry—13th, 63d, 65th, 80th, 91st, 140th. Light Artillery—15th Battery.
FORT DE RUSSY, Louisiana, March 14, '64.—Infantry—52d, 89th. Light Artillery—1st, 3d, 9th Batteries.
FRANKLIN, Tennessee, Nov. 30, '64.—Infantry—9th, 30th, 31st, 35th, 40th, 57th, 63d, 65th, 79th, 80th, 81st, 84th, 86th, 91st, 120th, 124th, 128th, 129th. Cavalry—Detachment of Eighth (39th) Regiment, Ninth (121st) Regiment, Eleventh (126th) Regiment. Light Artillery—15th, 18th, 22d, 23d Batteries.
FORT ANDERSON, North Carolina, Feb. 19, '65.—13th, 63d, 65th, 80th, 91st, 140th. Light Artillery—15th Battery.
FAIR GARDEN, Tennessee, Feb. 19, '65.—Cavalry—Second (41st) Regiment, Fourth (77th) Regiment. Light Artillery—18th Battery.
FORT PILLOW, Tennessee, June 5, '62.—Infantry—43d, 46th.
FORT DONELSON, Tennessee, Feb. 13-16, '62.—Infantry—11th, 25th, 31st, 44th, 52d.
FORT HENRY, Tennessee, Feb. 7, '62.—Infantry—23d.
FORT GILMORE, North Carolina, Sept. 29, '64.—Infantry—13th, 20th.
FISHER'S HILL, Virginia, Sept. 22, '64.—Infantry—8th, 11th, 18th. Light Artillery—17th Battery.
FORT McALLISTER, Georgia, Dec. 13, '64.—Infantry—83d, 90th. Light Artillery—19th Battery.
FOSTER'S FARM, Virginia, May 20, '64.—Infantry—13th.
FORT ESPARANZA, Texas, Nov. 27, '63.—Infantry—8th, 18th.
FUNKSTOWN, Maryland, July 10, '63.—Cavalry—Right Wing Third (45th) Regiment.
FALLING WATERS, Virginia, July 14, '63.—Cavalry—Right Wing Third (45th) Regiment.
FREDERICKSBURG, Virginia, Dec. 11-13, '62.—Infantry—7th, 14th, 19th, 20th.
FORT WAYNE, Arkansas, Oct. 28, '62.—Light Artillery—2d Battery.
FAIR OAKS, Virginia, May 31 to June 1, '62.—Infantry—20th.
FORT BLAKELY, Alabama, April 9, '65.—Infantry—24th, 52d, 69th, 93d. Cavalry—Tenth (125th) Regiment, Twelfth (127th) Regiment, Thirteenth (131st) Regiment. Light Artillery—3d Battery.
FREDERICKTOWN, Missouri, Oct. —, '61.—Cavalry—First (28th) Regiment.
FORT MORGAN, Alabama, Aug. 5-13, '64.—Infantry—67th. Heavy Artillery—1st (21st) Regiment.
FORT GAINES, Alabama, Aug. 5-8, '64.—Infantry—67th. Heavy Artillery—1st (21st) Regiment.
FARMINGTON, Tennessee, Oct. 7, '63.—Infantry—17th. Light Artillery—18th Battery.
FRONT ROYAL, Virginia, May 23, '62.—Infantry—27th. June 12, '62, 7th.
FIVE FORKS, Virginia, April 2, '65.—Cavalry—Right Wing Third (45th) Regiment.

LIST OF ENGAGEMENTS. 91

FITZHUGH'S CROSSING, Virginia, April 29, '63.—Infantry—19th.
FORT WAGNER, South Carolina, Sept. 7, '64,—Infantry—13th.
FORT SMITH, Arkansas, July 29-31, '64.—Light Artillery—2d Battery.
FRANKLIN, Missouri, Oct. 1, '64.—Infantry—52d.
GOLGOTHA CHURCH, Georgia, June 15, '64.—Infantry—33d, 85th.
GETTYSBURG, Pensylvania, July 1-3, '63.—Infantry—7th, 14th, 19th, 20th, 27th. Cavalry—Right Wing Third (45th) Regiment.
GREENBRIER, Virginia, Oct. 3, '61.—Infantry—7th, 9th, 13th. 14th, 15th, 17th.
GAINES' MILL, Virginia, June 27, '62.—Infantry—20th.
GAINESVILLE, Virginia, Aug 28, '62.—Infantry—19th.
GLENDALE, Virginia, June 28, '62,—Infantry—20th.
GRISWOLDVILLE, Georgia, Nov. 25, '64.—Infantry—12th.
GALLATIN, Tennessee, Aug. 21-27, '62.—Cavalry—2d (41st) Regiment.
GUNTOWN, Mississippi, June 10, '64.—Infantry—93d. Cavalry—Seventh (119th) Regiment. Light Artillery—6th, 14th Batteries.
GRAND COTEAU, Louisiana, Nov. 3, '63.—Infantry—46th, 47th, 60th, 67th.
GRAYSVILLE, Georgia, Nov. 27, '63.—Infantry—88th, 97th, 100th.
GOSHEN, Georgia, Oct —, '64.—Infantry—17th.
HATCHIE RIVER. Mississippi, Oct. 5, '62.—Infantry—25th, 53d.
HURRICANE CREEK, Mississippi, Aug. 13, '64.—Infantry—52d.
HARPER'S FERRY, Virginia, Sept. 13-15, '62.—Light Artillery—15th, 26th Batteries. July 6, '63, 17th Battery.
HOOVER'S GAP, Tennessee.—Infantry—17th, 68th, 72d (mounted), 74th, 75th, 82d, 87th, 88th, 101st. Light Artillery—4th, 18th, 19th, 21st Batteries.
HENDERSON'S HILL, Louisiana, Nov. 21, '64.—Infantry—18th. Light Artillery—9th Battery.
HARTWELL, Tennessee, Dec. 7, '62.—Light Artillery—13th Battery.
HENDERSON'S MILL, Tennessee, Oct. 11, '63.—Cavalry—Fifth (90th) Regiment.
HANOVER COURT HOUSE, Virginia, May 30-31, '64.—Cavalry—Right Wing Third (45th) Regiment.
HELENA, Arkansas, July 4, '63.—Infantry—43d.
HILLSBORO, Georgia, July 31. '64.—Cavalry—Detachment Fifth (90th) Regiment.
HUNTSVILLE, Alabama, Oct. 1, '64.—Cavalry—Detachment Twelfth (127th) Regim nt, Detachment Thirteenth (131st) Regiment.
HALLTOWN, Virginia, Aug. 24, '64.—Light Artillery—17th Battery.
HATCHER'S RUN, Virginia, April 2, '65.—Infantry—20th, 28th U. S. Col. Reg.
HURST'S STATION, Georgia, June —, '64.—Light Artillery—5th Battery.
IUKA, Mississippi, Sept, 19-20, '62.—Infantry—23d, 18th.
ISLAND No. 10, Mississippi River, March 10 to April 7, '62.—Infantry—31th, 43d, 46th, 47th, 59th.

LIST OF ENGAGEMENTS.

JACKSON, Mississippi, May 14, '63.—Infantry—8th, 23d, 47th, 48th, 59th, 93d.

JACKSON, Mississippi, (Siege) July 9-16. '63.—8th, 12th, 16th, 34th, 46th, 49th, 53d, 54th, 60th, 67th, 69th, 83d, 93d, 97th, 99th, 100th. Light Artillery—1st, 6th Batteries.

JONESBORO, Georgia, Sept. 1, '64.—Infantry—9th, 12th, 22d, 23d, 25th, 38th, 42d, 57th, 66th, 74th, 75th, 79th, 81st, 82d, 83d, 84th, 86th, 87th, 97th, 99th, 100th, 101st, 120th, 128th, 130th. Cavalry—Eighth (39th) Regiment., Left Wing Third (45th) Regiment.

JONESBORO, Georgia.—Light Artillery—5th, 15th, 19th, 20th Batteries.

KIRKSVILLE, Missouri, Aug. —, '62.—Light Artillery—3d Battery.

KINGSTON, Georgia, June —, '64.—Infantry—82d, 84th, 86th. Light Artillery—5th Battery.

KENESAW MOUNTAIN, Georgia, June 27, '64.—6th, 9th. 10th, 12th, 17th, 22d, 23d, 27th, 30th, 31st, 32d, 33d, 35th, 36th, 37th, 38th, 40th, 42d, 53d, 57th, 63d, 65th, 66th. 70th, 74th, 75th, 79th, 80th, 81st, 82d, 83d, 84th, 85th, 86th, 87th, 88th, 91st, 99th, 100th, 101st, 120th, 123d, 124th, 128th, 129th, 130th. Cavalry—Sixth (71st) Regiment. Light Artillery—5th, 7th, 11th, 15th, 19th, 22d, 23d, 24th Batteries.

KNOXVILLE, Tennessee, Nov. 17 to Dec. 4, '63.—Cavalry—Sixth (71st) Regiment. Light Artillery—15th, 23d, 24th, 26th Batteries.

KELLY'S ISLAND, Virginia, June 20, '61.—Infantry—11th.

KINGSTON, Tennessee, Nov. 7, '63.—Infantry—80th. Light Artillery—15th Battery.

LITTLE RIVER, Georgia, Oct. 26, '64.—Infantry—97th, 99th.

LOVEJOY'S STATION, Georgia, Sept. 2, '64.—Infantry—9th, 79th, 81st, 84th, 86th, 99th, 100th. Cavalry—Eighth (39th) Regiment.

LIBERTY GAP, Tennessee, June 26, '63.—Infantry—22d, 29th, 30th 32d, 81st. Cavalry—Eighth (39th) Regiment. Light Artillery—5th Battery.

LA MAVOO, Mississippi, Aug. 18, '64.—Cavalry—Detachment Seventh (119th) Regiment.

LOOKOUT MOUNTAIN, Georgia, Nov. 24, '63.—Infantry—9th, 38th, 40th, 42d, 80th, 88th. Light Artillery—4th Battery.

LITTLE OGEECHEE RIVER, Georgia, Dec. 8, '64.—Infantry—97th 99th.

LONE JACK, Missouri, Sept. 9, '62.—Light Artillery—2d, 3d Batteries.

LEXINGTON, Tennessee, Dec. 18, '62.—Light Artillery—Detachment 14th Battery.

LEWINSVILLE, Virginia, Sept. 11, '64.—Infantry—90th.

LAUREL HILL, Virginia, May 8, '64. Infantry—7th, 9th, 19th.

LAFOERCHE CROSSING, Louisiana, June 21, '63,—Heavy Artillery—Detachment 1st (21st) Regiment.

LOST MOUNTAIN, Georgia, June 17, '64.—Infantry—74th, 123d, 124th, 128th, 130th. Cavalry—Sixth (71st) Regiment. Light Artillery—18th Battery.

LOCUST GROVE, Virginia, Nov. —, '63.—Infantry—20th.

LEESBURG, Georgia, Aug. —, '64.—Infantry—17th.

LAVERGNE, Tennessee, Dec. 27, '62.—Infantry—58th.

LIST OF ENGAGEMENTS. 93

LITTLE HARPETH, Tennessee, Dec. —, '64.—Cavalry—Tenth (125th) Regiment.

MOORE'S HILL, Missouri, Aug. —, '62.—Light Artillery—3d Battery.

MOUNT HOPE, Tennessee, Dec. —, '64.—Cavalry—Tenth (125th) Regiment.

MUNFORDSVILLE, Kentucky, Sept. 14-16, '62.—Infantry—50th, 60th. Detachment (Recruits) 17th (mounted), 67th, 68th, 74th, 89th, Light Artillery—13th Battery.

MISSION RIDGE, Georgia, Nov. 25, '63.—6th, 9th, 10th, 12th, 15th, 22d, 32d, 35th, 38th, 40th, 42d, 44th, 57th, 58th, 59th, 68th, 74th, 75th, 79th, 82d, 83d, 86th, 87th, 88th, 97th, 99th, 100th, 101st. Cavalry—Left Wing Third (45th) Regiment. Light Artillery—4th, 7th, 8th, 10th, 11th, 12th, 19th, 21st Batteries.

MOBILE, Alabama, (Siege) March 27 to April 11, '65.—Infantry—24th, 26th, 47th, 50th, 52d, 67th, 69th, 89th, 93d. Cavalry—Tenth (125th) Regiment, Twelfth (127th) Regiment, Thirteenth (131st) Regiment. Light Artillery—1st, 3d, 14th Batteries. Heavy Artillery—First (21st) Regiment.

MARIETTA, Georgia, July 3, '64.—Infantry—6th, 9th, 17th, 33d, 70th.

MEADOW BRIDGE, Virginia, May 12, '64.—Cavalry—Right Wing Third (45th) Regiment.

MOSSY CREEK, Tennessee, Jan. 12, '64.—Infantry—79th, 80th. Cavalry—Fourth (77th) Regiment, Fifth (90th) Regiment. Light Artillery—18th, 24th Batteries.

MUSTANG ISLAND, Texas, Nov. 17, '63.—Infantry—8th, 18th.

MARYLAND HEIGHTS, Maryland, July 4, '64.—Light Artillery—17th Battery.

MINE RUN, Virginia, Nov. 30, '63.—Infantry—7th, 14th, 19th, 20th.

MORRISVILLE, North Carolina, April —, '65.—Cavalry—Eighth (39th) Regiment.

McMINNVILLE, Tennessee, Aug. 9, '62.—Cavalry—Second (41st) Regiment. Aug. 30, '62.—Light Artillery—8th Battery. Oct. 4, '63.—Infantry—17th. Light Artillery—18th Battery.

MARKS' MILLS, Arkansas, April 30, '64.—Infantry—43d, 50th. Light Artillery—2d Battery.

MADISONVILLE, Kentucky, Aug. 28, '62.—Infantry—65th. Oct. 5, '62—Cavalry—Fourth (77th) Regiment.

MORTON'S FORD, Virginia, Feb. 10, '64.—Infantry—14th.

MALVERN HILL, Virginia, July 1, '62.—Infantry—20th.

McDOWELL, Virginia, May 8, '62.—Light Artillery—26th Battery.

MILL SPRINGS, Kentucky, Jan. 19, '62.—Infantry—10th.

MULDRAUGH'S HILL, Kentucky, Aug. 28, '62.—Cavalry—Sixth (71st) Regiment.

MONTEREY, Kentucky, March —, '62 —Light Artillery—13th Battery.

MANASSAS GAP, Virginia, July 23, '63.—Infantry—20th.

MOORE'S PLANTATION, Louisiana, May 7, '64.—Infantry—52d, 89th. Light Artillery—1st, 3d, 9th Batteries.

MOORESVILLE, Alabama, Nov. 31, '63.—Infantry—72d (mounted).

MILTON, Tennessee, March —, '63.—Infantry—101st.

LIST OF ENGAGEMENTS.

MURFREESBORO, (Defense of) Dec. 7, '64.—Infantry—140th.

MACON, Georgia, April 20, '65.—Infantry—17th, 72d (mounted). Light Artillery- 18th, 24th Batteries.

NEW MARKET, Tennessee, Dec. —, '63.—Infantry—79th.

NASHVILLE, Tennessee, Dec. 15-16 '64.—Infantry—9th, 30th, 31st, 35th, 36th, 40th, 51st, 52d, 57th, 64th, 65th, 68th, 79th, 80th, 81st, 84th, 86th, 89th, 91st, 93d, 120th, 123d, 124th, 128th, 129th, 130th. Cavalry—Sixth (71st) Regiment Tenth (125th) Regiment, Eleventh (126th) Regiment, Detachment Thirteenth (131st) Regiment. Light Artillery—2d, 3d, 9th, 12th, 14th, 15th, 18th, 20th, 21st, 22d, 23d, 24th, 25th Batteries.

NEWNAN, Georgia, July 31, '64.—Cavalry—Second (41st) Regiment, Fourth (77th) Regiment. Light Artillery—18th Battery.

NEW HOPE CHURCH, Georgia, May 25, '64.—Infantry—6th, 9th, 12th, 17th, 27th, 31st, 33d, 36th, 40th, 57th, 70th, 79th, 83d, 91st, 97th, 100th, 128th. Light Artillery—5th Battery.

NEWTONIA, Missouri, Oct. 10, '62.—Infantry—26th.—Light Artillery 2d Battery.

NOTTOWAY C. H., Virginia, June —, '64.—Cavalry—Right Wing Third (45th) Regiment.

NORTH ANNA RIVER, Virginia, May 25, '64.—Infantry—7th, 14th, 19th, 20th.

NEW MARKET, Virginia, Sept. 23, '64.—Infantry—8th, 11th, 18th. Light Artillery—17th Battery.

NEW MADRID, Missouri, (Siege) March 3-14, '62.—Infantry—34th, 43d, 46th, 47th, 59th.

OLD OAKS, Louisiana, May —, '64.—Light Artillery—3d Battery.

OKOLONA, Mississippi, Feb. 22, '64.—Cavalry—Seventh (119th) Regiment.

OVERALL'S CREEK, Tennessee, Dec. —, '64.—Cavalry—Twelfth (127th) Regiment, Detachment Thirteenth (131st) Regiment.

OPELOUSAS, Louisiana, Oct. 21, '63.—Infantry—11th.

ORCHARDS, Virginia, June 25, '62.—Infantry—20th.

OPEQUAN, Virginia, Sept. 19, '64.—Infantry—8th, 11th, 18th. Cavalry—Right Wing Third (45th) Regiment. Light Artillery—17th Battery.

PHILAMONT, Virginia, Nov. 1, '63.—Right Wing Third (45th) Regiment.

PORT REPUBLIC, Virginia, June 9, '62.—Infantry—7th.

PICKETT'S MILLS, Georgia, June —, '64.—Infantry—86th.

PUMPKINVINE CHURCH, Virginia, June —, '64.—Infantry—17th.

PINE MOUNTAIN, Georgia, June —, '64.- Light Artillery—5th Battery.

PORT GIBSON, Mississippi, May —, '63.—Infantry—8th, 11th, 16th, 18th, 24th, 3 th, 46th, 49th, 54th, 66th, 67th, 69th. Light Artillery—1st Battery.

PLEASANT HILL, Louisiana, April 9, '64.—Infantry—46th, 47th, Detachment of 52d, 80th. Light Artillery—1st, 3d, 9th Batteries.

PALMETTO RANCHE, Texas, May 13, '65.—Infantry—34th.

PERRYVILLE, Indian Teratory, Aug. 28, '63.—Light Artillery—Detachment of 2d Battery.

LIST OF ENGAGEMENTS. 95

PORT HUDSON, Mississippi, (Siege) May 21 to July 8, '63.—Heavy Artillery—1st (21st) Regiment.

PEACH TREE CREEK, Georgia. July 20, '64.—Infantry—9th, 22d, 27th, 32d, 33d, 37th, 40th, 42d, 43d, 57th, 70th, 74th, 75th, 82d, 84th, 85th, 86th 87th, 88th, 91st. Light Artillery—5th, 19th Batteries.

PRAIRIE LEON, Arkansas, April 10, '64.—Infantry—43d, 50th. Light Artillery—2d Battery.

PULASKI, Tennessee, Sept. 27, '64.—Cavalry—Sixth (71st) Regiment, Tenth (125th) Regiment. Eleventh (126th) Regiment.

PERRYVILLE, OR CHAPLIN HILLS, Kentucky, Oct. 8, '62.—Infantry—9th, 10th, 15th, 22d, 35th, 38th, 42d, 44th, 57th, 79th, 80th, 87th, 88th. Cavalry—Second (41st) Regiment. Light Artillery—4th, 5th, 7th, 8th, 19th Batteries.

PETERSBURG, Virginia, (Siege) June 16, '64 to April 3, '65.—Infantry—7th, 13th, Detachment 14th, 19th, 20th, 28th U. S. Colored Regiment.

POWDER SPRING GAP, Tennessee, Dec. 15, '63.—Infantry—65th.

PEA RIDGE, Tennessee, April 15, '62.—Cavalry—Second (41st) Regiment.

PARKER'S CROSS ROADS, Tennessee, Dec. 31, '62.—Infantry—50th.

PRAIRIE GROVE, Arkansas, Dec. 7, '62.—Infantry—26th. Light Artillery—2d Battery.

PEA RIDGE, Arkansas, Nov. 6-8, '62.—Infantry—8th, 18th, 22d. Light Artillery—1st Battery.

PHILIPPI, Virginia, June 3, '61.—Infantry—6th, 7th, 9th.

PO RIVER, Virginia, May 10-12, '64.—Infantry—7th, 14th, 19th, 20th.

ROUND LAKE, Louisiana, May —, '64.—Light Artillery—3d Battery.

REYNOLD'S HILL, Tennessee, Dec. —, '64.—Cavalry—Tenth (125th) Regiment.

ROME, Georgia, May 17, '64.—Infantry—17th, 22d.

RAYMOND, Mississippi, May 12, '63 —Infantry—23d, 48th, 49th.

ROCK SPRINGS, Georgia, Sept. 12, '63.—Infantry—72d (mounted).

RED OAK STATION, Georgia, Aug. 20, '64.—Infantry—22d.

RED MOUND, Arkansas, April 17, '64.—Infantry—43d, 50th. Light Artillery—2d Battery.

ROCKY FACE RIDGE, Georgia, May 9, '64.—Infantry—22d, 57th, 63d, 81st, 84th, 86th, 87th, 99th, 123d, 130th. Light Artillery—5th, 14th, 19th Batteries.

RINGGOLD, Georgia, Nov. 27, '63 —Infantry—88th.

ROUND HILL, Arkansas, July 7, '62.—Cavalry—First (28th) Regiment.

ROWLETT'S STATION, Kentucky, Dec. 17, '61.—Infantry—Detachment 32d.

RHEATOWN, Tennessee, Oct. 11, '63.—Infantry—65th.

RICHMOND, Kentucky, Aug. 29-30, '62.—Infantry—12th, 16th, 66th, 69th. Cavalry—Sixth (71st) Regiment.

RUSSELLVILLE, Kentucky, Sept. 30, '62.—Infantry—70th.

RICH MOUNTAIN, Virginia, July 1, '61.—Infantry—8th, 10th, 13th.

LIST OF ENGAGEMENTS.

RAPPAHANNOCK STATION, Virginia, Aug. 4, '63.—Cavalry—Right Wing Third (45th) Regiment.

RIDDLE'S SHOP, Virginia, June 13, '64.—Cavalry—Right Wing Third (45th) Regiment.

ROANOKE STATION, Virginia, June —, '64.—Cavalry—Right Wing Third (45th) Regiment.

ROMNEY, Virginia, June 11, '61.—Infantry—11th.

RESACA, Georgia, May 15, '64.—Infantry—6th, 9th, 12th, 22d, 27th, 30th, 31st, 32d, 33d, 35th, 36th, 37th, 38th, 40th, 42d, 57th, 63d, 65th, 66th, 70th, 75th, 79th, 80th, 81st, 82d, 84th, 85th, 86th, 87th, 88th, 97th, 99th, 100th, 101st, 120th, 123d, 124th, 125th, 129th, 136th. Cavalry—Sixth (71st) Regiment. Light Artillery—5th, 7th, 11th, 15th, 18th, 19th, 22d, 23d, 24th Batteries.

RIVERS' BRIDGE, South Carolina, Feb. 2-3, '65.—Infantry—25th.

SUGAR CREEK, Tennessee, Dec. —, '64.—Cavalry—Tenth (125th) Regiment.

HONE MOUNTAIN, Georgia, July —, '64.—Infantry—17th.

SELMA, Alabama, April 2, '65.—Infantry—17th, 72d (mounted). Cavalry—Fourth (77th) Regiment. Light Artillery—18th Battery.

SPANISH FORT, Alabama, (Siege) March 27 to April 19, '65.—Heavy Artillery—21st. Infantry—26th, 50th, 52d, 93d. Cavalry—Tenth (125th), Twelfth (127th) and Thirteenth (131st) Regiments. Light Artillery—1st and 14th Batteries.

SNAKE CREEK GAP, Georgia, October 15, '64.—Infantry—25th.

SALEM CHURCH, Virginia, June 3, '64.—Cavalry—Right Wing Third (45th) Regiment.

SAILOR'S CREEK, Virginia, April 2, '65.—Cavalry—Right Wing Third (45th) Regiment.

STONEY CREEK, Virginia, April 2, '65.—Cavalry—Right Wing Third (45th) Regiment.

SKAGG'S MILLS, Tennessee, December 15, '63.—Infantry—65th.

SCOTTSVILLE, Alabama, April 2, '65.—Cavalry—Second (41st) Regiment.

ST. CHARLES, Arkansas, June 17, '62.—Infantry—40th.

SUNSHINE CHURCH, Georgia, July 31, '64.—Light Artillery—24th Battery.

STONE RIVER, Tennessee, December 31, '62 to January 2, '63.—Infantry—6th, 9th, 15th, 22d, 29th, 30th, 31st, 32d, 35th, 36th, 37th, 38th, 40th, 42d, 44th, 51st, 57th, 58th, 73d, 79th, 81st, 82d, 86th, 88th. Cavalry—Eighth (39th) Regiment, Left Wing Third (45th) Regiment. Light Artillery—4th, 5th, 7th, 8th and 10th Batteries.

SHILOH, Tennessee, April 6-7, '62.—Infantry—6th, 9th, 11th, 15th, 23d, 24th, 25th, 29th, 30th, 31st, 32d, 36th, 44th and 57th. Cavalry—Eighth (39th) Regiment. Light Artillery—6th and 9th Batteries.

SAVANNAH, Georgia, (Siege) December 10-21, '64.—Infantry—12th, 22d, 25th 42d.

SULPHUR BRANCH TRESTLE, Alabama, September 25, '64.—Cavalry—Detachment of Ninth (121st) Regiment.

SNICKER'S GAP, Virginia, November 11, '63.—Light Artillery—10th Battery.

SECOND BULL RUN, Virginia, August 28-30, '62.—Infantry—7th, 19th, 20th, 63d. Light Artillery—6th Battery.

LIST OF ENGAGEMENTS. 97

SPOTTSYLVANIA, Virginia, May 8-10, '64.—Infantry—7th, 14th, 19th, 20th. Cavalry—Right Wing Third (45th) Regiment.

STRAWBERRY PLAINS, Virginia, September 15, '64.—Infantry —13th, 20th.

SABINE CROSS ROADS, Louisiana, (or Mansfield) April 8, '64.— Infantry—16th, 46th, 47th, 60th, 67th. Light Artillery—1st Battery. Heavy Artillery—Twenty-First (1st) Regiment.

SUFFOLK, Virginia, (Defense) April 10 to May 3, '64.—Infantry— 13th.

SUMMERVILLE, Virginia, May 7, '62—Infantry—13th.

SOUTH MOUNTAIN, Maryland, September 14, '62.—Infantry— 19th. Cavalry—Right Wing Third (45th) Regiment. Light Artillery —16th Battery.

SAVAGE'S STATION, Virginia, June 29, '62.—Infantry—20th.

TAYLOR'S RIDGE, Georgia, May —. '64.—Infantry—9th.

TUSCUMBIA, Alabama, May 31, '62.—Cavalry—Second (41st) Regiment.

TALBOTT'S STATION, Tennessee, December 29, '63.—Cavalry— Second (41st) Regiment.

TUPELLO, Mississippi, June 14, '64.—Infantry—52d, 89th, 93d. Light Artillery—3d, 6th and 9th Batteries.

TUNNELL HILL, Georgia, May 7, '64.—Infantry—6th, 9th, 22d, 48th 84th. Light Artillery—5th Battery.

THOMPSON'S COVE, Tennessee, October 3, '63.—Infantry—17th. Light Artillery—18th Battery.

TRIUNE, Tennessee, June 11, '63.—Infantry—84th. Cavalry—Second (41st) Regiment.

THOMPSON'S HILL, Mississippi, May —, '63.—Infantry—23d.

TERRE NOIR, Arkansas, April 2, '64—Infantry—43d, 50th. Light Artillery—2d Battery.

TOWN CREEK BRIDGE, North Carolina, February 20,'65.—Infantry —13th, 63d, 65th, 80th, 91st, 140th. Light Artillery—15th Battery.

THOMPSON'S STATION, Tennessee, March 5, '63 —Infantry—33d, 85th.

THE WILDERNESS, Virginia, May 5-6, '64.—Infantry—7th, 14th, 19th, 20th.

UNION, Virginia, Nov. 2, '63.—Cavalry—Right Wing 3d (45th) Regiment.

UPPERVILLE, Virginia, Nov. 3, '63.—Cavalry—Right Wing 3d (45th) Regiment. June 21, '64—Right Wing 3d (45th) Regiment.

VINEGAR HILL, Kentucky, Sept. 22, '62.—Cavalry—Second (41st) Regiment.

VICKSBURG, Mississippi, (Siege.) May 18 to July 4, '63.—Infantry— 8th, 11th, 12th, 16th, 18th, 23d, 24th, 26th, 34th, 46th, 47th, 48th, 49th, 53d, 54th, 59th, 64th, 67th, 69th, 83d, 93d, 99th, 100th. Light Artillery— 1st Battery.

VERNON, Mississippi, Dec. 28, '64.—Cavalry—7th (119th) Regiment.

VANDERBURG, Kentucky, Sept. 12, '62.—Infantry—Detachment 65th Regiment.

LIST OF ENGAGEMENTS.

VARNELL'S STATION, Georgia, May 9, '64.—Cavalry—Second (41st) and Fourth (77th) Regiments.
VAN BUREN, Arkansas, Dec. 29th, '62.—Infantry—26th. Light Artillery—2d Battery.
VERSAILLES, Kentucky, Oct. 5, '62.—Light Artillery—13th Battery.
WILD CAT, Kentucky, Oct. 21, '61.—Infantry—33d.
WEST POINT, Georgia, April 16, '65.—Infantry—72d (mounted). Cavalry—Second (41st) Regiment. Light Artillery—18th Battery.
WALKER'S FORD, Tennessee. Dec 2, '63.—Infantry—65th, 116th, 118th. Cavalry—Fifth (90th) Regiment.
WILKINSON'S PIKE, Tennessee, Dec. —, '64.—Cavalry—Twelfth (127th) and Detachment Thirteenth (131st) Regiments.
WHITE OAK SWAMP, Virginia, June 30, '62.—Infantry—20th. June 13, '64.—Cavalry—Right Wing Third (45th) Regiment.
WINCHESTER, Virginia, March 22-23, '62.—Infantry—7th, 13th, 14th. May 25, '62.—Infantry—27th.
WILLIAMSPORT, Maryland, July 11, '63.—Cavalry—Right Wing Third (45th) Regiment.
WISE'S FORKS, North Carolina, March 10, '65.—Infantry—120th, 123d, 124th, 128th, 129th, 130th.
WATHEL JUNCTION, Virginia, May 7, '64.—Infantry—13th.
YELLOW BAYOU, Louisiana, May 18, '64.—Infantry—32d, 89th. Light Artillery—1st, 3d and 9th Batteries.
YELLOW HOUSE, Virginia, Aug. 19-21, '64.—Infantry—7th, Detachment of 19th.
ZOLLICOFFER, Tennessee, Sept. 20, '63.—Infantry—65th. Cavalry—Fifth (90th) Regiment.

REMINISCENCES.

INTRODUCTORY.

A number of reminiscences have been prepared by members of Company D, which are here presented for the purpose of preserving to their families the individual duties and experiences required in a more varied service than fell to the lot of most soldiers. The company took part in the active field campaign resisting the advance of the rebel army under Gen. Braxton Bragg on Louisville, in September, 1862, and in the advance from Murfreesboro of our own army under Gen. Rosecrans, in June, 1863, ending with the most terrible battle of the war, at Chicamauga, Ga., Sept. 19 and 20, our company losing more than half the number killed or wounded that were in the battle; then the siege of Chattanooga and its raising by the capture of Lookout Mountain and Missionary Ridge; the march to Knoxville immediately after, and the winter campaign without camp equipage and living principally off the country; after this, garrison duty at Chattanooga, protecting that most important place while Sherman moved forward to Atlanta and the sea -with his army, rush-

ing at an hour's notice to any point where an attack was made on our lines of communication; after this, in front at Decatur resisting the advance of the Rebel army under Gen. Hood in its last great effort to get North; and finally opening the great battle at Nashville by attacking on the right of the enemy, and following up in the pursuit until it was abandoned, and the war ended by the disbanding of their army.

BY J. H. MAUZY.

My first duty in camp was as officer of the day, on Aug. 14, 1862, and it was the first day that anything was done in Camp Logan in the way of sentinel and guard duty. The non-commissioned officers were appointed on this day. The most of them, and many of the commissioned officers, did not know the meaning of the commands or calls or even how to "fall into ranks," and the men who had any experience enjoyed making the confusion more confounded. Officers were called by their nick-names, and the men did not like to be stopped from going past their "chums" who were on guard duty with sticks for guns. My military experience was limited to the Zouave drill with the McReynold Guards at Rushville, and I knew nothing of actual camp life, so that I had a lively 24 hours' duty there in trying to get others to do what I knew nothing of. A soldier who had been out in the three-months or one-year service on duty as camp guard

would cry out "Corporal of the guard, beat No. 5." The Corporal would go to see what was wanted, when the guard would say that he wanted to get a drink of water; the Corporal would take his place and the guard would go off. Soon another guard would call out "Corporal of the guard, beat No. 9," and the Sergeant would go and find that the guard wanted to get some tobacco. He would take his place, and then "Corporal of the guard, beat No. 7," would be called out. The Sergeant and Corporal both being away, I went to Colonel Shaw and told him that I had run out of non-commissioned officers with whom to relieve sentinels who were calling. He gave me a "a pointer," and we soon stopped that game. The fact that it was the first time most of the men were ever restricted to certain bounds of a few acres, seemed to make them want to go outside the more, and it was a kind of adventure to get out. The difference in rank was a hard thing for all to learn, both in respect to the duties required and to the title. Tom, Dick or Harry were used when the soldiers should have said, Corporal, Sergeant, or higher rank. It was a regular picnic at Camp Logan. Day and night there was music, singing, dancing and story telling, when not on duty, and we were called to go before the novelty wore off.

In less than ten days from the time of leaving our homes we were trying the realities of war in Kentucky, and within thirty days from our muster into the United States service, we had campaigned over one hundred miles in that State and were prisoners at Munford-

ville, where we were surrendered with the "honors of war."

My first serious experience in the war was at Lebanon, Ky., September 6, 1862, where I had charge of a picket station over a mile south of that place. I had allowed one relief to go foraging, another was on duty at the outposts, and the third was with me at the station, about a quarter of a mile from the outposts. After noon an orderly dashed up and handed me a large envelope, which I opened and read: "Bring in your pickets immediately. E. DUMONT, Brigadier General." I still have the order. I was in a quandary, not knowing whether I was about to be attacked by a largely superior force, or what was going to happen. I sent men running to call out and try and get my foragers in. We waited, all of us nervously, a half-hour, but none came. We fell back a short distance, and waited again, and so for two hours, perhaps, when they came. But our astonishment was increased when we got back into the town and did not see a single soldier. The streets were deserted and the houses shut up. Finally some one called to us that our troops were down the railroad, getting on the cars, and that the rebels were coming in from the other side of town. We chose our direction quickly, and caught up with our troops in time to get on the cars for Lebanon Junction. There pressing duties came so fast that my detail was never looked after. A few days later we were at Munfordville and out of the way of a court-martial which I feared. It taught me a lesson—to keep my

command always ready for orders, although the temptation to relax rules was very great whenever there was a good prospect for a change of fare.

The day after our regiment changed camp into Wood's Division, at Chattanooga, October 21, 1863. Captain J. H. Mauzy, with Lieutenant John Reese, of Company C., was detailed to take charge of a guard of about fifty men, to escort a train of some fifty or more wagons to Stevenson, Ala., for supplies. At this time we were suffering much on account of short rations and heavy duties to perform. So we marched gladly away, thinking that by foraging we might better our condition. The Fall rains had begun, and the starved mules fell by the wayside until the road was lined with them nearly the entire distance of eighty miles; for we had to go the longest way to get there, the short route being controlled by the rebels. It was a sad sight to see our poor, faithful mules pull through the mud and over the mountains as long as they could stand up, and then fall in their tracks and die. We lived on parched corn until we got over Waldon's Ridge on the third day, and went into camp, twenty-seven miles out, having thirty mules dead and abandoned seven wagons. We sent out a forage train, which came back loaded, and we staid two days to feed up. Having no salt, our fresh meat, with persimmons, did not agree with us, and there were some very sick men for a few hours. The roads were so bad and the mules so weak, we could go only about twelve miles a day. October 29, we arrived at Bolivar, and went into camp to feed

up the mules we had left, (I think about half of them) for the return trip. Here I bought three tin plates at thirty cents each, three tin cups at twenty-five cents each, and a small tin coffee pot for $1.00, and our mess put on some style after that. November 8, we started back with our wagons loaded, and went the short route along the river, which had just been opened up; but for two miles in the gorge along the river the sight was horrible. The rebels had burned a large train of wagons, a few days previous, and shot the mules, and the stench from the partly burned animals was fearful. We got back to Chattanooga, November 12. A few days afterward, my bunk-mate on this trip, Lieutenant Reese, was killed in the charge on Mission Ridge.

The hardest march I ever endured, I think, was to East Tennessee, after the battles at Chattanooga. It was made in rainy, muddy, snowy, wintry weather, in light marching order, except that we had to carry everything we needed. It was the more disagreeable to me because I had been on staff duty with a horse to ride before this; and it was made still worse by my putting on a new pair of boots just before starting on the march. For days they remained on my feet and I suffered slow torture. I knew that if I took them off I could not get them on again, and so I suffered and plodded on. Captain Leeson was the only other captain along, and was the ranking officer and in command of the regiment. He had a horse which he often allowed the sick to ride, but as they were in a worse condition than myself, I did not feel envious.

At Marysville we struck the flour mills, and I will never forget the solid bread which we cooked in the ashes or on boards by the fire. It was not so heavy as solid shot, but made a similar impression when thrown. On the night march to Knoxville we ate parched corn. The rain poured down, and we rejoiced when, just before we got there, we heard the rebels had been repulsed there, at Fort Saunders, with great loss to them.

May 20, 1864, I was detailed by order of Major General Steedman to command a detail to guard to Nashville a train of box cars loaded with rebel prisoners, captured in the battle at Resaca, Ga. The trip was rendered dangerous by bushwhackers and guerrillas, who often fired into and captured trains. The engineer made it more so, by running very fast in the places where the woods were thickest. Nearly all the prisoners were satisfied to quit, freely saying that they considered their cause hopeless. But there was a Texan, and a Kentuckian, from Georgetown, who said they would "die in the last ditch." There was one boy, 18 years old, in whose story I took much interest, he seemed so honest and so homesick. He said his father was a graduate of West Point, and was a member of the Georgia convention that passed the ordinance of secession, and voted against it. He was then Mayor of Milledgeville, and his name was J. C. Haygood. The boy said he did not want to fight against the stars and stripes, and that he would take the oath of allegiance, and stay North and work until

the war was over. I gave him some directions and names to use when he got North, but never heard of him afterwards.

A military commission was in session at Chattanooga from July 29 to August 6, 1864, for the District of the Etowah. Captain William Glover was tried by it as a guerrilla. A band of desperadoes, under Gatewood, the noted outlaw, had terrorized all the country with a force of several hundred deserters from both armies, killing and robbing, so that it was not safe for soldier or citizen to be caught by them. So great was the fear of this gang that but little testimony could be got against them. General Bragg sent in by a flag of truce his testimony that Captain Glover was his Chief of Scouts and in the line of duty. The court believed from the evidence that he had been with the guerrillas, and sentenced him to eight years in the penitentiary. The trial lasted five days, and he had noted lawyers for his defense. About one hundred officers, soldiers, conductors on railroads, citizens and spies were tried by this court in a six months' session.

Dr. R. D. Mauzy was appointed a special surgeon to visit the army immediately after the battle of Chicamauga, September 19-20, 1863, and reported at Chattanooga a few days after. While there he was kept actively at work in the field hospital north of the river. But as soon as the wounded had all been cared for, he visited the 68th. In order to make him acquainted with the "Johnny Rebs.," he was taken out to the

picket lines, where at that time our front was on good terms. We met half way between the lines, which were not over 200 yards apart, and exchanged papers. At the same time the brigades next on our left would fire at each other whenever a head was shown above the rails that were used for protection. The doctor made his visit short, saying "they might take him for some prominent general, and not want to miss their chance, as they did with General Palmer, a few days before, when he was riding along the lines in citizen's clothes."

II.—BY LEE GOODWIN.

My first day's experience in camp at Greensburg taught me, by a lucky find of some potatoes, which I baked in the ashes, and which my mess enjoyed very much, while many others were growling around hungry, to always see after my own commissary supplies. And although at times the opportunity and place forbade any luxuries, my hunger made a sauce that supplied all deficiencies in that line. The pumpkin which we roasted on a pile of cedar rails, the first night after we were captured, failed to stew dry enough, but it was "Hobson's choice"—that or nothing. Further along on our march, at Rough Creek, I made a pin-hook and caught three small fish, fried them in tallow, and as my mate (J. H. Roberts,) did not like them cooked that way, I had a "square meal."

When we were exchanged and went South, Thomas Bosley said to me: "Lee, you do the foraging, and I will do the packing and cooking." So he made himself a haversack, which looked like a "pup-tent" sewed up into a haversack. He fulfilled the contract until the battle of Mission Ridge, where he was wounded in the leg. But before he was wounded, and on the first day on the line of battle, we advanced side by side to the rail pile, (all the boys will know what I mean by the rail pile) when a rebel shell went whizzing near. Bosley went spinning around on his feet, and in a moment fell. I stopped with him to see if he was badly hurt; but in an instant he opened his eyes as wide as they could be, and asked: "What in the h–ll was that?" He soon got up and moved on. Before this battle, rations ran so short that we stole the corn from the mules, parched it, and ate with a relish wormy crackers, and almost anything we could get. In the battle of Chicamauga I remember the remark of Frank Gisselbach, the Dutchman. When he was shot through the neck, the ball made a great number of holes through his rubber blanket, which was in a roll over his shoulders. He said: "The hole in his neck would grow up, but, by dam, the holes in his blanket would not." I also remember that if ever I wanted to see night come, it was on Sunday evening, in that battle, and I think most others felt in the same way.

Never will I forget a detail I went on with a wagon-train, to Stevenson, Ala., after supplies, while we

were shut up in Chattanooga, with only one way to get out and a long distance to go over the mountains. We camped in the Sequatchie Valley, to feed up our dying mules, and had to forage for all we got. George Smith and I went out, and found a hog. It was very poor, but we skinned it, and took it to camp. Poppino had gone in another direction, and brought in some potatoes. We cooked them together, and ate very heartily. Persimmons being ripe and very plenty, we finished up on them. A sicker lot of boys, with colic, you never saw. Our picket lines were very close together at this time, in Chattanooga, and were often relieved in fogs dark as night. One morning before daylight, General Willich, our brigade commander, came out to our reserve post (our captain was on duty at the time), and said: "Captain, do you know where all your pickets are stationed, and have you visited them all?" The Captain answered that he had visited nearly all of them. The General exclaimed: "My God! you should just so well know every man you got, as you know where you get your bread and butter." After the battle at Dalton, while we were eating our supper, a very small boy and girl came up, looking very wistful, and we asked them to eat with us. While eating they were telling how the "Johnnies" did while Bragg was camped about Dalton. The little girl said "One Johnny shot another Johnny." We asked her how that came. She said that he shot at a sheep, missed it, and killed a Johnny. It seemed to tickle the little ones very much. It was at this time that Ryland Bosley re-

marked, when he saw William Aldridge eating a hunk of ginger bread, which he had gobbled, "that the war was about over"—for it showed that luxuries were finding their way to the front.

I was never in a hospital during my term of service, and was in every engagement that the regiment was in except one. I was detailed on special duty at the time. I was not wounded while I was out. I I have a buckshot which I caught in my haversack at the battle of Chicamauga, and which a tin plate and some crackers stopped from hitting me in the hip.

I will close with William Innis' reply to the native: "Does Injeanny jine Tennessee?" "Yes, and laps half way over."

III.—BY JOHN M. FRANCIS.

The first impressions that I got of soldering were when Captain Innis, in his solemn way, swore me into the service, while standing on the sidewalk in the village of Milroy. I was only seventeen years old, and small of my age, and drew the attention of a large blacksmith in the crowd, by the name of Asbury Richey. He stepped up to my side and called the attention of the crowd by saying: "Boys, it is a tarnel shame to take such a small boy as this in the army, and break him down before he gets his set. What can he do a-soldering along by the side of me?" The con-

trast was so great it let me down from the height of thinking I was a man to that of being a small boy again. Only a few days elapsed until we were in Kentucky, marching from Bardstown to Lebanon. I saw my heavy-weight comrade limping and waddling like a duck in a thunder-storm. I stepped up to his side and began to look back, first over one shoulder, then the other, and drew his attention. Notwithstanding his piety and good nature, it was too much, and he blurted out: "What in the h—ll are you looking for?" Assuming as long a face as possible, I tried to make it appear that I had lost my knapsack; whereupon my burly comrade began to swear as only a tired soldier sometimes did. Mills Souder struck up "John Brown's Body," and sang and marched like it was fun. My heavy comrade soon found out that he could not stand the service, and had to be discharged. Years after I met him on the street in the same village. He took me by the hand and gave it a shake, such as you would expect from a grizzly bear, and turning to those about said: "Boys, this fellow is made out of hog's nose, and was the darndest toughest fellow in our regiment." It was a hard matter to determine by their looks who would stand the hardships the best. It was no uncommon thing to see men who were the very picture of health go down on a hard march, and young stripplings of boys in their teens turning hand springs or wrestling with a comrade after arriving in camp. Tom Patterson, Jeff. Trimble, Jim Richey, and myself have had to do extra-duty for such things. Not seeing

how the joke came in, we would sometimes try to get others into a little trouble. Sergeant Cohn was the left guide of the company on drill, and would call out, "Left!" with a peculiar accent, which the boys will all remember. My position was next to him. When marching by flank we would dress on him, and watching my chance, I would, with my elbow, throw him as far as I could in advance. The Captain would look down the line, and see his left guide out of position, and would give him such a reprimand as the strongest language would convey. The Sergeant, knowing it was my fault, did not think as much of me as a soldier would of his last "hard tack" on a long march, with no prospect of the supply train getting up. He watched to get me into trouble, but his peculiar tact got him details which kept him away from the company most of the time. He was a Jew, and made the service pay, and after the war went South into business.

I believe the worst trade I ever made in my life was when we were prisoners in Bragg's army. One of the long, lean, lank guards, seeing that I had a new canteen, said: "Hello, Yank, how would you like to trade canteens?" showing his, which was made out of cedar in the shape of a barrel, and with brass hoops. Its beauty and the thought of taking it home as a trophy, made me willing to trade without any further talk. Next day we started on our long, tiresome and dusty march, and I soon realized that hot pond-water in a new cedar canteen was one of the worst drinks I ever tackled.

Up to the time of the battle of Chicamauga (September 19, 1863,) my company had never been in what I considered a big battle, and boy-like, I had come to the conclusion that the "Johnnies" would be driven to the jumping-off place and the confederacy "busted" without my getting an opportunity to perform some daring exploit, in the midst of a great conflict. On Saturday, September 19, 1863, about 3 o'clock in the afternoon, our command marched by the right flank off of the road and into the woods, where we first struck the rebel lines. Poor Caleb Lee fell pierced by a minnie ball, the first one in our company. At his request Poppino and I took off his cartridge box and belt. Then it was that business commenced in earnest. There was the rebel line forming and dressing up on their colors as coolly, it seemed to me, as if they were on dress parade. We began to pour the balls from our rifles into their ranks as fast as it was possible for us to do so, and in return received their fire. For my life I could not tell how long we remained at the first stand we took. I am fully convinced of one thing, however, and that is, we remained long enough to take all the wish to be in a hard-fought battle out of your humble servant. I never expressed such wishes again while in the service, and now feel contented at home with wife and children without any feeling of shame for such a confession. I went into other hard-fought battles after that, but there was a change in my feelings from a fearless, thoughtless, reckless boy to those of a serious, nervous one,

fully realizing that my destiny was in the hands of an over-ruling Providence.

In next day's melee an incident occurred which was of much interest to me, and will illustrate how very much mixed things were. Sunday evening, after we had fallen back in irregular order, very much fatigued, I sat down by a tree to rest, when I noticed the regiment filing off to the left a short distance away, and going out of sight behind some willows which had grown up along a dry ditch. I thought to intercept them by angling across, but when I came to the willows and ditch, there lay a live Johnny on the rebel skirmish line, firing at our men. I was within six feet of him before either of us discovered the other. He had just emptied his gun, and as mine was loaded, I instantly brought it to bear on him. He threw up his hands, and exclaimed: "For God's sake, don't shoot." I never knew whether it was one of our batteries or one of the enemy's that began throwing shot and shell into those willow bushes at that moment. Such a storm of iron and leaden hail I never knew in all my experience, and with an instinct of self-preservation my companion and I shared the protection of a scrubby oak tree near by; and never did two kittens crowd into a warm nest on a cold night closer than we did between the spur-roots of that oak. Changes of position drew that terrible fire in another direction in a very short time, and I started with my prisoner for our lines, which were only a short distance away. I have thought since that no major-general, after a successful battle,

ever felt better toward himself than I did when I delivered over my captive.

While we were penned up in Chattanooga, with hunger gnawing at our vitals, I one day saw a couple of soldiers skinning a dog, preparatory to serving it up to satisfy their hunger. I stood by hoping they would invite me to a share in their feast; but, not receiving any, I had to satisfy my appetite by hunting among the mules of the corral, picking up grains of corn to parch. On the night march from Knoxville to Maryville, it was very dark and muddy. We were very weary, and in the night halted. I was no sooner down than fast asleep. There arose a wonderful commotion, and I awoke, thinking we were attacked. A long, lean old sow leaped over me, and Sam. Pegg, who was next, grabbed her hind leg, and was jerked out at full length, but held on firmly. The next morning Company D had fresh pork for breakfast. It was the pursuit of her which had made such a racket, and the one who caught her had the prize.

In the Spring of 1864, I was ordered to report to the Post Provost Marshal at Chattanooga, Tennessee. My first duty was in charge of part of the prison guard. The prison was on Main street, and had been a store room, twenty by seventy feet long, and our men had enclosed a space in the rear thirty by fifty feet with a fence twelve feet high. It was seldom we had less than 350 prisoners, and I have seen as high as 500 crowded into that small space. They were not rebels, but were made up of the worst characters—thieves,

deserters, bounty-jumpers, and representatives of every crime. There was a regular band of robbers inside its walls. It was an every-day occurrence to learn of the new arrivals being robbed by this gang of professional thieves, and it would have been worth the life of any inmate to testify against them. One fellow said he had "been in all the prisons from New York to Chattanooga, but had never met such a d—d set of scoundrels before." Balls and chains, hand-cuffs, and all such remedies were used on them. Sometimes they were taken to the front and put on the front lines of battle. Once Edward A. Junken went to guard some to the front, in the Atlanta campaign. When they arrived a battle was raging, and they were put in front. "Ep." said he was "glad to see them made to do duty, but did not enjoy being in such company in driving them into it." When General Sherman's army went on the Atlanta campaign, he ordered the sutlers back to Chattanooga, where they took up about twenty acres of ground; and the little city was called by the appropriate name of Sutlertown. It soon became necessary to detail a detective to work among them and in the city, to look after liquor selling, gambling and other violations of the laws of the post. The Provost Marshal selected me, and I was allowed to dress in citizen's or soldier's clothes, and to employ any means consistent with military rules to find the guilty parties. I never thought that my chances for getting hurt were reduced in the least by my duties at this time. The Provost Marshal dealt out justice similar

to the mayor of a city in time of peace; only his was military authority, and was very speedy in its execution. I have often seen as many as one hundred prisoners brought in during twenty-four hours, and they were tried as fast as the clerk could take down their names, crime and sentence in a book kept for the purpose. Commencing at 8 a. m., by noon the docket would be clear. Citizens were fined, and it was reported that over thirty thousand dollars of a fund was accumulated. My duties brought me into contact with all kinds of violators, and sometimes I would have to get the drop on them quickly with my revolver; but I had the military to back me, and now feel thankful that I did what I could to detect all robbers of the Government and disorganizers of our grand army in the field.

IV.—BY HARVEY CALDWELL.

The boys no doubt remember our forced march the night before the battle of Chicamauga, how the fences were burned to light us on our way, and how we stopped and made coffee, but did not get time to drink it. A few minutes after Lieutenant Beale was wounded, and Lieutenant Bailey took command of our company, he told me to go and tell Adjutant Goodwin that the enemy were flanking us on the left. I did so, and after coming back I laid down, and think

I was putting a cap on my gun when a ball struck me in the breast. Before this I saw Abram Billings throw up his hands, and thought I saw the blood, but it was only a glancing shot. I lay only a short time, when I got up and tried to walk to the rear, but did not go far till I suppose I fainted, as I knew nothing until some of the boys came and tried to carry me away. I was too heavy, and they left me on a gum blanket. This was after the regiment was driven back. Soon after, two or three Johnnies came up, and one of them took my canteen. I said: "Don't take it." He asked, "What is in it?" I said, "Water." He dropped it, and went on. Another one had two wool blankets, for one of which I traded my rubber one, thinking it would keep me warmer at night. In the evening another Johnny came and helped me back to a fire, and got me a rock for a pillow. He then asked me if I would trade my haversack and canteen for his. I told him I did not care, and I have the canteen yet. I have often thought I would like to have his name and address. On my way back I saw William Griffin, dead, on the first line. They had taken his shoes off, and cut open his pocket and taken his money. I suffered intensely during the two days and nights I lay there. It seemed that every hour would be my last, but I felt perfectly resigned to my fate, knowing that I had tried to do my duty and was dying in a good cause. Two or three wounded men lay near me. General Bragg and his staff rode close by me on Sunday morning.

Monday evening the rebels came with a wagon, and hauled us several miles to a field hospital, where they had seventy or eighty of our wounded. Here I got acquainted with Sergeant Taylor, of the 51st Illinois Regiment, who wrote the first word home, as he was paroled three weeks before I was; but not until I had been given up as dead for weeks by relatives and friends at home, as well as by my comrades in the army. We got a pint of unsifted corn meal for a day's ration. On Wednesday the rebel doctor examined my wound, and said the ball was in the lower part of my left lung. He said it was a very dangerous wound, and swore he did not believe they could kill a Yankee. I traded my knife to a rebel, and got two and a half dollars to boot in Confederate currency. Saturday evening they brought in a little buck sheep, and we thought we would get some meat; but the two or three bites given to each one only whetted our appetites for more. One or two of the men died every day, and the wagon would come. Piling them in, they would take them to a large hole, and dump them in and cover over with a little dirt. I got a hat off a dead man's head; I thought he did not need it, and I had none.

We remained at this place about three weeks, when we were taken in wagons to Ringgold, ten miles, and put on the cars for Atlanta. By some mistake I was on a train with rebel officers and soldiers, and when we got to Atlanta I inquired for a hotel, where I went and sat by the fire, and got a good breakfast, paying out my two dollars and a half for it. Afterwards I

met a rebel and traded some greenbacks for Confederate money, he giving me ten dollars for one, and then I returned to the hotel. Soon a rebel came and took me to the barracks where our wounded were, and I had to resume the pint of corn meal diet. In a day or two, as I was passing a shanty, some one called me. I went in and found William Danner. He was shot through the knee, and showed me the ball which had been taken out. He seemed quite cheerful. I never saw him after that time.

In two or three days we were put on the cars for Richmond, with five days' rations—five crackers and a piece of bacon as large as a man's hand. This we ate raw. We were nine days on the road, part of the time in crowded box cars. At Raleigh, N. C., I bought a dozen very small biscuits for two dollars. Arriving at Richmond, my first purchase was a sweet potatoe pie for twenty-five cents. We were taken to Libby prison, where we were kept forty-eight hours without anything to eat, and were so crowded that we barely had room enough to lay down on the floor.

After a few days I and a few others were taken to the Alabama hospital, where we had better quarters, but had the floor for a bed. The dead were carried out daily and put in the dead house, (where the rats were very numerous) until taken away for burial. I bought one sheet of paper and two envelops for a half-dollar, and wrote home. We were allowed to write a half-sheet and leave it unsealed. After a long time it was sent through and got home. Our ration

was a small piece of corn bread, with a quart of soup for twelve men, which we carefully divided by spoonsful, each man watching carefully to get his share.

After staying here a month, we were taken to the boat, and sailed to City Point, where next day we were exchanged, and went on one of our steamers for Annapolis, Md. One of the first men I met there was Robinson, of Company B, who showed me a list of the killed, cut out of the Cincinnati Gazette. Among the number was Harvey Caldwell, Company D, 68th Indiana. I told him I was like the Irishman, who, when he heard he was dead, "knew it was a lie as soon as he heard it." Here we were sent to the St. John Hospital, and there washed and given clean clothes—the first in two months—clean beds and plenty to eat. I cannot tell how happy we were for all this, and to be back again in "God's country." We left there December, 18, 1863, and in a few days were at home on Christmas day—happy.

V.—BY O. H. P. MOHLER.

In January, 1864, after the siege of Knoxville, Tenn., had been raised, our division marched to Strawberry Plains, where I was detailed with a squad to take charge of a large quantity of stock and provisions, on a plantation across the Holston River. The river was too deep to wade, and it was too cold and rapid to swim; so we tore down a log cabin near the river, made a raft out

of it, and crossed over. We found the rich old planter had everything he could wish—chickens, turkeys, potatoes, of both varieties, hogs, cattle, corn and hay, all in abundance. He also had a little water mill to crack corn for his negroes. We were a happy set of fellows, for it was the first good thing we had struck in this campaign. The first thing, was to get the mill going. We found an old darkey who could run it. And so we guarded and lived in good style, until orders came for us to load up and bring in the balance. There was enough to fill up ten or twelve wagons, and we were gladly welcomed back to camp by our hungry comrades there.

VI.—BY W. M. SOUDER.

It was in the winter of 1863, while in camp at Nashville, Tennessee, that some fourteen of the Rushville boys were messing together in one of those large bell tents. We had for our officer in charge, Sergeant Lester, whose duty was to draw the rations for our mess and see that we did our duty—policing, keeping our guns clean and everything in good order. The Sergeant was a real good fellow, but he had been a teacher, was a Yankee, and did not at all times understand our motives; and we thought him a little too strict in discipline for a volunteer. Nevertheless, all went along good-humoredly until, one day, he drew

from the commissary department a very poor piece of beef. The boys examined it, and were not hungry enough to eat it. The good Sergeant thought it might beat nothing in an emergency, and set it away in a camp kettle, just inside the tent door, to await such time as our hunger would make a demand for it. In the night some of the boys thought it would be a good joke to lay the Sergeant's boots on it for a cover. At reveille the Sergeant could not find his boots; but in marching out to answer to his name at roll call, he saw the boots on the kettle, and in his indignant way, not thinking they were his own, threw them over into an adjoining place, where they were "lost to sight and memory dear."

VII.—BY D. S. FLEEHART.

After the East Tennessee campaign, when we were detached for duty at Chattanooga, and had a permanent camp there from then on until the close of the war, it must not be supposed that we remained in camp doing guard duty all the time. While that was our home, we were not at home very much. When the regiment went out it was always in light marching order, sometimes with forty or sixty, and frequently one hundred, rounds of ammunition. A few men were left in camp—those who were not able to go, and they guarded our quarters while absent. I believe it was never my luck to be left in camp but once. Our duties

took us over many hundreds of miles; to Atlanta, to Knoxville, to Nashville, and into Alabama, to where Birmingham now stands. We had skirmishes with Forrest's, Wheeler's and Rhoddy's cavalry forces, and Hood's army, in battle at Decatur and Nashville; and after the last battle pursued them to near Tuscumbia, Alabama, and captured a part of the wagon train.

VIII.—BY A. W. EARNEST.

Up to a short time before the battle of Chicamauga, I was with the company in the performance of all the duties required in camp and field. During the campaign I was detailed as a cattle-guard at brigade headquarters, and was not in that battle; but my duties were so near and exciting that we felt the effects and did some very rapid manœuvering to escape capture. We were under great difficulties, for the long wagon trains and hundreds of stragglers filled the road, and the roar of the near conflict kept our nerves strung up to a high pitch. Soon after this, I returned to the company, and with the others endured the starvation siege at Chattanooga, and was with it in the advance and capture of Missionary Ridge. I was not well enough to go on the march to East Tennessee, immediately after, and remained with the convalescents of the 4th Army Corps.

About the middle of December we started with the

wagons and camp equipage to join our corps, near Knoxville, and on the 27th, while in camp near Calhoun, we were suddenly attacked by the Rebel General Wheeler and his cavalry. Colonel Laiboldt, of the 2d Missouri Infantry, was in command of our force of convalescents, and by a brilliant charge routed Wheeler and captured about 150 prisoners, with small loss to our force. Orderly-Sergeant James A. Smith, known as the tallest man in our regiment (he was six feet six inches), was in command of all the men of the 68th Indiana, and was conspicuous in this fight. He was carrying a sword of Captain Mauzy's, which had belonged to Colonel King, who had used it in the Mexican war. This he was waving in command, when a ball passed through his hand and through the sword and scabbard. But we came off victors, and the sword was soon restored to its owner, who now has it and shows it as a precious relic. We got to London with our prisoners on the cold New Year's day—January 1, 1864—and on the 15th, rejoined our commands at Dandridge. In February, I was detailed to go with Bridge's Battery of Illinois Light Artillery, and took part with Sherman's army in his advance to near Atlanta, where, on account of sickness, I was sent back, and soon rejoined the company at Chattanooga. I was in the fight at Decatur, Ala., resisting the advance of Hood's army on his way to Nashville, this being the last engagement I took part in. After the Nashville battle, I was furloughed for thirty days.

IX.—BY J. H. MAUZY.

It was my fortune to be called upon to perform nearly every kind of service that could fall to the lot of an infantry line officer. In the campaign of 1862 under General Dumont, in Kentucky, opposing the advance of General Bragg's army, there was almost continuous night and day work—on the march, constructing defensive works, or on the picket line, and finally a prisoner with nearly all the regiment at Munfordsville, followed by life in parole-camp, drilling. In January, 1863, I took part in the cold and perilous guarding of supply boats down the Ohio and up the Cumberland to Nashville, and there in tent-life in the slushy snow and mud, which brought on a fever and two weeks in a hospital.

After this, I was detailed as Brigade Inspector on the staff of Colonel Dan. McCook, whose command picketed the city to the south and east. This line of several miles I had to ride daily. I had, also, to report daily the condition of all the troops in the camps; every few weeks make an inspection of all the troops in the command (arms, accoutrements, camp and garrison equipage, etc.,) and, when on the march, put out the picket lines. Our regiment was detached from Colonel McCook's command in April, and sent to Murfreesboro. In May, at Colonel King's request, I gave up my position, and, on returning to the regiment, was appointed to the same position in the 2d Brigade, 4th

Division, 14th Corps, and was on duty with it during the whole of the campaign which ended with the battle of Chicamauga, where Colonel Ed. A. King, its commander, was killed, September 20, 1863. Colonel M. S. Robinson then commanded it until the reorganization of the army, in October, when the 68th Indiana was assigned to General Willich's (1st) Brigade, 3rd Division, General Wood, of the 4th Army Corps. I then returned to my company. Next day (October 21) I was ordered to take a guard of fifty men and escort about that number of wagons in a train for supplies, to Stevenson, Ala. We had a hard time on account of rainy weather, muddy roads, and, worst of all, so many mules perishing from starvation. But, after many vicissitudes, we got back to Chattanooga, November 12, and were kept busy during the next ten days preparing for battle. In the advance, on the 23d and 24th I was with the picket lines, and in the final assault, on the 25th, commanded companies A. and D.

During the night, orders were received to get ready to go to the relief of General Burnside, who was shut up in Knoxville by General Longstreet. We moved rapidly in light marching order, through the rain, and often in the night, and with little to eat, getting there after Longstreet had made his attack and been repulsed.

While in camp at Strawberry Plains, I was ordered to take a number of wagons, with a guard, and forage the country for supplies. I returned in the night with

only part of the wagons loaded. Next morning I was ordered to report at headquarters. General Willich asked me what were my orders the day before. I told him "They were to take the wagons and load them with forage off the country." "Did you do it?" he asked. I replied, "All that I could find that day. He said, "Did your orders specify any time to return?" I answered, "No, but thought that was the right thing to do." He then said, "You are a young officer, and I will give you another chance. Take these wagons and go again." We marched off in the direction of the North Carolina line, and were gone several days, until we got every wagon heaping full of anything we could find that was good for men or horses to eat. It so gladdened this old veteran of many wars and wounds to have plenty for his soldiers, that I received the place of Brigade Inspector on his staff, January 8, 1864.

General Wood soon after went home on a leave of absence, and General Willich, who was next in rank, commanded the division for a short time. About the middle of February he went to Cincinnati, to have a cancer cut out of his lip, and another officer and myself were appointed Aids-de-Camp, and accompanied him. Shortly after our arrival there, we received permits to go to our homes, and remain until further orders from him. In April, I was ordered to meet him at Indianapolis, and, after grand entertainments, which were given him by his German friends at Madison and Louisville, we returned to Chattanooga.

At the reorganization of the army, in April, 1864, the 68th Indiana was detailed for garrison duty at Chattanooga. In May, I requested to be relieved, and rejoined the regiment. May 20, I was detailed to the command of a guard and a train loaded with rebel prisoners, for Nashville. July 9, I was appointed by order of Major-General Steedman a member of a Military Commission for the District of Etowah, to try Thomas Jolly, a rebel spy, and such other prisoners as might be brought before it. We were in session until in January, 1865, and as the district extended from Stevenson to the front, there was no lack of cases.

February 14th, I was detailed by order of General Steedman as Judge Advocate of a general court martial. Among the celebrities ordered to our court for trial were General (and Prince) Felix Salm-Salm, Colonel Millington and Lieutenant Colonel Corbin. Previous to this (February 2) I was detailed by the commander of the post, Colonel C. H. Carlton, to take charge of the refugee camp, north of the river, which I visited daily, reporting its condition and requirements. The court occupied the "Dyer House," and sat until in May. Lee Goodwin and N. T. Ploughe were detailed as orderlies. June 1, I visited the Chicamauga battlefield, in company with Surgeon Wooden and Lieutenant Carson. June 20, 1865, I received an order to take charge of the rolls and records of the regiment and report to the A. C. M., 3d Division, 4th A. C., and we were mustered out of the United States service on that day.

X.—BY SAMUEL C. PEGG.

It is easy to tell over our trials and sports during the war, but to try to write them up in good connection is another thing.

I recollect that, shortly after we marched out as prisoners at Munfordsville, Ky., and laid down our arms, I filled my pipe and asked a "Johnny" for a match. He gave me to understand, with an oath, he "didn't carry Yankee tricks." When we got back to the Ohio river, after a series of long, weary marches, I told the boys I could swim that "creek" easy enough; and to show them that it could be done, I pitched in and swam across to the Indiana side, and then back again.

At the battle of Chicamauga I was anxious to be in a battle, and would not have staid out if I could have done so honorably; but after that I never had any hankering. Saturday night, Wesley Chalfant and I were put on picket, with orders not to fire unless the rebels advanced. When the fog began to rise, Sunday morning, then came the Johnnies, and Wesley said, "Sam, yonder they come, thick as hail." I don't think they were sixty yards off. Chalfant blazed away, and fell back in good order. I took good aim and fired. In getting back through a cornfield, it seemed to me they shot off about every stalk, but failed to bring me down. The next we knew we were

cut off with Negley's Division, and I did not get with my company until we reached Chattanooga. Then came a long siege of starvation, and then the battle of Missionary Ridge. We went up the Ridge with a will, but I doubt very much if any started on that memorable charge without a feeling of "Who will care for mother now."

I talked with a "Johnny" on top of the Ridge, who had both thighs broken by a musket ball. He said that when he saw our army forming by Ft. Wood he thought we were going to have review; but when he saw the colors unfurled and the advance made, he knew what was up. I asked him if he thought we would climb the Ridge. He said he "would have bet as much on it as on four aces;" that he had a notion to run, and he now wished to God he had.

After this came our march to Knoxville, that fearfully cold winter. One night while on picket I was relieved, and went back to the reserve, but they were gone. I hurried to camp, and found the regiment all in excitement with orders to "skin out" for Knoxville. I will always think a Johnny relieved me that night. After our return to Chattanooga, I was detailed at General Steedman's headquarters, where I had a very good time, for a soldier, until the war was over.

XI.—BY SAMUEL B. JONES.

September 19, 1863, in the battle of Chicamauga, I was knocked out of time on the first line occupied where our company suffered so terribly. While taking aim at a rebel color-bearer, I was struck by a musket ball, which passed through my left hand into my right arm, lodging in the elbow joint. Seeing I could do nothing more, I started to the rear. Just as I got in the rear, I looked up and down our lines, and I thought that half of our men were lying on the ground, dead. Working my way back, I saw some of our company being helped to the rear, and felt as if I had got off pretty well, as I was able to take myself. Going on (I do not know how far), I came to the headquarters of General Rosecrans. He and his staff were mounted, ready to start. I passed close by the General, and he, seeing my condition—the blood running down from my wounds, over my clothes to the ground; a pitiable sight, no doubt—turned to his surgeon, saying: "General, get down and bind up that man's wound, before we start; he is bleeding to death." This he did, gave me a drink of water, and then remounting they started on a gallop to the front. I lay down on the porch of the house and rested awhile. The blood being stanched, I felt somewhat better, and again renewed my journey toward the rear. After going some distance, I came to a large brick

house, which was used for a hospital. I went through it, and the sight of men shot to pieces in every conceivable shape was one which beggars description, and one I hope never to be called on to witness again. Thinking it was almost full enough, I went out in the yard. This was about full, also; but as night was coming on, I began to look for some place to roost. Finding a place where some men who were slightly wounded had built a fire, near the fence, I got a board, and putting one end through and the other on the ground, I sat astride of it, leaning against the fence, and so passed the night amidst the crying and groans of the suffering and dying ; for it was the last night on earth for many a poor fellow. Day at last dawned, to disclose sights more harrowing, if possible, than the evening before ; for the ambulances had been bringing in the wounded all night.

Shortly after daylight I came across Theodore Ploughe, who told me where our division hospital was. I made my way to it, and found there many of my own company. Soon we heard the booming of cannon and the rattle of musketry, which told that the conflict was still raging ; and so it was all through the day. In the evening it came closer and closer, the bullets striking the trees about us, and we began to think we were all to be slaughtered in a pile; but shortly the firing ceased, and General Wheeler and staff rode up, and demanded the surrender of the hospital. The surgeons were drawn up in line, relieved of their swords and pistols, and then they rode away.

Soon after, a spluttering Lieutenant with a squad of men rode up and ordered the surgeons to fall into line. Dr. Wooden begun to explain that he had surrendered to General Wheeler, when the Lieutenant jerked out his pistol, and with an oath ordered them to deliver up their overcoats and hats. We all expected to be robbed, but they left after robbing the surgeons. Right here I want to say that Surgeon Wooden and others then showed what kind of heroes they were; for they went for days bare-headed in the hot sun over the battle field, gathering up and caring for the wounded, and then worked all night in the hospital, assisting those who were suffering the most. All this time they endured the pangs of hunger. I got a little negro boy to hunt some corn and parch it, and with a few spoonfuls of boiled wheat I kept soul and body together. A great many died. It was my privilege to be with that brave and generous comrade, Caleb Lee, to the last. He was shot in the shoulder, the ball ranging into his chest. He lingered for four days in great suffering, and was buried near the tent in which he died. Day after day, for ten days, witnessed such scenes. Then an ambulance train came to take us to Chattanooga. There was joy then. The only sad thing was to leave our brave surgeons, who had voluntarily remained to care for us, to be marched off South as prisoners, while we were going to our friends. The man that was in the ambulance with me died in the night, and when daylight came I found my companion a corpse. After getting into Chatta-

nooga, the first man I saw was Dr. Mauzy, of Rushville, and soon my comrades found me, and did everything in their power to make me comfortable. I staid in Chattanooga until some time in January, 1864, when I was sent back to Nashville, then to Evansville by boat, and on June 29, 1864, I was discharged at Indianapolis.

XII.—BY GEORGE SMITH.

In the battle of Chicamauga, Isaac Dale, my intimate comrade, and myself agreed to stand by each other, if either should be wounded. In the first day's fight, he was severely wounded and fell. We were forced back. About sunset, I started to hunt him up. There were so many wounded who wanted water and help, that I gave all I had, and went on to where I thought we had engaged the enemy. While helping a wounded man to a better position there, I was attracted by voices crying, "Come over," "Come over." I looked up, and saw a line of rebels not over seventy-five yards away. My first thought was of Libby prison. The next was to run, and run I did. I struck out at right oblique, and it seemed to me like a whole regiment was firing at me, the air was so full of rebel bullets; but not one of them hit me. Up to this time it had not occurred to me that I was outside our own lines. I ran into Wilder's Mounted Infantry, who wanted to know the situation. I told them to go ahead, and in a few moments they were into the conflict.

XIII.—BY THOMAS T. PATTERSON.

After the battle of Hoover's Gap, I got sick, was sent to the hospital, and remained there until December, when I joined in the East Tennessee campaign with my company. At Chattanooga, I was detailed to go with the provision train of Sherman's army. Starting from Ringgold, Georgia, I was present at most of the battles fought from there to Atlanta. At Resaca, where General Willich was wounded, he had the band play when he was carried off the field of battle. We could forage and do a great many things that we could not do while with our regiment—our officer telling us not to let him see what we had. I was shooting hogs, one day, in a little woods, when an old lady hailed me, and said she had protection papers. I asked her, "Who from?" She answered, "General Bragg." I told her, "All right, you will get paid for your hogs."

XIV.—BY L. T. STEWART.

On the 15th of November, 1863, I was detailed as driver of an ammunition wagon, and ordered to report to General T. J. Wood. Our first duty was to bring up a pontoon bridge to throw across the Tennessee river, above the point of Mission Ridge, for Sherman's army to cross upon. After that battle we were

ordered to Knoxville with ammunition for Burnside's army. From there we drove a great deal, going as far as the Virginia line, and then to Cleveland, Tenn., where we recruited our teams and prepared for the Atlanta campaign. During the battle of Resaca, while delivering ammunition to the 66th Illinois Regiment, my two swing mules were shot. At the battle of Pumpkin Vine creek, myself and fourteen others, and their teams, were ordered to the front with ammunition. We had to drive through a very narrow place, in plain view of the rebels, and our white wagon covers made a good target for their batteries. They made it so hot we cut loose our mules and got back the best we could. That night, under cover of darkness, we succeeded in pulling our wagons out backwards. My wagon lost the two front wheels. At Marietta, I got a pass and returned to the regiment, and carried a gun until I was discharged. I was in the battle of Nashville and several skirmishes, but luckily received no wounds.

XV.—BY W. F. ALDRIDGE.

I was in the battle of Missionary Ridge, and in the East Tennessee campaign immediately after. We made a raft of logs, crossed the Holston river near Strawberry Plains, and went to a farmer named Vance. And what a good time we had on Christmas —old hen, potatoes and sorghum molasses. On "the

cold New Year's day" we gathered corn. We had a rough time marching and camping in the rain, mud and snow. I don't think I ever saw the rain fall as fast as it did when we routed Wheeler at Dalton. I was in the battles at Decatur and Nashville, and in the pursuit of Hood's army. After this I got a furlough. When I returned from home to the regiment, I was detailed to work in the gardens, the war being over.

XVI.—BY S. C. POPPINO.

At the crossing of Elk river, in the Tullahoma campaign, I borrowed a revolver and started on a foraging expedition. The first game I found was an old goat with two kids, upon which I took compassion, and passed her by. Soon after, I found a fine cow, which by her looks I knew to be fresh. I followed her to where her calf was, and it soon fell at the crack of my weapon. Soon George Ritchie came up, and I told him I would go to a cabin which was in the distance, across a deep ravine, get a bucket and milk the cow. I did not get the bucket, but captured two rebels. I have not space to give the details; but suffice it to say we had a feast when we returned to camp. On this campaign I contracted a chronic diarrhœa, and for it and the wound in my left knee, received at Chicamauga, I receive a pension. I partici-

pated in the battle of Nashville and the destruction of Hood's army. On this campaign we were forty-two days without a change of clothing, and had few overcoats and shelter tents. What did we look like when we got back?—dirty, ragged and lousey, and, I like to have said, God-forsaken; but He had blessed us with a crowning victory.

[Extract from letter of S. C. Poppino.]

CHANUTE, Kansas, July 3, 1887.

* * * Would to God we could meet and have a grand reunion of our old company. I cannot express in words the joy it would be to me. I want the boys, as many as can, to see this letter, and to know that I send my best wishes. Often do I think over our campaigns. I see the boys with the weary step, the still determined look, while some would swear at ill-luck, others would laugh it off with some droll expression. But, thanks be to God, a part of us are left to pay tribute to the memory of our dead comrades. I live in Southern Kansas, and my head, like many others, is silvered over; but every hair is patriotic. My constitution is gone, my legs are nearly played out, but, thank God, with my pension and the help of my boys we can and do run a quarter section farm, well stocked. Right here I want to say, when any of the boys come West, and feel a desire to call and see "Sile," they shall have the "best in the shop." I will be pleased to show them the great Neosho Valley, a country we are proud to claim as our home.

XVII.—BY MASON MAXEY.

On account of disability for field service, I was transferred to the Veteran Reserve Corps in January, 1864, and in the Winter and Spring was on duty guarding rebel prisoners at Indianapolis. The rebels had as good barracks to stay in as the guards, got as good rations, and actually fared better than we did; for we had to go on guard every other day and night during the worst kind of weather. We had from five to fifteen thousand to take care of, and it kept us busy all the time. The guards were made up from nearly all the regiments of the Union army. Many had been wounded, nearly all were in feeble health, and the hard duties required of us thinned out our number rapidly; but we did not grumble, and went where we were told and came when we were called, for we had no say so in the matter. I was on duty at the arsenal at the time President Lincoln was assassinated, carrying dispatches to the headquarters in Indianapolis. Washington street was draped in mourning from Pogue's Run to the river, and it was a grand, yet very sad sight to look upon, and to think of the President being murdered just when the war was over.

XVIII.—BY ED. A. JUNKIN.

In the Summer of 1861, while Sherman's army was battling its way to Atlanta, I was detailed with squads of men as train guards several times. It was our duty to see that none of the cars were opened, or anything taken from them, until we were relieved by the proper officers at the front. Our place was on the top of the box-cars, so that we could see plainly everything that was passing below; not a very desirable place in hot, rainy Summer weather, not saying anything about the exposure from the bullets of small parties of rebels and bushwhackers that frequently made targets of the train guards. Very often were the trains fired into, men killed and the trains captured. We would have to wait sometimes as long as two days, after we got to the front, before we would be relieved. On one of these trips, at Dalton, I think, while we were waiting, the hospital train came in from the front, loaded with wounded men from the battlefield of Kenesaw Mountain. It stopped close to the cars which we were guarding, and with a few others I went to see if we could find any acquaintances among the wounded. I think there were six or eight cars in the train. I went through several of them, and of all the sights I ever saw that was one of the saddest. Men were wounded in every imaginable way. Those that could not stand the jolting of the cars were

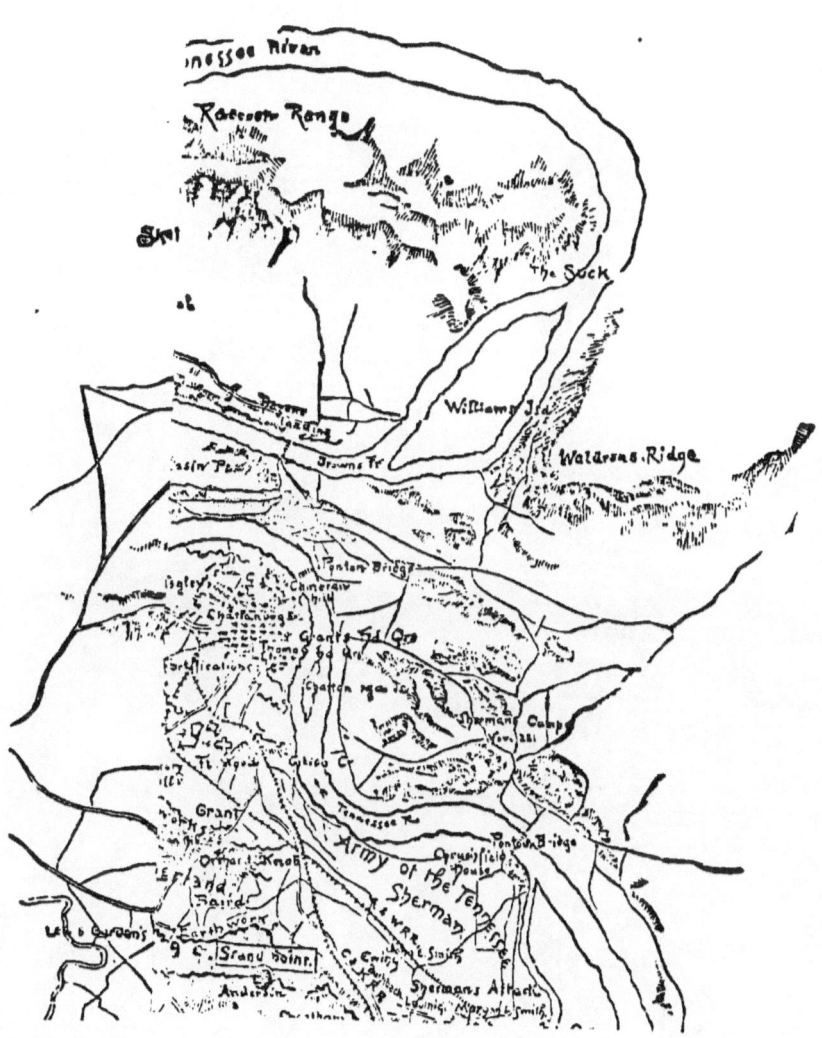

XIX.—COMPANY D AT CHICAMAUGA.

Lieutenant William Beale commanded Company D, 68th Regiment Indiana Infantry, at Chicamauga, until shot down, September 19th, 1863 (Captain Mauzy was in the battle as Brigade Inspector on the staff of Colonel King), and had with him thirty-six enlisted men of the Company. Of these one, William Griffin, was killed and twenty-one wounded, viz: Lieutenant William Beale, Abram S. Billings, James R. Bosley, William H. C. Buzan, Harvey Caldwell, Isaac Dale, James B. David, William H. H. Danner, Samuel B. Jones, Caleb Lee, James W. Richie, Jefferson E. Trimbly, and Payton H. Walters,. Thirteen were taken prisoners, as follows: Hugh Beetern, A. J. Gates, Frank Gisselbach, George T. Richie, S. C. Poppino, Fred. W. Short, John Simmons, and D. L. Thomas. Eight, though wounded, escaped capture.

Ten days after the battle Lieutenant Beale, Samuel B. Jones, and Jefferson E. Trimbly were exchanged. Jones' arm was amputated, and Trimbly's leg, (he died a few days afterward). Caleb Lee died in the rebel field hospital three days after he was wounded. He suffered such pain that he begged them all the time to kill him. The great numbers of wounded on both sides to be looked after, prevented much attention, and so they laid for days on the field; but the feeling of human sympathy prevailed, and the canteen

of water was divided with the wounded by the passing rebel, and kindly words spoken by those so recently in deadly conflict. The others, who were not hurt, were James A. Smith, Wesley Chalfant, John D. Brown, William Innis, Samuel Pegg, B. F. Cohee, John Francis, Samuel S. Bodine, William M. Souders, David S. Fleehart, Lee Goodwin, George Smith, Enoch Whiteley, Deliscus Lingenfelter, W. F. Aldridge, and Thomas Bosley—sixteen. Of this number, two months later, Samuel S. Bodine was killed, and Thomas Bosley, severely wounded, in the battle of Mission Ridge.

XX.—FIVE MONTHS' HOSPITAL LIFE—BY FIRST LIEUTENANT WILLIAM BEALE.

Little is known of hospital life, and how the sick and wounded were cared for during the war of '61, and many false impressions have been formed by some who have been in them only a short time, and who know very little of what the Government and loyal people of the North have done for them.

It was my lot to be wounded at the battle of Chicamauga, on September 20, 1863. I was captured and made a prisoner, but was exchanged on September 30, and was taken to Chattanooga, October 1st, where I was admitted to the hospital, which had formerly been a hotel. The first recollection that I had of be-

ing there was on the second morning after my arrival. Having slept twenty-four hours, I awoke to find a nurse feeding me on whisky with a spoon. As the hospital was crowded, and I was among the last getting in, my bed was made on the floor, along with many others. From the time I was admitted to the time my wife and kind friends sent Dr. Casterline to bring me home, I never had any cause to complain of of the treatment and care I received. The rising generation have but little conception of the magnitude of the war, and a great deal less of that of caring for the wounded; especially after a severe battle, where hundreds and sometimes thousands, were to be cared for at once. But the Government had everything in readiness for such occasions, so the wounded could be taken almost as much care of as if they had been at home. It is my opinion, from a careful observation, that they had more care and attention than if they had been at home. The patients had the best of food, trained nurses to attend them, and doctors who examined each one morning and evening.

But the question has often been asked: "How did the army get all the necessaries for its sick and wounded?" How little do we remember the loyal homes we left, how they toiled early and late, packing boxes of food and clothing for the hospitals. Never in this life will they know how much they have done to save the lives and sufferings of the ones they loved. There was one society that should ever be remembered with the kindest feelings, and that was the "Christian Com-

mission." It was established in every neighborhood of the loyal States, and prepared, collected, and forwarded everything that was of use to the sick soldiers, such as bedding, clothing, bandages, lint, fruits, jellies, meats, and every kind of stimulants, ready for use. I, for one, shall never forget the many good things which I received through their kindness. There was another beautiful deed which I must not fail to mention, though those who did it had but little conception of what it was worth. In almost every package which came to our hospital, though it was ever so small, was a kind letter of love and affection to the one that received it—such letters as only true patriot mothers, sisters, and friends could write. How it cheered the many sad hearts to know that they were remembered at home. For the five months that I was in the hospital, where there was no other commissioned officers, I am free to say that no other nation ever cared for her private soldiers as has our own. Well may the nations around us wonder at what has been done in the caring for the soldier in the late war. But when they remember that every soldier was a freeman and equal to the highest officer in command, then may they learn the strength of a government where every one is equal with his neighbor.

XXI.—FIGHT AT DALTON, GEORGIA, AUGUST 15th, 1864.—BY D. L. THOMAS.

August 14th, 1864 (while on garrison duty at Chattanooga), we received orders to move at a moment's warning. General Wheeler's cavalry had cut the railroad and captured Dalton, Georgia. At sunset, detachments from the 29th, 44th, 51st, and 68th Indiana Regiments, the 2d and 108th Ohio, the 78th Pennsylvania, and the 14th United States Colored Regiments, with a section of artillery, boarded the cars for the scene of action. The trains reached Tunnel Hill at midnight, and we marched to Buzzard Roost Gap, formed in line of battle, and waited for daylight. We met the rebel pickets two and a half miles from Dalton. Our skirmishers drove them half a mile, when their forces made a stand. We charged them, and soon put them to flight, and drove them through town at a rapid rate. Rain began to fall when the fight commenced, and by the time we reached the edge of town it was descending in torrents. A halt was made while a piece of artillery threw shells down the principal street. The storm soon abated, when many of our men were standing in water several inches deep. The line of battle moved through the town. Not a man, woman, or child was to be seen. The peaches we found in the yards and gardens were first-class. But the enemy had departed, and we were left in

peaceful possession. A wounded Confederate placed Wheeler's forces at four thousand cavalry and ten pieces of artillery. Their loss, not including the slightly wounded, who got away, was one hundred and fifty; our loss about forty. Our regiment had six wounded, two of them mortally. Our forces buried fifteen Confederates in a garden.

Two hours after the fight, some of us took a stroll over town, and, among other incidents, a young lady was singing and playing on a piano as though nothing had occurred. During the fight the women and children laid on the floors to avoid being shot.

We entered this fight with some degree of solicitude. The Confederacy had not recognized colored soldiers as prisoners of war when captured. In case we should be captured with colored soldiers in this fight, would our lives be spared? This question was discussed among us. The officers of the 14th Colored Regiment realized the situation. Hence, they recited their oft-repeated instruction to their men to neither ask nor give quarters. They impressed the fact that both colored soldiers and officers had been killed in every instance when captured. Hence, they would neither surrender nor take prisoners until the rights of prisoners of war were accorded to them. Consequently the few Confederates who fell into their hands met the same fate that had attended captured colored troops. Two Confederate surgeons were left to care for their wounded. While the enemy captured Dalton, the detachment of the 2d Missouri Regiment stationed

there still held the earthworks, and were rejoiced when we rescued them. On the 17th, our command started back by railroad. When we had passed Ringgold we found the road torn up by the raiders. In a few hours the construction corps had repaired the track, and we were again on our way to camp. But at Graysville we found the track torn up worse than the breach just repaired. But workmen from Chattanooga were repairing the road, so that we got back to camp at noon of the 18th.

Captain Henry Romeyn, 5th United States Infantry, thus describes the same incident in the National Tribune, of July 21, 1887. He was a Captain in the 14th United States Colored Infantry:

"Soon after passing Buzzard Roost Gap, the enemy's advanced guard was met and driven back on the main body. The Federal forces were at once deployed, the colored troops being given the left of the line, and the left company (B) thrown forward as skirmishers. No previous moment in the Captain's life had been so anxiously passed as was the next ten minutes. Would the men fight, or was their careful training vain? But as coolly as on drill the line pushed forward into a thick growth of timber and underbush. Reaching the farther side of this woods, the bullets were flying too thick for comfort, and as the left of the skirmish line had been unable to keep up with the right, that was halted for those in the rear to come up.

The fight was not severe, except in a limited space among some thickets lining the banks of a small stream, where a few of the enemy's skirmishers found themselves suddenly surrounded, and refusing to surrender to 'niggers,' were all killed.

"The colored soldier had fought side by side with his white fellow, had done his whole duty, and been commended for his steadiness and bravery. On the same line were two Indiana Regiments,—the 51st, Colonel A. D. Streight, and the 68th, Lieutenant-Colonel Espy—and for several months after we served together, and the longer we did so the stronger grew the soldierly tie between us."

D. S. Fleehart writes as follows of the fight at Dalton:

"The colored troops did nobly that day, as they did afterward; but the 68th was the first to enter the town right at the heels of the rebels, and in the hardest rain I ever saw. In the fight at Decatur, Alabama, two months later, when Hood attempted to cross the river on his way to Nashville, there were no troops to oppose them that had ever seen the smoke of battle, except the 68th and 73d Indiana, and the 14th United States Colored Infantry. We arrived there about 2 o'clock in the morning, and had just laid down to get a little rest when the rebels drove the pickets in. The pickets were the 10th Indiana Cavalry, dismounted, and were raw troops, having then only been in the

field a short time. A detail of one hundred men from our regiment and one hundred and fifty from the 14th United States Colored Infantry was ordered to re-establish the picket lines, which we did, although it was dark as Egypt, and not a man had ever seen the place in daylight. When daylight came we found we were within easy range of the rebel pickets. The remainder of our regiment was taken down under the bank of the river, and marched along until they got below the rebel pickets, and then, coming up on the the level ground with such "hallooing" as only Hoosiers can do, captured the pickets of the rebels, nearly half way up their line, in daylight and in plain view of the Johnneys, and in the range of fifty pieces of artillery. Nearly two months after this, at Nashville, we again fought in line with the 14th United States Colored Infantry, and were in at the "death," or general wind-up of the rebellion, so far as Hood's army was concerned. It just reminded me, after his defeat there, of the last day of our county fair. After the last big race is run, there is a general rush for the gates to get started home. So it was with the rebels. In the second day's battle they moved from right to left, and from left to right, to try and find a weak place in our lines; but "Pap" Thomas (God bless him!) had formed his lines to stay, and after repeated assaults their army just seemed to melt away, every fellow for himself. They wanted to go home, and I have no doubt they did go, for not half of their number recrossed the Tennessee when we followed them back

again, or, rather, their wagon train, down into Alabama. While we were on this pursuit, having gone across the country from Franklin to Murfreesboro to take the cars, via Stevenson, Alabama, and then via Huntsville, to try and head them off, the train stopped in the woods. We got off and started across the country toward Decatur, coming to a stream (I do not remember the name), where we camped that night. Early next morning, after breakfast, we disrobed, and tying our clothing to our guns, waded the river, the water reaching nearly to our arm-pits. During the day we crossed two more streams, or bayous, in the same manner. This was about Christmas, and the ground was frozen hard. Comrades who were on that trip, don't it make you shiver yet when you think of it? A day or two later, at Leighton Station, thirty-two miles southwest of Decatur, Alabama, we had our last Christmas dinner in the war. We had sweet potatoes and chicken for dinner. I was reminded of the one we had December 25, 1863, near Strawberry Plains, East Tennessee, at the farm of Samuel Vance, a loyal old gentleman, who gave us the potatoes and chickens, and loaned us a kettle to cook them in. On this occasion, our meal was confiscated, and "stolen fruits" never tasted sweeter. After this, our chief discomfort during the winter was that at three different times the river rose and covered our camp to the depth of from three to seven feet with water. We had to get out and get along the best way we could until the water ran down. Comrades, we will

never all meet together here again. We are scattered over the land. Some are buried in unknown and unmarked graves; some in the National cemeteries; while others rest in our home camps, where their comrades, relatives and friends can strew their graves with flowers. Boys, let us keep the history of the rebellion before our children, so that they may always point to us with pride, and say that 'My father was a soldier.'"

XXII.—BY CHARLES LESTER.

I was born in Onondaga county, New York, August 27, 1827; taught school in Ohio and Kentucky several years, and in the summer of 1852 attended Folsom Business College, at Cleveland, Ohio; taught several years in Kentucky and Indiana, where I married Emily R. Morgan, a daughter of Jesse Morgan, in Rush county, and began farming. When the rebellion came on, I felt it my duty to go. I volunteered, and was mustered into Company D, 68th Indiana. Soon after I was promoted Sergeant, and commissioned by Colonel King. I was with the company until it was called to Munfordsville. Being on picket there, I was left behind, and, with others, was attached to other troops, and went to Salt Creek; then to Louisville; from there to Elizabethtown, and back again to Louisville; and then rejoined the regiment, at Indianapolis, in parole camp. In April, 1863, while on picket

near Murfreesboro, one cold night, I took a severe cold, which developed into pneumonia, and I was sent to the hospital. The first morning that I got able to sit up, I was by the fire when the surgeon came in "tipsy." He ordered me to be sent at once to my regiment, and I was soon ready for the hospital again from a relapse. The Government lost much of the field service I was able to give, and I had to suffer, all because of that officer's morning dram. I was sent to Nashville, and when better I met Captain John Lakin, who had charge of the barracks there. He had me detailed as commissary sergeant, and I filled that position there until in March, 1864, when I started to join my company in East Tennessee. At Knoxville, I was put on duty in a drenching rain, and it again brought on sickness. I was sent to the hospital there, and after a long spell of sickness was furloughed home. I returned to the regiment at Chattanooga, and took my share of the skirmishing and fighting with Hood's army at Nashville, but gave out on the march in the pursuit, and shortly after was ordered to report at the headquarters of Colonel Morgan, commanding the 1st Colored Brigade at Chattanooga, where I wrote in the A. A. A. G.'s office until the end of the war. The duties of the position required accurate work, and I found much pleasure in it, and all the officials connected with my duties agreeable and intelligent men. During the last two weeks of my service there, the war being over, I was furnished a horse, and with others visited the battlefields and other places of in-

terest. The following order was issued, and I returned to my company, and with them was in a few days mustered out:

HEADQUARTERS COLORED BRIGADE, A. C.,
CHATTANOOGA, June 17, 1865.

Special Order, No. 42.

I. Sergeant Charles Lester and Private James H. Roberts, Company D, 68th Indiana Volunteers, detailed for special duty per Par. V., 30. No. 28, Headquarters District of the Etowah, are hereby relieved from said detail in order to be mustered out of the service of the United States by reason of the expiration of their term.

II. In relieving them, the Colonel commanding desires to express his highest satisfaction at the manner in which they have performed all their duties since their connection with these headquarters. In the Adjutant General's and Inspector's offices their services have been faithful, efficient and invaluable.

By order of Col. Thos. J. Morgan, Commanding Brigade.

JOHN E. CLELAND, Lieut. and A. A. A. G.

XXIII.—BATTLE OF NASHVILLE—BY SERGEANT CHARLES LESTER.

November 29, 1864, all the troops that could be spared from Chattanooga were sent to Nashville. All were taken except the sick and those on detached service. We went in box-cars, and on our arrival at Nashville were put on picket line, doing picket duty and digging trenches. Our Captain was on detached duty, our 1st Lieutenant had been permanently disabled, the 2d Lieutenant was sick in camp, and I, being the ranking non-commissioned officer present, had

command of the company. We were in the advance line of pickets when Hood's army first appeared, and part of Company D was out as infantry videttes. Some of us, who were anxious to see more, went on to the top of the ridge, and a shower of bullets was fired at us. We retreated in good order. After this the Johnneys wanted to see, and we returned the compliment. Neither party being disposed to receive the other in friendship, no further sight-seeing was sought. That day we left our trenches, by order, for the enemy to occupy, and falling back, went into camp near the railroad to Murfreesboro. Every morning, when not on other duty, we were drawn up in line of battle at three o'clock and remained there until daylight. Several days the ground was covered with snow and sleet, which froze hard and made it so slippery that one could hardly walk on the rolling ground. We were called out for drill once, at this time, which created some merriment, but was of no utility. Previous to the general battle, our regiment skirmished with the enemy at three different times. The first was to learn the position of the enemy in our front. We had the 14th United States Colored Infantry on our left, and several regiments in support in the rear. While the whole line was advancing and firing rapidly, some comrade called my attention to what we called a "gopher hole" (a vidette post), which we discovered to be occupied. I said, "Boys, let's go for them," which we did, and that post was silenced in a short time. A white rag

on a ramrod was hung out, and I said to the boys, "Cease firing," and called to them, "Leave your guns, and come out." Four Johnneys came forth. Just then "retreat" was given. Our Johnneys hesitated, as if to go back, but we stood and called to them to run. Three obeyed, and the other, being wounded, we left for their own men to care for. I sent them to the rear, and other regiments got the credit of their capture. At dress parade it was announced that we had captured twenty-one, and killed and wounded a number. In this charge the rebel fort was captured, and a number of our men were in their trenches; but a retreat was ordered, to avoid bringing on a general engagement at that time. On the morning of the 15th of December, 1864, we were ordered out with two days' cooked rations and eighty rounds of ammunition. Skirmishers were thrown out, and we advanced in line of battle, and soon the great battle began. Company D's position was on the left of the railroad to Murfreesboro, deployed as skirmishers, and we worked up near to the rebel lines, being in the woods. Some of us were behind a plank fence and some in the railroad cut. We kept up so much firing all day that the rebels concentrated their fire on us, and we soon found it convenient to seek cover a little farther to the rear, before dark. The snow had just gone off, the mud and water were deep, and in order to keep on top of the soft ground while sleeping, we gathered up sticks, brush and rails, and slept that night with guns and accoutrements ready for action. Early next morning,

we advanced for several hours without any resistance, passing over ground where many dead lay, stripped of their clothing, who had been killed the day before. At about 9 a. m., we came in sight of Hood's wagon train, going toward Franklin. Our artillery opened fire on them. In the afternoon they made a last stand at Overton Hill, and we made a charge through a thick undergrowth of woods and vines, and then down a hill. The rebels opened on us with grape and canister, but as we went rapidly down the hill it passed over our heads. Isaac Silvers, of Company D, was wounded in the arm by a minnie ball, and the breech of my gun was shot off. Before we got near enough to do much execution they broke and ran, every man for himself, and went over the ridge like a flock of quails. Our artillery threw shot and shell into them, and they were completely demoralized, throwing all away that would impede their progress. Then commenced a chase, and most of the rear guards were captured. After this, in the pursuit for twenty days, I could not keep up on account of debility, and returned to Nashville.

XXIV.—BY THOMAS E. BRAMBLETT.

Dear Comrades: I have been asked time and again what became of me after I left the regiment at Murfreesboro, Tennessee. I will tell you. I lay in

the field hospital two months or more; then I was sent to the hospital at Nashville; there I was examined, and my discharge ordered; then I was sent to the Convalescent Camp there, to the "Condemned Yankee Corps" (7th regiment). During the winter of '63, I was doing duty at Camp Chase, Ohio; was there when Morgan broke out of the penitentiary. I was one of the "boys" that crossed the Allegheny mountains on "the cold New Year's" week; was one of the "squad" that drew the barrel of whisky at Pittsburg; then I was sent to Washington City; was on guard duty there the remainder of my time; was on the skirmish line two days and one night with the 8th Illinois Cavalry, holding Early in check until the 22d Corps came up; then I was sent to the city; was on duty the night "Father Abraham" was shot, and remained on duty twenty-one days and nights. I was one of the "boys" that stole the Irishman out of the guard-house, and rowed him across the Potomac river, one stormy night, cheating the Colonel out of the fun of having him shot the next day. His offense was breaking a darkey's head with a rock. My next fun was in the riot with the boys and darkies' on 17th street. Now you know where I was and what I was doing. I am now trying to make a living by farming. It is true "Uncle Sam" is helping me some. I get two sandwiches per day, or its equivalent—thirteen cents. So, hoping this will satisfy all of my old comrades who are still on top, I shall bid you adieu.

XXV.—BY ENOCH WHITELY.

A camp for colored contrabands and white refugees was located on the hills, just back of our camp, while we guarded the military bridge at Chattanooga. The population of this camp was composed of all kinds of people. The colored folks were striking for freedom, the whites had lost all means of subsistence, the same being taken by the soldiers of the contending armies; and these people were of necessity, for the time being, pensioners upon Uncle Sam's bounty. Captain Mauzy was put in command of the camp. Of nights he would frequently take men from the regiment, and patrol the camp, arresting any soldiers found prowling about it or in the shanties or tents of the inhabitants. We soon "caught on;" and when the Captain was wrapped in slumber, we would take our muskets and patrol the camp, occasionally catching a stray soldier and scaring him for the fun. Of course, he believed the arrest legitimate, and after "pumping" him, and hearing his answers and his entreaties for release, we exacted a solemn promise and permitted him to escape. One night, when I was corporal of the guard, the Captain made the rounds with us, and retired. We then went back, on our own hook. In the refugee camp, we heard a male voice in one of the shanties. A hasty consultation was held. We decided that a soldier was in there, and that we would rush in, and

catch him before he could get out. Accordingly in we went, in the most unceremonious manner. Imagine our consternation when the armed guard stood in the midst of the family group, bowed at evening prayer! We had mistaken the good old man's voice in devotion, and supposed that a soldier had crept in clandestinely. Another night, two of our boys took a stroll in the contraband camp, and stepped into a shanty where a colored preacher was holding service. One of them discovered that the minister had a fine, new Burnside hat. When all bowed in prayer, one of the boys grabbed the hat and the other a towel, and slipped out into the darkness. In the run the leader struck a clothes-line, and was poised in mid-air, while the line, rebounding, struck the other soldier across the mouth, making a scar which remained for months. But it was a good hat, and lasted a year after the war.

XXVI.—EXTRACT FROM A LETTER BY JAMES W. RICHIE, MAY 18, 1866.

I was wounded in the battle of Chicamauga, September 19, 1863, being shot through the right lung. The ball passed through and out in the side, and so disabled me that I could not get away. On the evening of the 20th, the rebels took possession of the hospital, where I remained until the 27th, when I was

escaping capture several times, and were once pursued by blood-hounds, getting away by finding a small row boat, and the friendly aid of Union women in the mountains. Hansen got weary of trying to escape, and for fear he would surrender us both, I concluded to leave him, so that he could give himself up, if he wished. I then traveled about one hundred and fifty miles alone. One time I hid in a fence corner while some rebels rode by. When I got up, I found a large black snake close by where I had lain. I arrived in our lines at Strawberry Plains, East Tennessee, June 12th, twenty-six days after my escape from the cars. To tell all my adventures and escapes while a prisoner would make a book.

XXVII.—BY N. T. PLOUGHE.

I was born in Rush county, Indiana, March 12, 1840. When about twelve years old, my father sold his farm, moved to Kokomo, and bought a farm near there, and in about a year traded it for hotel property in Kokomo. For the next five years, I was mail-carrier and clerking in the postoffice there. When the war began, I was working in a saw mill in Rush county, and I remember distinctly that on August 7, 1862, before breakfast, and before the sun was up, Manlius W. Pierce and I put down our names as volunteers, so as to get an early start. There are many

removed to Ringgold, Georgia. I was kept there until October 1st, when three hundred of us were sent to Richmond, Virginia, via Atlanta, Augusta, Charlotte and Raleigh, arriving at Richmond on the 10th, and I was then taken to a hospital. On the 18th, I was sent to Libby prison, and from there to Castle Pemberton, where I remained until November 13th, when I was sent to Danville, and kept until the 15th of May, 1864. I was one the unfortunate five hundred selected from the Danville prison to be held as hostages, and to be executed in case our government retaliated on their prisoners for the Fort Pillow massacre. My name came ninth on the list. A number of us dug a long tunnel with an old case-knife, and we were almost ready to escape when some of the prisoners informed on us. We were put on the cars to be sent to prisons further south. Left Danville on the 15th, and about 11 o'clock of the night of the 16th, four of us made our escape by cutting a hole in the bottom of the car, large enough to slip through. We dropped down through, and lay between the tracks while the cars stopped at a station about thirty miles from Columbia, South Carolina. After the train had passed on, and the citizens had left the station, we ran back on the railroad, and held a council. We concluded the best way would be to go two and two together; so we separated, two going in the direction of the sea. My comrade (Hansen) and I concluded to try and make our lines in East Tennessee. We traveled together nearly two hundred miles, narrowly

incidents in a soldier's life which are indellibly written in his mind; yet, when it comes to writing them down after a quarter of a century has passed, and without notes or dates, it would be strange if there are not some mistakes. At Louisville, Kentucky, I was detailed as company drummer, although I voluntarily took a musket for guard duty, on several occasions. At Bardstown, we rested awhile in the fair grounds, and a chicken found its way into my haversack. I had to wring its neck, for at that early date in our soldier's life we had to keep shady on our pressed dainties. The weather was so warm I did not get much good of my chicken, for by the time we went into camp it had begun to get old. While in camp at Nashville, the musicians became somewhat neglectful of their duties, and did not get out to "drummer's call" in the morning promptly. The Colonel, I think, got up unusually early one morning, to "drummer's call," and seeing that most of us were absent, thought he would see if he could not bring about a better attendance. So he ordered us to bury a dead horse that lay unpleasantly close to our camp. We went, did a good job, and thought we got off easily. We were out at calls on time after this. For fourteen days and nights, after leaving Murfreesboro for Tullahoma, in June, 1863, I did not have my clothes off, and my feet were wet all the time. I think the blackberries we ate saved half of Rosecrans' army. The night of September 18, 1863, we were on the march all night. We halted every little while, and the boys would drop

down and fall asleep in the road in no time. Then the word "Forward!" spoken low, would come, and we would plod on. We halted about daylight, to make coffee and read our letters; for the mail carrier had come, and made glad the hearts of many a poor fellow who did not live to see the setting of the sun. I was back and forth from the line of battle to the the field hospital, helping the wounded, all the afternoon and night of the 19th. The next day (the 20th), I saw that the hospital was in danger, and told all those that could march, and got them started toward Chattanooga. I got in there about 12 o'clock that night, with the division ambulance. The next two months was spent there behind the breastworks, having the monotony relieved by the enemy throwing shot and shells at us quite often. One night, they came so thick that my bunk-mate and I thought it best to go to the trenches. When we went back to our tent, next morning, a piece of shell had passed down through where "Doc" Earnest would have been lying. At Mission Ridge, we lost one of our company, who was every inch a soldier—Samuel S. Bodine. The last words I heard him say, before he started on the last charge up the ridge, was, "I don't like to, but I guess I will have to," in his peculiar all-ready way. In a short time I found his lifeless body near the top of Mission Ridge. Our regiment was immediately ordered to go to East Tennessee, and I was detailed to stay and care for the company baggage at Chattanooga, until a wagon train could be sent with it, about

two months latter. While we were crossing the Holston river, the rebel General Wheeler thought he would take us in, but the boys gave him a set back. Orderly Smith was wounded in the hand. He had our ration of coffee in his haversack. A ball cut the bottom out, and we lost our coffee, much to our regret. After many marches and counter-marches, we got back again to Chattanooga. I participated in the battle of Nashville, and in the pursuit of Hood to Decatur, Alabama. We had no change of linen for about six weeks. When we crossed the river there, the enemy showed a little fight, and a new recruit of some regiment had a full knapsack, which he threw away. I spied it, and made my toilet then and there, right under fire. After this campaign was finished, I was detailed as clerk of a court-martial. I have a silver dollar which Captain Mauzy gave me then, of the date of 1782. After my discharge, in June, 1865, I emigrated to Kansas, and in 1871 was married, and am now farming.

XXVIII.—BY JOHN L. T. WILSON.

I started into the service as teamster; broke three teams of mules, of six mules each, that never had been haltered, and had plenty of work from the beginning. At Munfordville, the night before we surrendered, I helped Colonel King wrap our flag around his body, to

save it from being captured. Month after month passed, of hardship, mule driving, in the rain and mud and swamps. On the trip from Murfreesboro, James Hood, Luther Stewart, and I got into Tullahoma about midnight, passing about fifty stalled teams, and were the first of the train there. We lay there the next day, which gave me a chance to recruit my team, by finding a couple of large black mules, and donating to the boys two of my smallest. I now had a team I took great pride in, but it made extra duty for me, as I was selected to go often, because I had such an extra outfit. On we went, up and over the mountains, having many adventures, and down to Pond Springs. The fight at Chicamauga was coming on. We marched after night with the train, it being so dark we had to build fires to light the train on its way, and camped, late in the night, in a little valley by a little brook, where we were surrounded by plenty of ripe corn; and you bet we knew what to do with it. The next day, the battle was raging hotly, and the next (Sunday) the storm of the battle was still more constant. That evening, as our teamsters were in the cornfield, laying in a supply, orders came to hitch up quick, and get out, for we were five miles behind the rebel lines. "Bill" Aldridge rolled the camp kettles in lively, and hadn't even time to put his finger in the bean soup while we were hitching up. We drove in a fast trot about two hours, which brought us to where Wilder's cavalry was guarding the road for our benefit. There we were attacked by a small squad of rebel cavalry,

but they were soon driven off, and we went on in the direction of Chattanooga, near which we went into camp about midnight, and next day pulled the train across the river opposite the town. We immediately went to hauling rations from Stevenson, Alabama, over the mountain road. The train was moved over on to the Chattanooga side shortly afterwards, and feed got so scarce that many mules starved to death haltered to the wagons. Immediately before the Mission Ridge battle, I assisted in hauling pontoons for our troops to cross the the river on, to attack the rebels on their flanks. When the Atlanta campaign began, I was given command of the 3d Division, Fourth Corps, ordnance train. We had several close calls on our way, but luck was with us, and we got there in good condition. We lay in front of Atlanta several days, having a jolly time, with the exception of a few times when the rebels spied us, and then we would get a lively shelling from their artillery. Just before we flanked Atlanta, Sherman put me in charge of all the ordnance trains of the army, which I ran successfully until we had possession of the city. We lay there about thirty days, when our corps (the 4th) was sent back to look after Hood. We were hotly pursued by his army all the way back to Nashville, marching nearly day and night. The "rebs" got so determined to have our train, that I had to double it up, two wagons abreast, so that our guards would have a better chance to protect them. While the hard-fought battle of Franklin was raging, I emptied the fort of

all the extra ammunition, and took it away to Nashville. At Spring Hill, we were attacked, and I lost my horse in the fight. Twice during the night they came upon us, but were repulsed. About 8 o'clock the next morning, we were surrounded by rebel cavalry; but, with the assistance of a battery, cut our way out—the drivers and train-guards fighting like tigers. We were all armed, either with guns or revolvers. When we arrived at Nashville, men and mules were nearly played out from fatigue and loss of sleep. After the battle of Nashville, we again started back over the same road, to Pulaski, and from there went to Huntsville, Alabama. On that march was the first time we had a wagon to sink down as low as the bed in the mud. We had to pull the mules out one at a time, in the "Twelve-mile Bearings," a swampy country, twelve miles wide, between the two places. This was our last hardship, and the next five months were rather quiet about Nashville.

XXIX.—BY ARTHUR J. GATES.

No man who never witnessed it can have anything like a correct understanding of the state of affairs in the rear of an army during a battle. When it was found, at the battle of Chicamauga, that the enemy was going to capture our hospital at Crawfish Springs, our surgeons gave orders for every man who was able

to make his escape to Chattanooga, ten miles distant. Rebel prisons, like the nightmare, always haunted Union soldiers, and when this danger was announced the scare of crippled wounded men, trying to get away, cannot be described. Since time has allayed the horrors of that time, many amusing incidents are recalled. I commenced hobbling away (my wound being in my leg), aided by a stick which is still in my possession. I was overtaken by a teamster, who kindly permitted me to ride. Surgeon Wooden told Luther Stewart to save the headquarter wagon, and the camp equipage was piled in indiscriminately. Having participated in the bloody carnage of Saturday, when nearly three-fifths of our company engaged had been killed or wounded, it made a feeling of horror prevade me. All day Sunday, as I heard the dreadful roar of cannon and musketry, the thought kept coming to me, what is the fate of my comrades who are engaged to-day? It seemed that life could not endure in the midst of so great destruction. I could not help mourning my comrades as dead. When I reached Chattanooga, and was crossing the bridge, I never was so surprised and overjoyed, when my messmate, D. L. Thomas, whom I never expected to see again, met me. Those who could walk, marched to Bridgeport, Alabama, to take the train for Nashville. I crossed the mountains in a wagon. At Tullahoma, I met my cherished friend and neighbor, George Thomas, coming to our aid. His tender acts of kindness to me at Nashville cannot be forgotten.

He sought our regiment every time a battle was imminent. At Lebanon Junction, Kentucky, he was with us, and, armed with musket and accoutrements, lay with us in line of battle all day when an attack was expected. I went from Nashville to Evansville, thence to Indianapolis, and did not rejoin the regiment until the Spring of 1865.

XXX.—BY D. L. THOMAS.

On the 26th of October, 1864, our regiment returned to camp at Chattanooga, after several days' riding and marching along the Nashville railroad, to prevent Forrest from cutting the road. We were hoping for a few days' rest, but orders were in waiting for us to go on to Dalton, Georgia, to intercept other raiders that were threatening the Atlanta road. But, at midnight, orders came to draw rations, and be ready at a moment's notice to march to the depot and board the cars for Decatur, Alabama. The order was obeyed, and we sat with all our accoutrements on until the morning was well advanced, when we boarded the cars with sixty men and equipments to each box-car. There were no seats, as usual, so that a portion of each company took passage on top. As the trains ran by telegraph orders from headquarters, many delays occurred at stations on the way. During the day the sunshine was intense, which caused us to vacate the tin roofs

when the train was not moving. It was a poor regiment that, with experience, could not board a train of freight cars after it started. The boys who lost hats always stocked up by snatching hats from the unsuspecting bystanders, as the train started from stations. At 2 o'clock next morning, our train halted on the banks of the Tennessee, opposite Decatur. The railroad bridge was burned in 1862—said to have been done by order of General Mitchell. The Confederates, under General Hood, had a line of battle, with pickets in front, around the town. By 3 o'clock we had marched across the pontoon bridge and lain down inside the earthworks. As everything was still as death, we were ready for a much-needed rest and sleep. But, alas! the Confederate yell broke in upon the stillness, as they charged and drove in our pickets. Our batteries opened with a few rounds, and we were ordered into the works to receive the expected assault at daybreak. And again the stillness of a cemetery prevailed. Morning dawned with a heavy fog. Half of our regiment was ordered on the skirmish line in front of our works, to drive back the enemy and re-establish the picket line. It was a most reluctant duty when the writer made the detail from Company D, naming who should go, as all regarded the position as one of imminent peril. But as the Confederate pickets saw ours approaching through the fog, they receded, and our line was re-established. When the fog disappeared, the picket fight began, and continued nearly all day. Our boys had learned so well how to

"hug the ground," and take advantage of every obstacle, that they rested in comparative safety. Their greatest danger came from our own men in the works, firing at the enemy, and the balls falling among our own men. Isaac Rodgers, of Company D, was painfully wounded. As George Smith carried him on his back to the fortification the "Johnnys" enjoyed the target practice, but without hitting their mark. During the day a Confederate battery disabled our wooden gunboats, and opened on our pontoon bridge from a bend in the river below our works. The 14th United States Colored Regiment passed out of the works along the water's edge, and when in position climbed the bluffs, charged, captured, and "spiked" the battery, while the artillerymen in amazement ordered, and in some cases tried to lead, the "niggers" to the rear. It was their first introduction to colored troops. As the 14th boys were starting to dump the guns into the river, the infantry support rallied from their surprise, and drove our boys back. The 14th lost fifty-odd, killed and wounded, in that successful assault. Late in the day, our skirmishers were all withdrawn. After nightfall, our whole brigade was put on picket, with two men at a place, with a shovel. They took turns standing guard and digging "gopher holes," for protection the next day. If mortals ever suffered for sleep, we were the boys, after losing so much sleep and being shipped like cattle. We could hear the rebel pickets talking in an undertone within a stone's throw. But what was that to exhausted, weary men?

It excited no more fear than the lowing of kine or the dog baying at the moon. We dared not sit down, else we would be entirely overcome with sleep. We would go to sleep upon our feet, and awake when falling. Then, between us and the earthworks was a line of small trees, placed with the tops pointing outward, and the limbs trimmed with the sharp points toward the enemy, to check them when they were assaulting the works, so that for the moment, under a galling fire, they would become confused and retreat. But what about our situation? Should they assault at daybreak, as we anticipated, we would be in front of this obstruction, and between two fires. This caused some concern. But before day we had sought out the "gates," so, should necessity require, we could get back in, by running a quarter of a mile down the line. Morning dawned, and the enemy gradually withdrew. In the meantime new troops had been coming from the north—several regiments from Michigan. The beardless youths had just drawn big bounties, bought officers' suits, kissed their sweethearts good-bye, and were ready to put down the rebellion. To say they were gullible, as new troops are among "old" soldiers, is putting it mild. And the big stories related to them of the great battle are too wonderful to repeat. But Hood was gone, and the new soldiers sent on picket, while we drew our blankets around us upon the ground for sweet repose more refreshing than homefolks could have enjoyed upon a bed of roses. But those "band-box" soldiers got in their work. Our

exaggerated reports of the battle had possessed them so completely that they fancied they saw rebels every hour of the night. And their fusilade upon the picket line often broke in upon our quiet slumber. But they paid for their credulity. The way our boys stole from them, right before their eyes, was a wonder. Finally their officers put guards over everything, with instructions to allow no old soldier to come near. "But," said the guards, "how will we know who are the old soldiers?" The officers forcibly rejoined, "Why, them soldiers with dirty clothes on!" Not knowing that Sherman was going to march to the sea, every one supposed he was following close after Hood. In fact, we expected every hour to see "Old Billy" (Sherman) coming. The second morning after Hood retired, our regiment was sent out at 3 o'clock on a reconnoisance. The other troops were not aware of the fact. About 8 o'clock, we came marching in with banners flying. The camp was alive with interest. Then the questions! "What command is yours?" "Sherman's advance" came from all sides. "We've followed Hood from Atlanta." Then hats waved and the air was rent with cheers. "Bully for Sherman," and kindred ejaculations came from the late arrivals. "But, what regiment?" "68th Colored Regiment," "4th Calcutta," and so on, *ad nauseam*, came from our boys. A new officer desired definite information, and did not think a private soldier would dare to give an officer a disrespectful answer. Plucking one of our boys, he earnestly asked, "Mister, please what regi-

ment is this?" He retired feeling doubtless that war was demoralizing, after getting the bland response, "3d Ireland!" We pitched our "dog tents," and awaited further developments. One morning a cold drizzly rain was falling. We had scarcely any camp equipage. The lack of comfort caused several of the boys to report sick. The writer escorted them to the surgeons, and reported. The apothecary was supplied with quinine only. At least that was all the drug in sight. "Let me see your tongue. How is your pulse?" was propounded to each sick man in turn. "Well, have you anything to get your medicine in?" "No, sir." "Well, hold your hand," and a portion of quinine was poured into the palm. "Now"—showing with point of pocket-knife—"You take about this much every two hours." Poor fellows had to crawl under their "dog tents" and deposit their medicine on their tin plates or some other article from their scanty supply. But it was not often our doctors were without paper to wrap the medicine. Early November 10th, we reached Chattanooga again, a distance of 120 miles, and enjoyed a short rest.

A MUCH greater variety of incidents, adventures and duties performed by members of Company D would have been presented, if their experiences could have been obtained. A number are dead, and the present address of others is unknown. How we should like to have read Orderly Sergeant James A.

Smith's experience while an officer in a colored regiment! George Snider's long experience as Hospital Steward afforded him unequaled opportunities to see that important department of war. But he writes (July 2, 1887,) that he had been two months at Hot Springs, and was yet too weak to write more than a few lines. "Dan" Simpson's adventures while with Sherman's army on its great march to the sea, and through the Carolinas to Washington, as one of the "bummers" who achieved celebrity, would have added spice to our collection. Sergeant Cohn might have told us many headquarter secrets, learned while tailoring for the generals who commanded our armies. Ryland Bosley and Payton Walters might have told the story of their many changes, long travels, and duties, after they were wounded and taken prisoners at Chicamauga; and so might Oliver Sailors, when he was captured by Forrest. Thomas Bosley could have told of his wound at Missionary Ridge, and his other service; John D. Brown of all the war to the end; Charles F. Junken could have written of many incidents which happened while he was a train guard for several months, on trains running from Chattanooga to Knoxville. Others could write of guard duty at the "Suck" (a narrow place in the Tennessee river, a few miles below Chattanooga), where they assisted the steamboats through by windlass and ropes. It is doubtful if any of the company could equal Frank Cohee for continued service. He was scarcely ever unable for duty, and being with the company at all

times, could have written an interesting history. Isaac Hurst, a good writer, could have told us of many important events which happened in and about Nashville, where he performed the clerical duties assigned him. Lingenfelter, Brown, Beetem and Silvers could have told of much service. "Billy" Buzan was born August 3, 1848, and when mustered was only a few days over fourteen years old. He is probably the youngest man who was in the ranks in 1862, carrying a musket and with his company in all its marches and duties, until severely wounded in the battle of Chicamauga, Georgia, September 19, 1863. We should liked to have some of his experiences, and are sure that he would have looked on the bright side, for he seemed to enjoy active soldier life.

THE DEAD.

Since our return home, nine—James A. Smith, Gabriel Cohn, George T. Richie, Isaac Dale, Charles Eagy, Manilus W. Pierce, John Simmons, Jerry and Sanford Widner,—have gone to join "The armies of the Lord," and each year may add to their numbers from our ranks. Let us who remain remember their virtues, forget their faults, and do what we can to prosper the country they helped to save.

IN MEMORIAM.

Dead of Company D, 68th Indiana.

JAMES W. INNIS.
JAMES A. SMITH.
GABRIEL COHN.
GEORGE T. RICHIE.
SAMUEL S. BODINE.
ABRAHAM S. BILLINGS.
JOHN CALLENDER.
HENRY CONRAD.
ISAAC DALE.
JAMES B. DAVID.
WILLIAM H. H. DANNER.
CHARLES EAGY.
WILLIAM GRIFFIN.
WALTER S. LANGE.
CALEB C. LEE.
MANLIUS W. PIERCE.
LLEWELLYN PIERCE.
JOHN SIMMONS.
JEFFERSON E. TRIMBLY.
JEREMIAH A. WIDNER.
DAVID S. WIDNER.
MATHIAS CHALFANT.

THE DEAD.

Major James W. Innis was born in Anderson township, Rush county, Indiana, November 17, 1831, where he remained until the war began, excepting three years which were spent in learning his trade of carriage trimming in Cincinnati. He was manufacturing carriages when the first call for troops was made, and laid aside his apron, saying: "I have nothing to contribute but my service, which I freely give." He enlisted in Company F, of the old 16th Indiana, and served one year as orderly sergeant, the most trying office in the army. Captain Beachbard, says: "He was the best one I ever knew." At the expiration of his time, he returned home, and recruited for the 68th Indiana. He was elected captain of Company D. June 8, 1863, he was mustered as major, but his health was so broken by exposures and privations that he resigned soon afterward, and returned home, where he lingered through much suffering until April 24, 1867. Major Innis was a strict disciplinarian, kind and generous, of a jovial disposition when not on duty. He was known as a worker in the Masonic order, and the last rites and ceremonies at his grave were attended by large number of that fraternity and his comrades of the war. We mourn his loss as a comrade, friend and citizen.

Samuel S. Bodine, son of W. A. and Matilda Bodine, was born at their home, in Rush county, Indiana, October 29, 1842, and was killed in the battle of Chattanooga, November 25, 1863. He was a young

man, reared in our county, possessed in a high degree those amiable traits of character which attract us to our friends, and was beloved by a large family circle. Educated in the principles of christianity, he honored his father and mother and loved his fellow-men. He was a patriot, and when his country called for aid in suppressing the rebellion and maintaining her integrity, he stepped forward as a volunteer. As a member of Company D, 68th Regiment Indiana Volunteers, he shared with that regiment their trials and hardships. In the battle of Chicamauga, he passed safely through, though many of his comrades fell or were disabled. With the remnant of the company he entered the conflict for the possession of Missionary Ridge, and fell as victory was perching on their standard, in the front line and near the summit in the last charge. The bullet cut the jugular vein in the neck, and he died without speaking a word. Mournfully his comrades gave him a soldier's burial next day. Several weeks after, his brother, William A. Bodine, who had been a soldier in the 37th Indiana, got permission to bring his remains home, and an impressive funeral service was held in the Presbyterian church in Rushville, Sabbath, January 24, 1864, in the presence of a large assembly. The interment was made in East Hill cemetery, where sleeps the soldier dust of Hackleman, Wolfe and Wallace.

Rev. D. M. Stewart.

JEFFERSON E. TREMBLY.—The following extract is from a letter of Orderly Sergeant James A. Smith to S. B. Trembly, an uncle who raised Jefferson, (who was an orphan):

"CHATTANOOGA, Tenn., October 23, 1863.—I am a stranger to you, but I thought a few lines concerning the death of your nephew would be acceptable, even from a stranger. He died yesterday (October 22) at 10 o'clock p. m., from a wound he received in the battle of Chicamauga, September 19. He was wounded in the left knee, and twenty-one days after mortification took place below the knee; so his leg was amputated, but he could not be saved, although I know he was cared for. I know this to be the case by what I have seen. When visiting him in the hospital he told me that his nurse waited on him and treated him like a brother. To-day I went to the hospital and his nurse and I placed him in his coffin. I have been in the service with him fifteen months, and am happy to say he was a good, honest, upright boy, and was always ready to do his duty as a soldier, and his death will be lamented by every member of Company D."

His comrades carved a beautiful monument out of the mottled stone found where we dug out a fort, and placed it above his grave. He was about nineteen years old, and was born in Butler county, Ohio.

WILLIAM H. H. DANNER.—The following, *in memoriam*, was written for the Rushville papers by Rev. D. M. Stewart on the news of the death of William H. H. Danner, of Company D, 68th Regiment Indiana Volunteers, who was wounded at Chicamauga, and taken prisoner, and died in prison at Richmond, Virginia, February 25, 1864, of small-pox:

"He was the youngest son of Mrs. N. E. Danner, and a youth of remarkably kind and amiable disposition, moral and correct in all his habits. He was a christian. Very early in life he sought

THE DEAD.

the God of his fathers, and gave his heart to Christ. He was a patriot. One brother was already in the service of the country, and his mother and sister were by his absence left entirely alone; yet he felt it to be his duty to answer the call for aid, and go to save his country. After his capture, he was indirectly heard from at Atlanta on his way to Richmond, and from thence, in January last, he was permitted to send through a very short letter to his mother. From that time until a few days past no word was received from him. His anxious mother received the tidings and particulars of his death through a fellow-prisoner, from St. Lawrence county, New York, who has since been exchanged. He gave to his wife (Mrs. Sayles) the particulars of the case, and she has written to Mrs. Danner. Thus another of our young men has fallen in defense of our homes and country. He sent, as his dying request, the charge to his friends to meet him in heaven. How singularly the conflict between hope and fear has been settled in the heart of this anxious family. While no word came, hope still lingered that he might live. The Lord reigns, and he brings to pass whatsoever he will."

MANLIUS W. PIERCE will be remembered by all the members of Company D as a man who always was ready to do his duty. His disposition was cheerful, and kindness to his comrades was a virtue which he practiced whenever any opportunity offered. Very few musicians in the service attended to more calls than he, for he was seldom off duty. The exposures and hardships then endured sowed the seeds of disease, and several years after his return home his health gradually failed, and he was an invalid until relieved by death. He was a brother of Llewellyn Pierce, a good, faithful comrade, who shrank to a skeleton before he would quit his duties, and died at Murfreesboro, Tennessee.

MEMORIAL ADDRESS.

A quarter-centennial reunion of the 68th Regiment Indiana Infantry was held at Greensburg, Indiana, August 19, 1887, at which Comrade Rev. E. H. Wood, of Company K, delivered the following address:

To the Surviving Members of the 68th Indiana Volunteer Infantry:

MY DEAR COMRADES:—Since the announcement of this reunion, and more especially from the time I was solicited to speak to you on this occasion, I have anticipated this time with great interest and pleasure.

We have reached the quarter-centennial (twenty-five years) since that memorable day, August 19, 1862, when at the capital of our grand old State, on an adjoining commons, we were mustered into the service of Uncle Sam to serve for a period of three years, if not sooner discharged by the expiration of the war, or indefinitely should the necessities of the case require.

We enlisted in the midst of war and national commotion and insecurity; the clouds hung dark and heavy about us; with a united South and a divided North environing our armies with alternating defeats and

victories, we marched bravely and steadily forward, conquering as we went a bitter and determined foe. having knowledge of the country, and protected in their well selected and almost invulnerable fortifications. Some of us had been to dream-land and had visions of volunteer service, preparations, drill, camp-life and dress parade. So under the inspiration of martial music and an impulse of duty, we enrolled our names in the home company, and prepared to enter camp. A trunk was provided and supplied with well selected articles, from which a complete toilet might be arranged; perhaps a change of clothing throughout, especially a good supply of white collars and shirts, fancy neckties, gloves, etc.; and Greensburg being our rendezvous, we expected to spend many a leisure hour with the good and fair amid the refreshing shades and beautiful surroundings of this loyal and to us memorable city.

With a good-bye to father, and a kiss for mother and sisters, we hied away to camp, sure the trunk was not forgotten, with but little other thought than of entering a military academy, to spend weeks or months in careful, painstaking preparation for war, and thus by gradual transition pass from the citizen to the soldier, full-fledged.

But as it has been said that dreams are realized only in their opposites, so this vision proved to be a baseless fabric. But four days passed from the original enlistment, when on Sabbath evening, seated in the various churches of the city, listening to the gospel

dispensed by God's chosen and appointed servants, and others in camp becoming acquainted with their new surrounding, not a few raw recruits were startled by the cry, "marching orders;" and such a sensation followed as Greensburg had not known. Before Monday morning light had dawned, visions of pleasure and quiet camp-life had vanished, trunks were left behind, and all were speeding on to the arms of a more military character.

General Bragg, in command of the Confederate forces, had invaded Kentucky, and was threatening Louisville and our own border. A necessity was forcing us, and all available troops were to be ordered to the front. On Tuesday, August 19th, 1862, the Indiana regiments then assembling at the capital, and being equipped for war, were hastily called into line to listen to words of loyalty and courage from O. P. Morton, the war horse and war Governor of Indiana; and the words which that day fell from his lips were full of sympathy and proved an inspiration to the boys who were about to don the blue and shoulder the musket, to drive back the invader who threatened our own firesides. Could the veil be withdrawn that hid the inner feelings of some whose bones had scarcely hardened into manhood, it might have disclosed some fluttering hearts as the examining officer passed down the line, each one waiting in almost breathless suspense the decision, fit or unfit for war; but perhaps at that stage of the war the tests were less rigid, as the necessities were more pressing.

But with each returning day, the urgency of the case seemed to increase. Rumors of war grew more fearful. The hoofs of the war steed could almost be heard. Distant mutterings as a battle afar, by vivid imaginations were brought into closer proximity. All seemed to crave the onset, and soon amid flying banners and the rumbling of drums we were actually off to the war.

The soil of Kentucky, our neighbor, that State memorable for neutrality, witnessed the first scenes of the military service of the 68th Indiana Regiment.

Many lessons were to be learned before the citizen soldier could master the art of war. Some say he was loth to learn, and his pride rebelled, but in war they became a military necessity. But we dare not tarry at too great a length on details. A full month was consumed in marching and camping, aching and fretting, eating and sleeping, guarding and picketing, praying and cursing, and scarcely a dozen days of September had passed, and less than a month from that memorable 19th of August, when from Lebanon Junction marching orders were given to move forward into the last gap. The fate of the 68th at Munfordville is fresh in your memory, and the letters written by the boys to fond friends at home, might have read thus: "We have met the enemy, and we are theirs."

But what of that old flag, which as by a miracle was saved from the hands of its most bitter foe? The flag was made by the brave and loving hands of the patriotic ladies of Greensburg; some of them are here

to-day, God bless them. That flag was never dishonored, that flag was never a prisoner. Are those wrinkles erased, does it still bear the impress of that body, noble martyr, Edward A. King, who folded it about his own person beneath his clothing, to save it from dishonor and disgrace, and bore it back in triumph to the old Hoosier State? I love and honor it. It was my lot and honor to be one of the six color guards to defend the flag in the time of danger. Should we ever reach that time in the history of our country when it shall be thought advisable to exchange or return flags that may have been captured, this one bearing the name of the 68th Indiana Volunteers will not be of that number.

This sudden interruption in our onward military history, caused by General Bragg's obstinacy and unyielding disposition, justified a return to our State and homes, and a brief visit to mothers, sisters, wives and sweethearts. Only, however, to be re-equipped, drilled and pushed again to the front to prosecute the war with still greater vigor.

It was now clearly to be seen this was no child's-play. Men and supplies must be provided equal to the emergency. "All quiet on the Potomac" would not fight the battles nor gain the victories. A desperate disease required a desperate remedy. Rebel foes were to be fought both in our front and rear, and at that time, if ever, it was true that eternal vigilance is the price of our liberties. Overtures had been made but refused, war seemed inevitable and the arbiter to settle

the impending troubles. Men had cried peace, peace, but peace came not. The war was a decided failure, but still, like Banquo's ghost, it would not down; and with every battle almost the Federal lines were lengthened and borders enlarged, while those of the Confederates were shortened and circumscribed. The failure was mostly on one side, especially in the culmination.

Our Southern brethren found it was more than a common wrestle or breakfast spell, and that the boys in blue were not to be trifled with. So we pushed onward. The battle of Stone River only crowded the enemy farther south, and opened up a new line of march.

Hoover's Gap was entered in June, 1863, to culminate in the battle of Chicamauga in September, and the possession of Chattanooga, Tennessee.

The victory of Mission Ridge and Lookout Mountain was the key to unlock the middle South, and the release of Knoxville, which followed, only drove the enemy over into North Carolina and Virginia; and by rapid successive movements the war of conquest went on, until finally the most gigantic expedition was inaugurated known in the annals of the war, viz.: "Sherman's March to the Sea," which completely broke the backbone of the Confederacy, and following this dismemberment, dissatisfaction and demoralization settled down upon them.

The surrender of Lee and his whole army, and the capitulation of Johnson's army in the southwest, were the finishing touches and a signal for a speedy dis-

bandment of our own armies, and a return to our homes and secular pursuits.

The battle of Nashville was the last engagement in which the 68th participated, and side by side with the colored troops our army under command of the indomitable and persistent "Pap Thomas," added another victory to its already illustrious history.

Many incidents in army life were calculated to furnish variety and destroy the monotony, which, if left unbroken, would have proved disastrous to our soldiery. A greater calamity could not befall a soldier than downright home-sickness. Some of you may have passed through such an experience. Many a soldier has sickened, wasted away and died, when if the true cause had been written upon his head-board, it would have been, "Died of home-sickness."

Some little license must be shown to the tricks, pranks and amusements in camp and on march, and General Turchin recognized this fact, and the boys understood it, when he made the announcement to his command that he would sleep for one hour. There was a great significance in the order that only the top rails were to be appropriated, and all with one accord proceeded to keep themselves warm and broil their fat pork, which was not healthy to be eaten raw. Uncle Sam's boys claimed a silent partnership in all the chicken roosts along their march, and would peer with delight into the potato pits, cellars and smoke-houses on the way.

Some things appeared to become a military neces-

sity, and attended the precipitation and prosecution of a cruel, bloody war, as when on "Sherman's March to the Sea" the main army cut loose from the principal source of supplies, and cast upon the favors and frowns of the people through whose country they passed, were compelled to seek subsistence as they marched.

Mills were found and appropriated, and grists were awaiting our coming. Engineers, millers and mechanics were detailed from the ranks of the army, for it was created from the industrial pursuits. A grander army of men was never marshaled upon the field of battle than marched forth to the defense of this Union. They were invincible, and the cause for which they contended they knew was just.

War at times has been cruel and unrelenting, and would seem unwarranted amid its devastations and inhuman slaughter of unprotected and helpless innocents, and unlimited appropriation of precious life and treasure; but in these throes great principles affecting man's destiny have been settled, and a new impetus has been given to the onward march and development of human civilization.

Not the smallest of the issues that crowned the war was the emancipation of four millions of slaves in these United States of America, giving a more forcible emphasis to the couplet, ours is, "The land of the free and home of brave." "The emancipation proclamation" by Abraham Lincoln, was one of the most grandly inspired productions issued in this coun-

try of ours since the Declaration of American Independence by our patriotic fathers.

Human slavery stood up as a mighty Gibralter to obstruct the onward progress of American enterprise and civilization. So enormous had grown the evil of this institution that it was becoming intolerable, and the anti-slavery sentiment rapidly increased in strength and courage.

For thirty years the trouble had been brewing and the clouds gathering, and the storm rolled on; and our American Congress was the chief scene of the controversy. Pro-slavery men demanded protection and more territory, while the advocates of anti slavery principles yielded at times for the sake of peace; but by and by patience ceased to be a virtue; the question could not be settled by arguments in debate, or conciliatory measures. We had reached the culmination; the lovers of freedom resolved thus far shalt thou go and no farther, "and let thy proud waves be stayed."

At the close of 1860, Fort Sumpter was still incomplete, but few guns being mounted. A United States garrison, numbering 109 men, of whom only sixty-three were combatants, under Major Robert Anderson, occupied Fort Moultrie.

On the night of December 26th, Major Anderson, learning that the secessionists had made preparations to capture Fort Moultrie and seize the other fortifications near Charleston, transferred his force to Fort Sumpter. Here he mounted fifty-two of his lighter guns. South Carolina assumed the air of Plenipoten-

tiary, and demanded the surrender of all the forts in the State. This President Buchanan refused, and Fort Sumpter was virtually in a state of siege.

On April 11th, General Beauregard demanded the immediate surrender of the fort.

Major Anderson at once refused to comply, hoping reinforcements would reach him by the 15th, when Beauregard responded that he would open fire upon the almost helpless band at half-past four on the morning of the 12th of April, which he did; causing serious damage, but no one hurt. However, provisions and ammunition being almost exhausted, the evacuation of the fort was agreed upon on the afternoon of the 13th, and on the 14th Major Anderson marched out with flying colors. This was in fact the first real engagement of the war. But after many marches and battles, and months and years had passed, we look again, and on April 15th, 1865, just four years after the surrender, the Union flag, the same which had been lowered in 1861, was again formally raised over the dilapidated walls of Fort Sumpter.

How often were the hearts of the Union soldiers cheered, when news came from the distance of victory to our arms, and the music broke out along the line, when foot sore and weary from severe and long continued marches, loss of sleep, and short rations, well nigh driving them into an indifference as to whether they survived or not.

Do you not remember the 4th of July, 1863, while marching along the banks of Elk river, perhaps about

mid afternoon, the moving army was ordered to halt; many of us knew not why, but the suspense was soon relieved, as the orderlies swept by on their flying steeds announcing in their flight the victory at Vicksburg, that Pemberton had surrendered to Grant, thus opening up the Mississippi river for navigation to the Union army. A more potent victory could hardly have attended our noble army in the southwest. It was the key that unlocked the Mississippi river, according to the words of General Pemberton himself, who in reply to General Johnson, who advised the evacuation of Vicksburg, said: "I have decided to hold Vicksburg as long as possible, with the firm hope that the government may yet be able to assist me in keeping this obstruction to the enemy's free navigation of the Mississippi river. I still conceive it to be the most important point in the Confederacy."

Yet, notwithstanding his cherished hopes, on the morning of that memorable 4th of July, he declared himself to be free and independent of Vicksburg, and he was quickly superseded by General Grant; and his army of 27,000 gray coats gave place to the Boys in Blue.

An incident or two recurs in which our own regiment was interested, in regard to General Willich, whom we all regarded as a brave and faithful soldier and commander. Like General Grant, his speeches were not very numerous nor lengthy. Our regiment was encamped at Fort Wood, Chattanooga; preparations were being made for the attack upon Mission

Ridge, lying immediately in front of us. The brigade was ordered into line by regiments. The old General was urging the great necessity of courage, that the lines be well closed up, and that no man desert his post; and in his quaint German way, he said, "If any man runs, shoot him down; better one man die, than all go to the dogs."

Again, after the desperate fight at Mission Ridge, when we had gone on and on, scaled and taken the ridge, to the surprise and beyond the expectation of the commanding officers, (according to the congratulatory letter of General T. J. Wood to the troops the following day), the boys were seated in groups reviewing the events of the day, and rejoicing over the victory gained, surrounded both by the rebel and our own dead and dying. Willich passed along, visiting one group and then another in succession, and said, "Well, boys, cheer up, the war is almost over now; a little while and we'll all go home; then I'll come around and drink coffee with you and your vives."

Much of the important military history of the 68th is connected with the battles of Chicamauga, Mission Ridge and Lookout Mountain. The former took place September 19th and 20th, 1863, which inducted us into Chattanooga by the skin of our teeth. The latter, November 23d, 24th and 25th, which raised the siege and opened our way to Knoxville and East Tennessee, and cleared our entire front on the south and east.

A grander and more imposing scene perhaps was never witnessed, than that seen upon the summit and

slopes of Lookout from dusk until midnight, as Hooker with his 10,000 stealthily pushed his way up the hights, over craggy cliffs. On, on, went the forlorn hope. The God of nature had provided a dense fog, which covered the sides of the mountain, concealing our movements from the enemy, and the Confederates were completely taken by surprise; and after the evening's entertainment and fireworks, they abandoned their position with a loss of 2,000 prisoners; while Hooker and his troops encamped for the night upon the upper part of the slope which he had won, and lay down to pleasant dreams. This was one of the most hazardous and yet successful strategic feats of the war.

We recall the days of Thermopylæ with its narrow defile, and Leonidas with his chosen band of 300 Spartans, and a few hundred Thespians and Thebans. This small host fought till Leonidas and well nigh all his followers were killed, and none left to tell the story. But a different sequel attaches to the "battle above the clouds," for these, too, bravely fought, and stood their ground and triumphed gloriously, and lived to fight another day.

Sad duties and experiences to the soldier were not uncommon. Yet it was necessary to nerve himself for the most unpleasant task. The evening shades of November 25, 1863, terminated the battle of Mission Ridge. A comrade brave and true had fallen. The materials and conveniences for burial were not at hand, as we could wish, and as the noble dead deserved.

To bury a comrade dear as we would a dumb brute seemed repulsive and horrible, but as there was no other choice, and necessity is the mother of invention, we gathered about our dead comrade who had fallen near the summit of the ridge and close on to the enemy's fortifications, bore him away in the arms of his associates to the newly-made grave, wrapped in his own soldier's blanket, as a winding sheet; not even a rude box could then be obtained, in which to place the lifeless remains; so we lowered him into the grave with feelings of deep sorrow over the loss of so brave a soldier, and slowly covered the body out of sight. No display, nor military honors, muffled drum, reversed arms and burial salute were afforded upon the occasion. We had no time for this.

> "The soul of one had fled;
>   Tread lightly, comrades, ye have laid
> His dark locks on his brow,
>   Like life, save deeper light and shades;
> We'll not disturb them now.
>
> Slowly and sadly we laid him down,
>   From the field of his fame, fresh and gory;
> We carved not a line, we raised not a stone,
>   But left him—alone in his glory."

In a quarter-centennial address I should not dwell simply upon the events and experiences during the war; yet I confess to you, when I turned my mind to it, the entire three years service and many events of the war open out before me like a panorama. And out of the many things that could be told I hardly

knew what to select, where to begin, and still more embarrassed where to end.

The passing from civil life to the military was a transition involving great importance, and weighed largely not only in deciding the destiny of a Nation, but in moulding the destiny of the individual as well.

Some seemed to regard the soldier's life as necessary demoralization, and hence an abandonment of all principles and course of conduct true and noble. Some dared even to predict for the citizen soldiery the life of wholesale murder and highway robbery, and that the disbandment of the army would be but the liberating of a band of unmerciful cut-throats, pirates and thieves, libertines and drunkards. A more unkind, shameful and unworthy prophecy was never conceived.

Never did any country under the shining sun in so short a time marshal an army to the defense of her flag, her borders and her firesides, composed of men so full of downright manhood, loyalty and devotion to a country, nor perhaps where so large a per cent. maintained their moral integrity. And when the time came for discharging the army and returning those who survived to their homes and peaceful pursuits, it was effected with as much ease as the dismissing of a public school. The soldier again became the citizen; the sword was beaten into a plow-share and the spear into the pruning-hook; the anvil and the plane, the counting-room and the various industrial pursuits now became their occupation.

And many a noble brave, like a bird let loose after a long confinement, fairly flew to your retreat, where his mind had mostly been during the intervening months and years, and many a maiden's heart did bound with joy in posssesion of her soldier boy.

You are well aware that the three or four years service in the war occupied the best and most important period in the history of many of our countrymen.

Homes, families, business, preparations for life's work, pursuit of studies—all these could not well be forsaken, even temporarily. But what were all these without a country? Patrick Henry, in the closing sentence of that memorable speech, exclaimed "give me liberty, or give me death." Hence, at one general signal went forth the farmer, mechanic, merchant, lawyer, physician, student, artist, miner, poet, banker, philanthropist and christian, to offer their lives, if need be, to save their country, or

"To fight till the last armed foe expires,
Fight for their altars and their fires,
Fight for the green graves of their sires,
God and their Native Land."

Hence the interruption in life's plans, and results could never be atoned for, and the majority perhaps physically are not to-day what they would have been, only for the exposure and extreme military service; and the $60,000,000 annually disbursed to our suffering heroes is worthily bestowed, and perhaps our government will not have done full justice to her brave

defenders until the entire roll of Federal soldiers is embraced in the pension list.

But what hath been wrought in this quarter of a century? Every one of us is just twenty-five years older. Many of us have a wife; we hadn't then. An interesting family; we hadn't then. Some of you are grandfathers; you weren't then. You eyes were bright, clear and strong. You could take deadly aim on a rebel 1,000 yards away; you are wearing spectacles now. Your faces and heads were covered then with hair, raven black or blood red, but you are getting badly frosted now. So changed are we all that it is with difficulty we recognize each other. You are not fit for war now; your eyes are too dim. You could not bear a musket; your teeth are gone, and you couldn't bite a cartridge. The heads of some of you are too bare to endure the winters, such as that New Year's day of 1864, at Strawberry Plains.

A new generation has been born, grown up to manhood and cast a vote for President of these United States, since you and I were mustered into the military service of this country. A reconstruction of all the States in rebellion has been effected, and the stars and stripes is the national ensign over every foot of land in this broad domain. The West and South have opened their doors, and emigration has poured in by the multiplied thousands, homesteads have been entered, and claims laid and proven, and the resources of the far West are being developed by the persistent toil of ex-soldiers. Turn where you will, into every

line of business, trade and profession, and you will find those who have a military record of which they are proud, and influential members of society.

An organization has sprung up, composed of honored veterans, the Grand Army of the Republic, which is a potent factor in this country, and should open rebellion break out, would stand ready any morning at the sound of the bugle to wheel into line and quell the invader.

I appeal to you, are these men found to be the demoralizing elements of society, let loose upon the country to poison and devour? Nay, verily; but rather the bones and sinew, the brains and heart, the warp and woof of this Republic.

As Bartholdi's statue representing the Goddess of Liberty stands proudly upon its pedestal in Bedloe's Island, guarding the entrance to New York harbor, exhibiting the extraordinary genius and enterprise of our age, and expressive of the international fraternity which now prevails, so stand the Union soldiers. Noble sentinels, harmless, yet true by their past heroism in war and devotion to law and order in peace, seem to reflect the sentiment—" Peace on earth, good will to men." Comrades, at our first quarter-centennial I greet you, but not all. Arrange yourselves as for an evening dress parade. Every man from colonel to private in his proper place. Now shall the roll be called. No, no; a scene would be presented too sad for contemplation. How many are missing! Only think, Colonel King has dropped out from the head of the

column. Espy is missing. Wooden no longer ministers to the sick, and the low but sincere prayers of Monfort are hushed in death. Wheeler, quick as a flash and brave enough for any danger, fills a soldier's grave. What of the other commissioned officers? Some are gone. Then follows a longer list of sergeants and corporals, who are numbered with the dead; and last, but not least, the many in the ranks who bravely fought, evincing a courage and determination equal to any in ancient warfare. Their bodies rest in different cemeteries North and South. Do we say of them they are dead? Are they not only sleeping? They speak to us to-day; they are too noble to die. They are ever remembered by what they have done. A soldier brave and true, who now himself has gone, conceived the thought of perpetuating the memory of the Union soldiers by an annual decoration of their graves with choice and beautiful flowers, and now this day, of all the days in the year, in our Nation is the most interesting. We spend one day at least in every twelve months with our departed heroes. Thus are

> "Covered the thousands who sleep far away—
> Sleep where their friends can not find them to-day;
> They who in mountain and hillside and dell
> Rest where they wearied, and lie where they fell.
> Softly the grass blades creep round their repose.
> Sweetly above them the wild floweret blows;
> Zephyrs of freedom fly gently o'er head,
> Whispering prayers for the patriot dead;
> So in our minds we'll name them once more,
> So in our hearts we'll cover them o'er.

Roses and lilies and violets blue,
Bloom in our hearts for the brave and true;
Think of those far-away heroes of ours,
And cover them over with beautiful flowers.

When the long years have rolled slowly away,
E'en to the dawn of earth's funeral day,
When the archangel's trumpet and tread,
Raise up the faces and forms of the dead,
When the great world its last judgment awaits,
When the blue sky shall swing open the gates,
And our long columns march silently through,
Past the Great Captain for final review,
Then from the blood that has flowed for the right,
Crowns shall spring upward, untarnished and bright;
Then the glad ears of each war-martyred son
Proudly shall hear the good tidings, well done;
God will reward these dead heroes of ours,
And cover them over with beautiful flowers."

Comrades, we soon again shall give the parting hand and enter upon another quarter-centennial. Some may reach that distant mile stone, and a few trembling and time-worn veterans may surround this old flag, to recount their victories and cheer each other onward; but to most perchance, when August 19, 1912, shall come, they will be silently sleeping the sleep of death; but let us not grow melancholy on this account. Ever remember life is real, life is earnest. Let us make our lives sublime, and, departing, leave behind us footprints in the sands of time. Stand by the old flag of the Union. Never permit it to be trailed in the dust by the hand of vile traitors; ever be faithful to the highest principles of true manhood, which will add

strength and perpetuity to our goverment, giving power at home and influence abroad, against communism, anarchism, socialism and nihilism, which would seek to undermine and destroy good government. Thus may we be in all the future a beacon light to the nations of the world, the land of the free and home of the brave.

ARMY OF THE CUMBERLAND.

The following was the organization of the Army of the Cumberland before the battle of Chicamauga, Georgia, September 19 and 20, 1863:

MAJ.-GEN. W. S. ROSECRANS, Commanding Army.

Headquarters Guards.—15th Pennsylvania Cavalry, 10th Ohio Infantry, 1st Battalion Ohio Sharpshooters.

TWENTIETH ARMY CORPS.
MAJ.-GEN. A. McD. McCOOK.

FIRST DIVISION.
BRIG.-GEN. JEFF. C. DAVIS.

First Brigade.—Col. P. S. Post, 22d Ind., 59th Ills., 74th Ills., 75th Ills. *Second Brigade.*—Gen. W. P. Carlin, 21st and 38th Ills., 15th Wisconsin, 101st Ohio. *Third Brigade.*—Col. H. C. Heg, 81st Ind., 25th and 35th Ills., 8th Kan. *Artillery.*—5th Wis., 8th Wis., 2d Minn. Batteries.

SECOND DIVISION.
BRIG.-GEN. R. W. JOHNSON.

First Brigade.—Gen. Aug. Willich, 15th and 49th Ohio, 32d and 39th Ind., 15th Ohio, 89th Ills. *Second Brigade.*—Col. J. B. Dodge, 77th Penn., 29th and 30th Ind., 34th and 79th Ills. *Third Brigade.*—Col. P. P. Baldwin, 6th Ind., 1st and 93d Ohio and 5th Ky. Cavalry. *Artillery.*—Battery A, 1st Ohio, 20th Ohio, 5th Ind.

THIRD DIVISION.
MAJ.-GEN. P. H. SHERIDAN.

First Brigade.—Gen. W. H. Lytle, 36th and 88th Ills., 24th Wis., 21st Mich. *Second Brigade.*—Col. B. Laiboldt, 2d and 15th Mo., 44th and 73d Ills. *Third Brigade.*—Col. L. P. Bradley, 22d, 27th, 42d and 51st Ills. *Artillery.*—Battery H, 2nd Ind., G, 1st Mo., C, 1st Ills.

ARMY OF THE CUMBERLAND.

FOURTEENTH ARMY CORPS.

Maj.-Gen. George H. Thomas.

Escort.—Co. L, 1st Ohio Cavalry. *Provost Guard.*—9th Mich. Infantry.

FIRST DIVISION.
Brig.-Gen. A. Baird.

First Brigade.—Col. B. F. Scribner, 38th Ind., 2d, 33d and 94th Ohio, 10th Wisconsin. *Second Brigade.*—Gen. J. C. Starkweather, 1st and 21st Wis., 24th Ills., 79th Penn. *Third Brigade.*—Gen. J. H. King, 15th, 16th, 19th U. S. Infantry; 1st Battalions 18th, ditto, 1st and 2d. *Artillery.*—1st Michigan, 4th Ind., Battery H, 5th U. S. A.

SECOND DIVISION.
Maj.-Gen. J. S. Negley.

First Brigade.—Gen. John Beatty, 42d and 88th Ind., 3d Ohio, 15th Ky., 104th Ills. *Second Brigade.*—Col. T. R. Stanley, 18th and 69th Ohio, 19th Ills., 11th Mich. *Third Brigade.*—Col. W. Sirwell, 78th Penn., 21st and 74th Ohio, 37th Ind. *Artillery.*—Batteries A and M, 1st Ohio, Bridge's Battery Ills. Light Art.

THIRD DIVISION.
Brig.-Gen. J. M. Brannon.

First Brigade.—Col. John M. Connell, 17th, 31st and 38th Ohio, 82d Ind. *Second Brigade.*—Col. John P. Croxton, 4th and 10th Ky., 10th and 74th Ind., 14th Ohio. *Third Brigade.*—Col. F. Vanderveer, 9th and 35th Ohio, 2d Minn., 87th Ind. *Artillery.*—4th Mich., Battery C, 1st Ohio, Battery I, 4th U. S. A.

FOURTH DIVISION.
Maj.-Gen. J. J. Reynolds.

First Brigade.—Col. J. T. Wilder, 17th and 72d Ind., 92d, 98th and 123d Ills. *Second Brigade.*—Col. Ed. A. King, 68th, 75th and 101st Ind., 80th Ills., 105th Ohio. *Third Brigade.*—Gen. J. B. Turchin, 11th, 36th, 89th and 92d Ills. *Artillery.*—18th, 19th and 21st Ind. Batteries.

TWENTY-FIRST ARMY CORPS.

Maj.-Gen. T. L. Crittenden.

FIRST DIVISION.
Brig.-Gen. T. J. Wood.

First Brigade.—Col. Geo. P. Buell, 26th Ohio, 58th Ohio, 13th Mich., 100th Ills. *Second Brigade.*—Gen. G. D. Wagner, 15th, 40th, 51st, 57th Ind., 197th Ohio. *Third Brigade.*—Col. C. G. Harker, 3d Ky., 64th, 65th and 125th Ohio, 73d Ind. *Artillery.*—8th and 10th Ind., and 6th Ohio Batteries.

ARMY OF THE CUMBERLAND.

SECOND DIVISION.
MAJ.-GEN. J. M. PALMER.

First Brigade.—Gen. Charles Craft, 1st and 2d Ky., 31st Ind., 90th Ohio. *Second Brigade.*—Gen. W. B. Hazen, 41st and 124th Ohio, 6th Ky., 9th Ind., 110th Ills. *Third Brigade.*—Col. W. Grose, 36th Ind., 6th and 24th Ohio, 23d Ky., 84th Ill. *Artillery.*—Battery B and 21st Ohio, and M and H 4th U. S. Art.

THIRD DIVISION.
BRIG.-GEN. H. P. VAN CLEVE.

First Brigade.—Gen. S. Beatty, 9th, 17th Kentucky, 19th Ohio, 79th Ind. *Second Brigade.*—Col. Geo. F. Dick, 44th, 86th Ind. 13th, 59th Ohio. *Third Brigade.*—Col. S. M. Barnes, 51st, 99th Ohio, 35th Ind., 8th, 21st Ky. *Artillery.*—26th Penn., 3d Wisconsin, 7th Ind.

RESERVE CORPS.
MAJ.-GEN. GORDON GRANGER.

Escort.—Co. F, 1st Mo. Cavalry.

FIRST DIVISION.
BRIG.-GEN. JAMES B. STEEDMAN.

First Brigade.—Gen. W. C. Whittaker, 40th Ohio, 84th Ind., 96th and 115th Ills. *Second Brigade.*—Col. J. G. Mitchell, 98th, 113th and 121st Ohio, 78th Ills. *Third Brigade.*—Col. John Coburn, 33d, 85th Ind., 22d Wis., 19th Mich. *Artillery.*—9th and 18th Ohio, M 1st Ills.

SECOND DIVISION.
BRIG.-GEN. J. D. MORGAN.

First Brigade.—Col. R. F. Smith, 10th, 16th, 60th Ills., 10th, 14th Mich. *Second Brigade.*—Col. Dan. M. McCook, 52d Ohio, 85th, 86th and 125th Ills. *Third Brigade.*—Col. C. C. Doolittle, 18th, 22d Mich., 106th, 108th Ohio, 10th Tenn. *Artillery.*—10th Wis., E 1st Ohio, I 2d Ills.

THIRD DIVISION.
BRIG.-GEN. R. S. GRANGER.

First Brigade.—Col. S. D. Bruce, 83d Ills., 13th Wis., 71st, 102d Ohio, 28th Ky. *Second Brigade.*—Gen. T. D. Ward, 70th Ind., 79th Ohio, 102d, 105th, 129th Ills. *Third Brigade.*—Gen. J. G. Spears, 3d, 5th and 6th Tenn. *Artillery.*—H, 2d Ills., 5th Mich., 1st Tenn.

CAVALRY.
MAJ.-GEN. D. S. STANLEY, (Absent).
BRIG.-GEN. ROB'T. B. MITCHELL, (Commanding).

FIRST DIVISION.
COL. E. M. McCOOK.

First Brigade.—Col. A. P. Campbell, 1st Tenn., 2d Mich., 9th Penn. *Second Brigade.*—Col. O. A. LaGrange, 2d, 4th Ind., 2d, 3d Tenn., 1st Wis. *Third Brigade.*—Col. L. D. Watkins, 4th, 5th, 6th, 7th Ky., and Battery D, 1st Ohio.

SECOND DIVISION.

Brig.-Gen. George Crook.

First Brigade.—Col. R. H. G. Minty, 7th Penn., 4th Mich., 4th U. S., 3d Ind. (Battalion.) *Second Brigade.*—Col. Eli Long, 1st, 3d, 4th Ohio, 2d Ky. *Third Brigade.*—Col. W. Lowe, 5th Iowa, 10th Ohio, 5th Tenn. Chicago Battery.

UNASSIGNED TROOPS.

Pioneer Brigade.—(Brig.-Gen. J. St. Clair Morton.) 3 Battalions.—1st Mich. Engineers and Mechanics; 2d Ky. Battery with Engineers and Mechanics; 1st Ky. Battery at Murfreesboro, Tenn.; 12th and 20th Ind. Battery at Nashville, Tenn.; 13th Ind. Battery at Gallatin, Tenn.; Battery C, 2d Ills. at Fort Donelson, Tenn.; 4th Tenn. Cavalry at Nashville, Tenn.; Battalion 5th. Ky. Cavalry at Clarksville, Tenn.

CONFEDERATE ARMY.

Organization of the Confederate army, Gen. Braxton Bragg, commanding, at the battle of Chicamauga, Georgia.

RIGHT WING.

Lieut.-Gen. Leonidas Polk.

CHEATHAM'S DIVISION.

Maj.-Gen. B. F. Cheatham.

Jackson's Brigade.—Brig.-Gen. J. K. Jackson, 1st Confed. Battalion, 5th Ga., 2d Ga. Battalion, 5th Miss., 8th Miss., Scogin's (Ga.) Battery. *Maney's Brigade.*—Brig.-Gen. Geo. Maney, 1st Tenn., 27th Tenn., 4th Tenn., 6th Tenn., 9th Tenn., Maney's (Tenn.) Battery, Smith's (Miss.) Battery. *Smith's Brigade.*—Brig.-Gen. Preston Smith, Col. A. J. Vaughn, 11th Tenn., 12th Tenn., 47th Tenn., 13th Tenn., 29th Tenn., 154th Tenn., Scott's (Tenn.) Battery. *Wright's Brigade.*—Brig.-Gen. M. J. Wright, 8th Tenn., 16th Tenn., 28th Tenn., 38th Tenn., 51st Tenn., 52d Tenn., Carnes' (Tenn.) Battery. *Strahl's Brigade.*—Brig.-Gen. O. F. Strahl, 4th Tenn., 5th Tenn., 19th Tenn., 24th Tenn., 31st Tenn., 33d Stanford's (Miss.) Battery.

HILL'S CORPS.

Lieut.-Gen. D. H. Hill.

CLEBURNE'S DIVISION.

Maj.-Gen. P. R. Cleburne.

Polk's Brigade.—Brig.-Gen. L. E. Polk, 1st Ark., 3d Confed., 5th Confed., 2d Tenn., 35th Tenn., 48th Tenn., Calvert's (Tenn.) Battery. *Wood's Brigade.*—Brig.-Gen. S. A. M. Wood, 16th Ala., 33d Ala., 45th Ala., 32d Miss., 45th Miss., Hankin's Battalion, Semple's (Ala.) Battery. *Deshler's Brigade.*—Brig.-Gen. James Deshler, Col. R. Q. Mills, 19th Ark., 24th Ark., 6th Tex., 10th Tex., 15th Tex., 17th Tex., 18th, 24th Tex., 25th Tex., Douglas' (Tex.) Battery.

BRECKINRIDGE'S DIVISION.

Maj.-Gen. John C. Breckinridge.

Helm's Brigade.—Brig.-Gen. B. H. Helm, Col. J. H. Lewis, 41st Ala., 2d Ky., 4th Ky., 6th Ky., 9th Ky., Cobb's (Ky.) Battery. *Adams' Brigade.*—Brig.-Gen. Dan'l Adams, Col. R. L. Gibson, 32d Ala., 13th La., 20th La., 16th La., 25th La., 19th La., Austin's (La.) Battalion, Slocomb's (La.) Battery. *Stovall's Brigade.*—Brig.-Gen. M. A. Stovall, 1st Fla., 3d Fla., 4th Fla., 47th Ga., 60th N. Car., Mebane's (Tenn.) Battery.

CONFEDERATE ARMY.

WALKER'S DIVISION.
Maj.-Gen. W. H. T. Walker.
Brig.-Gen. S. R. Gist.

Gist's Brigade.—Brig.-Gen. S. R. Gist, Col. P. H. Colquitt, 46th Ga., 8th Ga. Battalion, 16th S. Car., 24th S. Car., Ferguson's (S. Car.) Battery. *Ector's Brigade.*—Brig.-Gen. M. D. Ector, Ala. Battalion, (Stone's), Miss. Battalion, (Pound's), 9th Tex., 10th Tex. Cavalry, 14th Tex. Cavalry, 32d Tex. Cavalry, Battery. *Wilson's Brigade.*—Col. C. C. Wilson, 25th Ga., 29th Ga., 30th Ga., 1st Ga. Battalion, 4th La. Battalion, Battery.

LIDDELL'S DIVISION.
Brig.-Gen. S. J. R. Liddell.

Liddell's Brigade.—Col. D. C. Govan, 2d Ark., 15th Ark., 5th Ark., 13th Ark., 6th Ark., 7th Ark., 8th Ark., 1st La., Sweet's (Miss.) Battalion. *Walthall's Brigade.*—Brig.-Gen. E. C. Walthall, 24th Miss., 27th Miss., 29th Miss., 30th Miss., 34th Miss., Fowler's (Ala.) Battery.

LEFT WING.
Lieut.-Gen. James Longstreet.

McLAW'S DIVISION.
Maj.-Gen. Lafayette McLaw.
Brig.-Gen. J. B. Kershaw.

Kershaw's Brigade.—Brig.-Gen. J. B. Kershaw, 2d S. Car., 3d S. Car., 7th S. Car., 8th S. Car., 15th S. Car., 3d S. Car. Battalion. *Wofford's Brigade.*—Brig.-Gen. W. T. Wofford, 16th Ga., 18th Ga., 24th Ga., 3d Ga. Battalion, Cobb's (Ga.) Legion, Phillip's (Ga.) Legion. *Humphreys' Brigade.*—Brig.-Gen. B. G. Humphreys, 13th Miss., 17th Miss., 18th Miss., 21st Miss. *Bryan's Brigade.*—Brig.-Gen. Goode Bryan, 10th Ga., 50th Ga., 51st Ga., 53d Ga.

HOOD'S DIVISION.
Maj.-Gen. J. B. Hood.
Brig.-Gen. E. M. Law.

Law's Brigade.—Brig.-Gen. E. M. Law, Col. Sheffield, 4th Ala., 15th Ala., 44th Ala., 47th Ala., 48th Ala. *Robertson's Brigade.*—Brig.-Gen. J. B. Robertson, 3d Ark., 1st Tex., 4th Tex., 5th Tex. *Anderson's Brigade.*—Brig.-Gen. Geo T. Anderson, 7th Ga., 8th Ga., 9th Ga., 11th Ga., 59th Ga. *Benning's Brigade.*—Brig.-Gen. H. L. Benning, 2d Ga., 15th Ga., 17th Ga., 20th Ga. *Artillery.*—Maj. Frank Huger, Fickling's (Va.) Battery, Jordan's (Va.) Battery, Moody's (La.) Battery, Parker's (Va.) Battery, Taylor's (Va.) Battery, Woolfolk's (Va.) Battery.

HINDMAN'S DIVISION.
Maj.-Gen. T. C. Hindman.
Brig.-Gen. Patton Anderson.

Anderson's Brigade.—Brig.-Gen. Patton Anderson, Col. J. H. Sharp, 7th Miss., 9th Miss., 10th Miss., 41st Miss., 44th Miss., 9th Miss. Battalion, Garrity's (Ala.) Battery. *Deas' Brigade.*—Brig.-Gen. Z. C. Deas, 19th Ala., 22d Ala., 25th Ala., 39th Ala., 50th Ala., 17th Ala. Battalion, Dent's (Ala.) Battery. *Manigault's Brigade.*—Brig.-Gen. A. M. Manigault, 24th Ala., 28th Ala., 34th Ala., 10th S. Car., and 19th S. Car. consol., Water's (Ala.) Battery.

CONFEDERATE ARMY. 211

BUCKNER'S CORPS.

MAJ.-GEN. S. B. BUCKNER.

STEWART'S DIVISION.

MAJ.-GEN. A. P. STEWART.

Johnson's Brigade.—Brig.-Gen. B R. Johnson, Col. J. S. Fulton, 17th Tenn., 2d Tenn. 25th Tenn., 44th Tenn., 9th Ga. Artillery, Battery E. *Brown's Brigade.*—Brig.-Gen. J. C. Brown, 18th Tenn., 26th Tenn., 32d Tenn., 45th Tenn., Newman's (Tenn.) Battalion, Dawson's (Ga.) Battery. *Bate's Brigade.*—Brig.-Gen. W. B. Bate, 58th Ala., 37th Ga., 4th Ga Battalion, 15th Tenn., 37th Tenn., 20th Tenn., Oliver's (Ala.) Artillery. *Clayton's Brigade.*—Brig.-Gen. H. D. Clayton, 18th Ala., 36th Ala., 38th Ala., Humphrey's (Ark.) Battery.

PRESTON'S DIVISION.

BRIG.-GEN. WILLIAM PRESTON.

Gracie's Brigade.—Brig.-Gen. A. Gracie, Jr., 43d Ala., 1st Ala. Battalion, 2d Ala. Battalion, 3d Ala. Battalion, 63d Tenn. Battery. *Trigg's Brigade.*—Col. R. C. Trigg, 1st Fla. Cavalry, 6th Fla., 7th Fla., 54th Va., Peeple's (Ga.) Battery. *Kelly's Brigade.*—Col. J. H. Kelly, 65th Ga., 5th Ky., 58th N. Car., 63d Va., Battery.

JOHNSON'S DIVISION.

BRIG.-GEN. B. R. JOHNSON.

Gregg's Brigade—Brig.-Gen. John Gregg, Col. C. A. Sugy, 3d Tenn., 10th Tenn., 30th Tenn., 41st Tenn., 50th Tenn., 1st (20th) Tenn. Battalion, 7th Tex., Bledsoe's (Mo.) Battery. *McNair's Brigade.*—Brig.-Gen. E. McNair, Col. D. Coleman, 1st Ark. Rifles, 2d Ark. Rifles, 4th Ark., 25th Ark., 35th Ark., Culpeper's (S. C.) Battery.

CAVALRY.

MAJ.-GEN. JOSEPH WHEELER.

WHARTON'S DIVISION.

BRIG.-GEN. JOHN A. WHARTON.

First Brigade.—Col. C C. Crews 7th Ala., 2d Ga., 3d Ga., 4th Ga. *Second Brigade.*—Col. T. Harrison, 3d Confederates, 1st Ky., 4th Tenn., 8th Tex., 11th Tex., White's (Ga.) Battery.

MARTIN'S DIVISION.

BRIG.-GEN. W. T. MARTIN.

First Brigade.—Col. J. T. Morgan, 1st Ala., 3d Ala., 51st Ala., 8th Confederate. *Second Brigade.*—Col. A. A. Russell, 4th Ala., 1st Confederate, Wiggins' (Ark.) Battery.

RODDEY'S BRIGADE.

BRIG.-GEN. P. D. RODDEY.

4th Ala., 5th Ala., 53d Ala., Forrest's (Tenn.) Regiment, Ferrell's Ga.) Battery.

CONFEDERATE ARMY.

FORREST'S CORPS.
MAJ.-GEN. N. B. FORREST.
ARMSTRONG'S DIVISION.
BRIG.-GEN. F. C. ARMSTRONG.

Armstrong's Brigade.—3d Ark., 1st Tenn., 2d Tenn., McDonald's Battalion. —— *Brigade*—4th Tenn., 8th Tenn., 9th Tenn., 10th Tenn., 11th Tenn., Freeman's (Tenn.) Battery, Marion's (Tenn.) Battery.

PEGRAM'S DIVISION.
BRIG.-GEN. JOHN PEGRAM.

Davidson's Brigade.—Brig.-Gen. H. B. Davidson, 1st Ga., 6th Ga., 65th N. Car., Rucker's Legion, Huwald's (Tenn.) Battery. *Scott's Brigade.*—Col. J. L. Scott, 10th Confederate, 1st La., 5th Tenn., 13th Tenn. Battalion, 16th Tenn. Battalion, Louisiana Battery (1 section).

RESERVE ARTILLERY.

Barret's (Mo.) Battery, Darden's (Miss.) Battery, Havis' (Ala.) Battery, LeGardewi's (La.) Battery, Lumsden's (Ala.) Battery, Massenburg's (Ga.) Battery.

FOURTH ARMY CORPS.
MAJ.-GEN. G. GRANGER.

FIRST DIVISION.
MAJ.-GEN. J. M. PALMER.

First Brigade.—Brig.-Gen. Chas. Cruft, 21st Ill., 38th Ills., 29th Ind., 31st Ind., 81st Ind., 1st Ky., 2d Ky., 90th Ohio, 101st Ohio. *Second Brigade.*—Brig.-Gen. W. C. Whittaker, 96th Ills., 115th Ills., 35th Ind., 84th Ind., 8th Ky., 40th Ohio, 51st Ohio, 99th Ohio. *Third Brigade.*—Col Wm. Grose, 59th Ills., 75th Ills., 84th Ills., 9th Ind., 30th Ind., 36th Ind., 24th Ohio, 77th Penn. *Artillery.*—5th Ind. Battery, 4th U. S. Artillery, Co. H; 4th U. S. Artillery, Co. M.

SECOND DIVISION.
MAJ.-GEN. P. H. SHERIDAN.

First Brigade.—Brig.-Gen. J. B. Steedman, 36th Ills., 44th Ills., 73d Ills., 74th Ills., 88th Ills., 22d Ind., 21st Mich., 2d Mo., 15th Mo., 24th Wis. *Second Brigade.*—Brig.-Gen. G. D. Wagner, 100th Ills., 15th Ind., 40th Ind., 57th Ind., 58th Ind., 13th Mich., 26th Ohio, 97th Ohio. *Third Brigade.*—Col. C. G. Harker, 22d Ills., 27th Ills., 42d Ills., 51st Ills., 79th Ills., 3d Ky., 64th Ohio, 65th Ohio, 125th Ohio. *Artillery.*—1st Ills. Artillery, Co. M; 10th Ind. Battery, 1st Miss. Artillery, Co. G.

THIRD DIVISION.
BRIG.-GEN. T. J. WOOD.

First Brigade.—Brig.-Gen. A. Willich, 25th Ills., 35th Ills., 89th Ills., 32d Ind., 68th Ind., 8th Kan., 15th Ohio, 49th Ohio, 15th Wis. *Second Brigade.*—Brig.-Gen. W. B. Hazen, 6th Ind., 5th Ky., 6th Ky., 23d Ky., 1st Ohio, 6th Ohio, 41st Ohio, 93d Ohio, 124th Ohio. *Third Brigade.*—Brig.-Gen. S. Beatty, 44th Ind., 79th Ind., 86th Ind., 9th Ky., 17th Ky., 13th Ohio, 19th Ohio, 59th Ohio. *Artillery.*—Bridge's Battery Ills. Artillery, 6th Ohio Battery, 26th Penn. Battery.

www.ingramcontent.com/pod-product-compliance
Lightning Source LLC
Chambersburg PA
CBHW022143300426
44115CB00006B/324